The Nine Lives of
MICKEY
ROONEY

Also by Arthur Marx:

The Ordeal of Willie Brown
Life with Groucho
Not as a Crocodile
Son of Groucho
*Everybody Loves Somebody Sometime (Especially
    Himself)*
Goldwyn
Red Skelton

Plays

The Impossible Years
Minnie's Boys
My Daughter's Rated X
Groucho

The Nine Lives of

MICKEY ROONEY

Arthur Marx

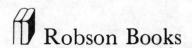 Robson Books

First published in Great Britain in 1987 by Robson Books Ltd,
Bolsover House, 5-6 Clipstone Street, London W1P 7EB.

British Library Cataloguing in Publication Data

Marx, Arthur
   The nine lives of Mickey Rooney.
   1. Rooney, Mickey   2. Actors—United
   States—Biography
   I. Title
   791.43′028′0924   PN2287.R75

ISBN 0-86051-421-8

Printed in Great Britain by Billing & Sons Ltd., Worcester.

To:

Scott Meredith

ACKNOWLEDGMENTS

My sincerest thanks to the following people and organizations for their help in the gathering of material for this book.

Norman Abbott
Frank Arno
Greg Bautzer
Mort Briskin
Marcy McGuire Cassell
Wally Cassell
Jack Carter
Joe Cohn
Jimmy Cook
Jackie Cooper
Elaine Mahnken Davis
Red Doff
Maurice Duke
Bullets Durgom
Bill Gardner
Kitty Kelley
Howard Koch
Margaret Lane
William Ludwig

Arthur Malvin
Les Martinson
Sam Marx
Sidney Miller
John Fenton Murray
Robert Neeb
Herb Nussbaum
Jack Paar
Richard Quine
Bonita Granville Rather
Marshall Robbins
Timothy Rooney
Al Rosen
Ann Rutherford
Nick Sevano
Simon Taub
Rudy Tronto
Alan Wasser

And special thanks to:
Les Peterson,
The Marvin Paige Motion Picture and TV Research Service,
    all the people who work at the Academy of Motion Picture Arts
    and Sciences Research Library,
and to Roger Kahn, who collaborated in Mickey's 1965 auto-
    biography, *i.e.*, which was useful for information about Mickey's
    early days.

PHOTOGRAPHS

Mickey at age three
Mickey and Coleen More, 1932
Mickey as Mickey McGuire
Mickey's doting mother, Nell, playing nurse to him
Judy Garland and Mickey
Esther Williams and Mickey
Bob Hope, Mickey, Judy Garland, and Jackie Cooper at the Coco
Mickey and Judy Garland, 1940
Mickey and top banana father Joe Yule
The wedding party for Ava Gardner and Mickey
Mickey and his new bride, Ava
Mickey and movie father Lewis Stone
MGM's famous "stock company" on Lionel Barrymore's birthday
Mickey entertaining the troops in Belgium
Mickey and his second wife, Betty Jane Rase, 1946
Mickey and his radiant third bride, actress Martha Vickers, 1949
Mickey and fourth bride, actress Elaine Mahnken, 1952
Barbara and infant son Michael Joseph Kyle Rooney, 1962
Mickey, following Barbara's funeral
Mickey with sixth wife, Margie Lane, 1966
Mickey going through a car wash
Mickey and seventh wife Caroline Hackett, 1969
Mickey with eighth wife Jan Sterling on "This Is Your Life"
Mickey opening *Sugar Babies*
Ann Miller and Mickey doing their schoolroom sketch
Mickey and Ann Miller in finale of *Sugar Babies*
A mature Mickey Rooney

PROLOGUE

I've known Mickey Rooney off and on since the mid-thirties when we were kids and taking tennis lessons together on Marion Davies's court in Beverly Hills. Our instructor was Eleanor "Teach" Tennant who later won prominence as the coach of two Wimbledon champions, Alice Marble and Bobby Riggs.

At the time I didn't know anything about Mickey except that he was playing the role of Puck in the Max Reinhardt production of *A Midsummer Night's Dream* at the Hollywood Bowl and was supposed to be very good in it. I was not impressed by the fact that Mickey was an actor. My father was an actor, too, with a lot more credits than my tennis-playing companion had. To me, Mickey was just a brash, freckle-faced kid, about my own age and size, who had an amazing amount of energy and who talked a better game of tennis than he played.

Several years later, after Mickey signed a contract at Metro-Goldwin-Mayer and was on the threshold of stardom, my father, who was also making pictures there, would bump into him on the lot. Occasionally, he'd bring Mickey home to dinner as a favor to my sister Miriam who had a crush on him. He seemed to like her, too. At the end of the evening, as Mickey was about to leave, he would kiss Miriam on the cheek and promise to send her a box of candy the next day. Miriam would wait eagerly for the candy, but it would never arrive. The next time he met my father on the lot he would say, "Hey, Grouch, did Miriam ever get that candy I sent her?"

"Not yet, Mick."

"That's strange. I'd better call the shop and get after them."

Miriam's still waiting for the candy.

9

THAT'S THE WAY that Mick was—all mouth and a bit of a show-off—
even in those days. But nobody minded it: He was personable and
always entertaining.

Later on, Mickey would show up to dinner at our house with Judy
Garland. She was about sixteen, shy and unspoiled, fresh from her
success in *The Wizard of Oz*. After dinner, everyone would gravi-
tate to the piano in our living room. There Mickey would play
(strictly by ear), Judy would belt out a few songs, and my father
would play his steel-stringed guitar.

The first time my father unveiled his instrument and started to
strum it, Mickey boasted, "I can play that."

"You can?" My father handed the guitar to him. "Let's see you."

Mickey responded to the challenge by wrapping his left hand
around the frets and strumming a simple C chord.

"That's all?" said my father as Mickey handed the guitar back to
him. "I thought you could play."

Mickey shrugged, unembarrassed. "I didn't mean a six-stringed
guitar," he replied.

Of course, there is no other kind. But that's Mickey Rooney for
you.

By the time Mickey scored his initial success in the Andy Hardy
series, I was out of his league socially (although we still played tennis
occasionally). He was a major movie star now, making $2,500 a
week; I was just a schoolboy on an allowance. The economics of our
situations placed us in different worlds.

After that, we lost contact for a number of years. Mickey went on
to become the number-one male box-office attraction in America,
replacing Clark Gable, and I sank into oblivion as a tennis bum and
struggling writer.

Our paths didn't converge again until the sixties when, with my
partner, I created, wrote, and produced a television sitcom for
Mickey—called "Mickey,"—which lasted seventeen weeks on ABC
before being axed because of abysmally low ratings.

During this period I got to know all the different Mickey
Rooneys—the star, the fine dramatic actor, the comedian, the prima
donna, the masochist, the philandering husband, the conscientious
father, the composer, the scriptwriter, the sportsman, the animal
lover, the philosopher, the hedonist, the stalwart friend, and the
God-fearing churchgoer. One thing was always evident: Mickey's
enormous talent as a performer whenever he was in the mood to
apply himself to the task. Which wasn't always.

Following the demise of the television series, I had no more personal contact with Mickey until I met him at a party at the Beverly Hills Hotel some years after his success in *Sugar Babies*. In the interim, through the newspapers, I followed the highs and lows of his tempestuous life. His frequent trips to the altar and the divorce court (his fifth wife, Barbara Thomason, the one he was married to when we were doing the series, was murdered by a family friend); his financial disasters; and his problems getting his career back on track again. All of which I thought would be grist for an interesting biography of him.

At the party, which was attended by a number of celebrities, I managed to corner Mickey and offer congratulations on his smashing success in *Sugar Babies*. He was almost bald, with something of a potbelly and shaggy white eyebrows, but his blue eyes were as clear as ever and his grin just as disarming.

Mickey hugged me warmly. Apparently he harbored no grudges about the failure of our TV series, so I used the opportunity to broach the subject of our collaborating on his autobiography, which I'd read he was thinking of writing on his own.

Mickey admitted he was in the throes of setting his story down on paper. In fact, he said, he had already written about a hundred pages covering his early years.

"You're so busy," I pointed out, "you'll never finish it yourself. Why don't you let me work on it with you? I've had a lot of experience writing biographies." And I rattled off the five previous ones I had perpetrated.

Mickey's blue eyes peered at me suspiciously. "I don't know," he finally replied. "I'll have to think about it."

We exchanged telephone numbers, and he promised to get back to me as soon as he'd given my proposition some thought.

The very next day he called.

"How would we do this thing?" he asked.

"What do you mean?" I said.

"I mean, er, the business arrangements." It was obvious from his tentative tone that that was a subject he was not eager to talk about but felt he must. "I suppose you'd like your name on the cover."

"Well, I would like my name to appear somewhere," I said. "It can either be, 'by Mickey Rooney as told to Arthur Marx,' or 'Mickey Rooney with Arthur Marx.'"

"I see," Mickey replied thoughtfully. "And what about the financial arrangements?"

"I've never done a book with anyone before," I informed him. "I'll

11

take whatever is the usual collaborator's cut . . . I think it's somewhere around forty percent."

"That wouldn't do," Mickey said. "I wouldn't want your name on my autobiography. And I couldn't give you anything like forty percent of the royalties. It would have to be a flat fee."

"In that case, I wouldn't consider it," I said. "I don't 'ghost' books or do it without some royalty arrangement."

"I figured that," Mickey said. "So I guess we can't do it."

"I guess so," I said. "But would you mind if I do it without you?"

"Go ahead,' Mickey suggested in a friendly tone. "It couldn't be anything like the one I'm writing, anyway."

Thank God for that! I thought, as the two of us exchanged goodbyes and hung up. I intended to write a truthful biography of Mickey Rooney. Not a hatchet job, because I liked him too well and respected his talent, but one that revealed a few warts. Mickey, on the other hand—unless he had changed considerably since we'd last worked together—had a tendency to overstate or understate, or not state at all, if it was to his benefit. He could never tell the real truth about himself.

Not that many people could, or would. Actors, particularly, spend too much of their lives pretending to be other people to be able to be very introspective about themselves. Many of them don't know *who* they are.

So in a way I was relieved when Mickey turned me down, for I knew I would have nothing but trouble trying to persuade him to tell the truth and nothing but the truth.

By not wanting to share either the credit or any of the spoils, Mickey Rooney had made the complete transition from successful movie moppet to adult superstar.

The Nine Lives of

MICKEY ROONEY

1

O N A WARM July evening in 1951, Mickey Rooney and two of his
closest friends, Marcy and Wally Cassell, were riding along
Ventura Boulevard on their way to dinner at a restaurant in the San
Fernando Valley. That year was not the best of times for the thirty-
one-year-old former box-office king. Since his Andy Hardy days,
Mickey had gone from number one draw to being a virtual has-been
and pariah in Hollywood. Whether it had been a wise move or egre-
gious blunder, Mickey had cut his ties with MGM, the studio responsible for turning him into a star. He'd done so in order to make a
million in independent production, but the money didn't roll in.

His personal life was a shambles, too. The most recent of Mickey's
three marriages—to three of the world's most beautiful women—
had just ended in failure, burdening him with alimony and child
support payments that would have broken a man more wealthy
than Mickey had ever been. He was too fond of gambling; he'd also
liked the sauce and some other chemicals; and he was hounded by
creditors day and night. All of which added up to a reputation so
tarnished, even in a town like Hollywood, that after Mickey was
invited to present an Oscar at the 1951 Academy Awards clambake,
the Board of Governors thought better of it and at the last minute
withdrew their invitation while Mickey was still at home getting into
his tuxedo.

Such was the chaotic state of Mickey Rooney's life as he was being
driven to dinner by the Cassells.

As Cassell stopped his car for a red light, Mickey glanced out the
window and noticed a 24-sheet billboard with a huge picture of his

pal Judy Garland on it. With a compassionate shake of his head, Mickey clucked his tongue sympathetically and exclaimed, "Boy, has *she* screwed up *her* life!"

The thought process that led Mickey to that conclusion about his best friend Judy while totally ignoring how he might have been responsible for screwing up his own life is a real clue to what makes the man tick. His resiliency is remarkable and is probably what has sustained him, even more than his enormous talent, through a string of failures and comebacks that would make Rocky's pugilistic career pale in comparison.

In his sixty-six years of getting himself in and out of more tight spots than James Bond, Mickey Rooney has never lost faith in himself—well, hardly ever—with the result that in the twilight of his career he achieved an astonishing new success on Broadway as the star of the smash hit musical *Sugar Babies* that would have seemed a pipe dream a year earlier.

The Mickey Rooney Story, in fact, is so improbable it would make a great movie. It even has a happy ending. So far. The only trouble is, as one film producer replied when it was offered to him, "Who would believe it?"

Well, Mickey Rooney would. Mickey has been believing in himself ever since he first set foot on the stage of a burlesque theater at age fifteen months and knocked the audience dead with a rendition of "Pal of My Cradle Days." Not that Mickey ever slept in anything so mundane as a cradle. A theatrical trunk is more like it.

If ever a person had the right to claim he was born in a trunk, it's Mickey Rooney.

Mickey was born Joe Yule, Jr., in a roominghouse at 57 Willoughby Avenue, in Brooklyn, New York, five minutes before noon on September 23, 1920.

Willoughby Avenue was slightly south of Greenpoint, the tough Brooklyn neighborhood where Mickey's father, Joe Yule, Sr., grew up. Contrary to popular belief, Mickey's father was not Irish. He was born in Edinburgh, Scotland, five years before the turn of the century, and migrated to Brooklyn with his parents when he was still a toddler.

Mickey isn't quite sure how his father spent his formative years in Brooklyn, nor exactly what kindled his interest in show business. However, Bernard Sobel, in his excellent *Pictorial History of Burlesque*, writes that Joe Yule began his "stage career when he was a child performer in old-fashioned melodramas like *The Slaves of New York* and *The Volunteer Organist*." Before becoming a come-

16

dian he worked as a property man at Percy Williams's vaudeville theater in Brooklyn. When America entered World War I in 1917, Yule joined the army. He served as a doughboy in France, where he somehow managed not to get his head blown off in the trenches. Which was a lucky thing, for he was not too tall as it was. After the armistice, Yule got a job as a property man for *Jack Reid's Record-Breakers*, a touring burlesque show that was in Manhattan for a short stand. Burlesque when Joe Yule went to work in it was just a bawdy variety show, consisting of dancing girls, comedy sketches on the order of Abbott and Costello's "Who's on First?" routine, and hawkers in the audience selling candy for a dime a box.

IT WAS WHILE working as a property man for Jack Reid that Joe Yule met Kansas-born Nell Carter, a short, aggressive, and ambitious young lady who was working as an "end pony" in the chorus line. The twelve tallest girls in the chorus would dance in the back row, and the twelve shortest in the front line. The tall ones were called show girls, and the short girls, ponies. Because Nell Carter was about the size of five-foot-three-inch Joe Yule, she was made a pony; and since she danced at the end of the front line, she was an end pony.

According to Mickey Rooney's 1965 published autobiography, *i.e.*, *Jack Reid's Record-Breakers* was nothing like the burlesque of a later period, when all the emphasis was on bare flesh. Mickey writes that he remembers his mother boasting to him, "In *Jack Reid's Record-Breakers* you had to be able to dance. You couldn't just go out and show off your body."

Jack Reid's Record-Breakers was larger than the show in which the inexperienced Nell Carter got started. That show, the one Nell had abandoned Kansas City to join while still in her teens, was called *Bobby Barker's*. Bobby Barker, a small-time comic, commanded a company consisting of himself, his brother who played the piano, and six dancing girls, one of whom was Nell Carter. There were skits, songs, and a four-piece band. The show wasn't important or good enough to obtain work on any of the major circuits, so Nell spent her first couple of years as an entertainer touring the sticks of Oklahoma and Utah for $14 a week. Eventually Nell was able to dance her way out of Indian country and into *Jack Reid's Record-Breakers*.

Because in burlesque and vaudeville one had to travel to find new audiences, Nell Carter still led the life of a vagabond. The only differences were that the cities she played now were larger, her salary was a few bucks higher, and there were sidewalks instead of cow paths and Indian trails around the theaters.

Joe Yule's and Nell Carter's paths crossed backstage shortly after Yule assumed his duties as a property man for the show. Their initial meeting started off in conflict—like a Rock Hudson-Doris Day comedy. A short time before she had to go on stage, Nell sought out the property man and told him she needed a costume. But all Yule managed to dig out of his trunk was an evening dress large enough to fit a much heftier woman.

Nell shook her head. "That's no good. I need a costume I can dance in—not get buried in."

Yule shrugged and said rather indifferently, "Sorry, lady, that's all I can find. Take it or leave it."

She left it, stomping off in a rage.

Yule laughed and said to himself, "Imagine bringing *that* home to Mom."

The spunky Nell grew on Yule, however, and after their first brief and stormy encounter, he started asking her for dates. Nell, whose first impression of Yule hadn't altered much, turned him down with monotonous regularity. However, as a result of their frequent confrontations backstage, some sort of relationship developed.

Perhaps it was Niagara Falls, where their show was playing a split-week, that brought out the romantic in Joe Yule, for it was there, with the spray from the falls hitting him in the face, that he popped the question to Nell Carter. Nell, surprised and pleased, accepted him, and the two were married by a judge in the Rochester courthouse a few days later.

Even in burlesque there were social strata. Jack Reid didn't like the idea of a gorgeous end pony being married to a lowly property man. When he mentioned this to Nell, she told him to mind his own business—he wasn't going to tell her whom she could marry.

Realizing he wasn't getting anywhere with the pugnacious Nell, Reid turned to the new groom and reiterated his feelings to him. "It's too late, we're already married," Yule shouted. "What's the use of talking about it?"

"You're right," agreed Reid. "You're both fired!"

SOON AFTER, NELLIE got a job as an end pony with Pat White's *Gaiety Girls*, and Joe was hired on as the property man.

Pat White not only liked Yule, he thought he had ability as a comedian—especially after Joe dropped a heavy prop on his own

18

foot one night and reacted in an especially comic way. A few days later, the top banana of the show died unexpectedly, and White asked Yule to step in for him.

Since Yule knew the routines, as well as bits he'd seen in other shows, he agreed to substitute. History doesn't record that Yule's first appearance as a burlesque comic was a smash because it was too minor an event to have been reviewed. However, he must have done a creditable job. Pat White made him the company's permanent top banana.

IT WASN'T LONG after Joe made his stage debut that Nellie felt kicking inside her distended belly. Excited as any expectant mother would be, Nellie informed the man responsible for this miracle. Yule couldn't—or at least didn't want to—believe it. To turn him into a believer, Nell placed his hand on her belly so that he, too, could feel the kicks.

Anything but pleased, for it was expensive to have a baby, not to mention it being a helluva inconvenience when you were traveling in vaudeville, Yule felt like kicking, too. Instead, he celebrated by getting drunk.

Because they couldn't afford to give up her salary, Nell remained in the chorus line until August, six weeks before the baby was due. At that point she retired to the rooming house on Willoughby Avenue in Brooklyn to await the baby's arrival. Fortunately, *The Gaiety Girls* was playing Brooklyn at this critical time in their lives, so Joe could continue to do his thing for Pat White without leaving his family in the lurch. But the family's income was virtually cut in half. As a result, there wasn't much money to prepare for the coming baby. Nellie couldn't afford maternity clothes, so she fashioned a maternity skirt out of three large black neckerchiefs given to her by Joe's brother who had recently been discharged from the Navy. Somehow they managed to raise the deposit—$150—for the room in the lying-in hospital. The deal, which they had to agree to in writing, was that they'd have two weeks following the birth of the baby to pay the balance of the hospital bill. If they couldn't pay, the hospital kept custody of the baby until they came up with the necessary cash.

As Mickey tells it, he might have spent months as an infant prisoner of the lying-in hospital if his mother hadn't been frightened by a newspaper article about a hospital where two newborn babies had been accidentally switched.

Scared of getting the wrong baby, Nell exclaimed "I'm not going to have my baby at any hospital. I'll have it at home, so I can be sure I get the right one."

And Joe—whose gift of gab had earned him his top banana spot—fast-talked the hospital into returning his hundred and fifty dollars.

Not long afterward, Joe Yule, Jr., was born in the back room of the brownstone on Willoughby Avenue, three flights up. The baby, a look-alike for Joe Yule, Sr., weighed in at five pounds seven ounces. Nellie was excited and thought Yule would be proud. When they finally located him, he was sitting amidst a pile of clothing at the bottom of a laundry chute, with a bottle of Scotch in his hand, warbling "Glasgow Belongs to Me."

The day after Mickey was born, Pat White's *Gaiety Girls* finished its run in Brooklyn and moved on to Newark, New Jersey. Since the Yule family couldn't afford to have two people out of work, Joe joined the company in Newark, leaving Nell to fend for herself. However, the family finances weren't strong enough to have Nell lying around, convalescing and nursing her infant, very long either. So fourteen days after Mickey's birth, Nell packed up him, herself, and the baby paraphernalia and joined her husband in Newark, where she resumed her duties in the chorus line.

Joe Yule Junior's traveling days had begun.

His cradle during his early infancy was a drawer of a wardrobe trunk in his mother's and father's tiny dressing room, wherever they played. When he outgrew the drawer, his bed became a padded Indian basket Nell had picked up during her travels in Oklahoma.

Yule père wasn't pleased to have a baby in his dressing room. Not only was the place constantly cluttered with bottles, diapers, rattles, bottle warmers, and other such apparatus, but he had to sit with Sonny—their nickname for Joe Junior—when Nell was in front of the footlights. This cut into Yule's favorite backstage sport—chasing the pretty girls in the cast around the wings. Now he was busy warming up Sonny's milk bottles or changing dirty diapers and washing them in the sink, hardly a fitting pastime for the show's top banana.

"You and that kid are going to drive me crazy yet," Yule would complain.

At ten months, Sonny began to walk—mostly around the backstage.

Backstage in a burlesque house—with its colorful costumes,

strange pieces of scenery, funny props, baggy-pants comics, and beautiful but tough-talking show girls—was the only nursery school Sonny ever knew. Who needed a sandbox? Or toys? He played with props and got to try on the leftover costumes. While other kids his age were home in their cribs, Sonny was standing in the wings watching a comic drop his pants or hit a colleague over the head with a turkey bladder, or ogling a lineup of beautiful girls doing the cancan in skimpy costumes. It was training like that that no doubt nurtured Mickey Rooney's great appreciation of statuesque, beautiful women.

By the time he was a year old, Sonny was beginning to talk. One of the first sentences he learned to put together was, "I can do that."

He was ready to make his debut as an entertainer at about a year and a half. One night, he followed the musicians into the orchestra pit. While Sid Gold, a comic, was doing a monologue, Sonny crawled onto the kettledrum and went through the motions of playing. The audience began to snicker at his cute little antics. Sonny responded by drumming a little more energetically. The audience signaled its appreciation by filling the theater with laughter. The orchestra leader had no choice but to go along with Sonny's antics: No one in the theater was paying any attention to Sid Gold's monologue. The comic left the stage and admitted defeat.

Joe Yule was afraid that Pat White would fire him and Nell for not keeping their kid in the dressing room where he belonged. But White was so pleased with the audience's reaction that he decided to make Sonny a regular part of the show. He even spent fifty dollars on a custom-made tuxedo for the pint-sized performer to wear while doing his stuff on the drum.

Ham that he was, even at that age, Sonny wasn't content for long just to sit on a kettledrum in a tuxedo and pantomime drumming. One night, when a tenor was about to sing a maudlin ballad called "Pal of My Cradle Days," Sonny stood up on the drum and yelled out, "Pardon me, sir. I bet I can sing that song too."

That brought down the house and put the tenor in the kind of spot you wouldn't even want your worst enemy in. If he got tough with the kid and told him to get lost, the audience would hate him. And if the kid hung around and sang, no matter how amateurishly, he'd steal the show right out from under him.

"All right, how much do you want to bet?" said the condemned actor, forcing a smile.

With a disarming little shrug, Sonny turned to the orchestra leader for help. Realizing that the audience had been eating up the banter and wanted the contest to proceed, the orchestra leader handed Sonny a five-dollar bill.

Sonny launched into the number with the confidence of a seasoned trouper. And why not? He'd heard the song every night for three months and knew the eighteen lines of music, lyrics, and even the tenor's gestures by heart.

By the time Sonny finished delivering the tear-jerking lyrics on one knee, à la Al Jolson, there wasn't a dry eye in the house. After the sniffling subsided, there were cheers, laughter, and enough applause to convince Sonny that he had won. With a grin, he tore the five-dollar bill in two, gave half to the conductor and pocketed the rest. He'd learned already not to have much regard for money.

"We win," Sonny exclaimed. "How about that?"

The audience roared and clapped their approval again.

It was evident that Joe Yule, Jr., was a born performer. He had everything it took to make it in show business: chutzpah, talent, and a seven-foot-tall competitive instinct.

"Mickey was a natural-born pirate," Joe Yule recalled years later in an interview about his son. "He swiped laugh lines from everybody's act, and when he'd get down on one knee on the runway and sing about his gray-haired mother, you needed a bucket to collect all the tears."

Taking note of Sonny's various talents, Pat White promoted him from the kettledrum to the stage, teaming him with Sid Gold. They did songs, patter, and corny jokes, with Sid feeding Sonny straight lines such as, "Why does a fireman wear red suspenders?"

The jokes weren't very new, even for the early 1920s, but with a toddler like Sonny supplying the punch lines, the audience ate up the act. For a finale, Sonny would break into "Pal o' My Cradle Days," which made even the toughest burlesque audiences reach for their handkerchiefs.

Despite the success of their routines, Sonny found he was getting bored doing the same thing performance after performance. One Ladies' Matinee he decided to do some ad-libbing. Some of the more off-color material that was used at night was toned down during the day, in regard for the sensibilities of the small contingent of naughty ladies who'd sneak off and buy a ticket to the matinee just to see what it was that was titillating their husbands when *they* sneaked off to see the show in the evenings.

Sonny Yule decided to liven things up.

When Sid Gold asked Sonny, "Why does a fireman wear red suspenders?" the tuxedo-clad midget riposted with, "To keep his jockstrap up!"

Sid Gold s jaw dropped to the tops of his two-toned shoes. Pleased with his bon mot, Sonny broke into a wide grin, but there were no smiles in the audience. The silence was deafening.

It's hard to believe that times could ever be so innocent that people would be shocked by the mention of the word jockstrap. But Sonny's parents, standing in the wings, could hardly wait to get their hands on their smart-aleck son. Sonny simply stood his ground, just as if he'd given the straight man the correct punch line, and waited calmly for the next straight line to come out of Sid Gold's mouth.

GOLD: Sonny, why did the man put the puppy in the icebox?
SONNY: Because it was a hot dog!

Sonny's parents and Pat White sighed with relief. The show was back on track again.

Although Sonny learned his lesson about ad-libbing and didn't stray from the script again for a long, long time, he soon found he had another problem to contend with. It seems he was legally underage to be working on the stage, and he and his parents were beginning to be hounded by an organization called the Children's Society, which had been formed to be the watchdog against child-labor-law violators.

For a time, the Yules managed to fool the society by claiming that Sonny was a midget. (What two-year-old would be wearing a fifty-dollar tuxedo?) But eventually the truth came out, and it looked as if Sonny's career was over—until someone in White's organization thought of contacting Alfred E. Smith, then governor of New York State. Smith, who'd always been fond of people in show business, came through by giving Sonny a special work permit.

With the age problem successfully circumvented for the time being, the management felt free to give Sonny an act of his own. Dressed in his forty-inch grown-up tuxedo, Sonny sang a song and told a few childish jokes. The audiences adored every bit of it, and called him back for encores.

As the months passed, Sonny added a few imitations to his act. His favorite takeoff was of the Two Black Crows—a highly successful comedy team of the day named Moran and Mack, who worked in blackface. Sonny had their routines down pat. A sample:

23

MACK:	Understand you're raisin' pigs.
MORAN:	Thas right. We buy pigs for three dollars apiece in the fall, fatten them up all winter, and sell them in the spring for three dollars.
MACK:	You can't make any money that way.
MORAN:	No, but we have the company of the pigs all winter.

One evening while he was doing his Moran and Mack imitation, Sonny, for the first time, forgot a punch line. He froze for a moment, then repeated the feed line. When he still couldn't think of the reply, he twisted his little face into a merry grin and exclaimed, "I guess the record's stuck."

The theater rang with laughter and applause at the youngster's ability to think on his feet. Showman that he was, Sonny repeated the boo-boo and the ad-lib at every performance after that, with consistently successful results. Before long, he had every grown-up actor in the show wishing he'd never been given that special work permit.

2

A PSYCHIATRIST WOULD probably find much to criticize about the way Joe Yule, Jr., was raised. No doubt the doctor'd be able to trace most of Mickey's problems as an adult—financial, marital, and professional—to those impressionable years when he traveled the burlesque circuits with his parents.

Mickey would probably disagree. To him it was an exciting way to grow up. Not only was the basic ham in him satisfied by his nightly stint on the boards, but his parents' travels took him all over the East and Midwest, and even up into southern Canada. Mickey got to learn about the United States firsthand, not out of a dull geography book.

Of course, their life-style on the road was anything but deluxe. The Yules lived in cheap show-business boardinghouses, with mother Nell sometimes having to cook on a Sterno stove in the room. There was a boardinghouse rule against cooking in your room, for using a Sterno stove violated the fire laws. When caught, the three Yules would be tossed out on the street. This happened more often than one would imagine, for when you're cooking Irish stew or corned beef and cabbage in a poorly ventilated boardinghouse, it's impossible to keep the pungent odors from escaping to the other parts of the dwelling. On the train, there was usually money for just one berth, which the three of them were forced to share. If money was scarcer than usual, they'd have to sit up all night in a parlor car. Taking care of the laundry was difficult, too. Nell washed the family's clothes in the room they lived in; they'd dry on a clothesline run from the window. If they were in a seaport town, and there were a lot of gulls in the neighborhood, sometimes the laundry would be dirtier when Nell hauled it in than when she'd hung it out to dry.

Yet Sonny was spoiled. If there was money for just one steak dinner in the dining car, Nell would insist that Sonny—not her husband—get it, while she and Joe would dine on cheese sandwiches. If Sonny tore his suit, they'd splurge for a new one for him. No matter that their clothes were getting threadbare.

One of the rewards for Sonny of traveling on the road was that he was given his own small valise. It was about the size of a doctor's satchel, but Sonny adored it and carried it everywhere—except in a train station. There the Yule family made a strange sight. Yule Senior would be carrying the heavy suitcases, and Nell would be holding all of Sonny's toys. But, though they could ill afford it, Nell acquiesced to Sonny's request that a porter carry his valise, while he walked ahead of the entourage like the heir apparent.

When Sonny was about four years old, his parents decided to separate. Yule didn't enjoy the role of a family man. As fond as he was of Sonny, being the head of a household cut into his carousing and woman chasing. By the same token, Nell was discovering that it took too much of her energy to be both an end pony and a good mother. It was making her ill, and a doctor advised her to quit the show.

They agreed to go their separate ways for a while. Yule took a job in a stock company in Chicago, and Nell packed up her things and Sonny and went to live with her sister in Kansas City.

There were a number of reconciliations and separations before the Yules divided up the forty dollars they had, kissed each other goodbye for old times sake, and filed for a divorce.

It would be a long time before Sonny would see his father again.

IN KANSAS CITY Sonny was exposed to normal childhood for the first time—normal, that is, except that he didn't have a father. He got to live in a house with a yard and a kitchen, and to play games with the neighborhood children. And it was no longer necessary to cook and do the washing in the bedroom.

Sonny's costumes were put carefully away, along with the Sterno. At four years old, Sonny was washed up in show business, a has-been with nothing to look forward to but kindergarten.

Since she couldn't mooch off her sister forever, Nell had to think of a way to make some money. After a while, she and a friend named Myrtle Sutherland opened a restaurant that featured home-cooked chicken and hot biscuits. The restaurant was a moderate success. Not because Nell was such a good cook, but because the price was right. At her restaurant, you could get a whole chicken dinner, including a glass of beer, for twenty-five cents.

But the smell of fried chicken with country gravy couldn't compare with the smell of greasepaint. Both Nell and Sonny missed show business more than they would admit to anyone but each other—Sonny probably more than Nell, for at least she was busy frying chicken and baking biscuits. *He* was doing nothing, except playing hide-and-seek with a bunch of kids.

To fill the void of civilian life, Nell, instead of putting Sonny to sleep with bedtime stories, read aloud to him from *Variety*. One evening she read that a West Coast movie producer named Hal Roach was looking for child actors for the *Our Gang* series. That was the break Nell had been waiting for. She immediately buttonholed her partner in the restaurant and showed her the item in *Variety*. Nell said she had a hunch that Sonny might make it big in the movies. "He's a natural."

Myrtle didn't disagree, so the next day they closed the restaurant, packed up all the leftover fried chicken, bought a used car with a torn convertible top, and hit the road for Hollywood.

It was the same wild territory Nell had covered when she was dancing with *Bobby Barker's Gaieties*, so she was familiar with the roads as well as the dangers. However, after paying for the car and gas, there was no money left for hotels or boardinghouses. As a result, throughout their three-and-a-half-week trip, they cooked on an open fire under the stars and slept in a tent. The car broke down several times, but somehow Nell managed to find a mechanic to repair it for a price.

By the time they arrived in Hollywood they had twenty-five dollars left. Nell found a cheap hotel in the cheapest section of Hollywood and hoped that Hal Roach would put Sonny to work immediately.

However, it was mid-December when they arrived, and nobody did any work during the Christmas season. Consequently, it was after the first of the year before the persistent Nell wangled an interview for Sonny with one of Hal Roach's assistants.

The assistant was impressed and offered to hire Sonny for five dollars a day. Nell was experienced enough in show business to know that you never took the first offer. Especially five dollars a day! That was an insulting price.

She told the man that her Sonny was worth three times that and rattled off his burlesque and vaudeville credits.

The assistant wasn't impressed. It was five dollars a day, take it or leave it. Nell didn't take it, telling the man that she didn't need charity, she could always go back to work as an end pony. She figured she could bluff him into giving Sonny more. But the bluff didn't work. The assistant turned around and went back into his office, slamming the door loudly behind him.

For a time Nell found work in a chorus line in the city of Oakland for twenty-five dollars a week. Two other aspiring stars in the chorus were Joan Blondell and Glenda Farrell. Miffed that Nell had turned down the Roach offer, Sonny pointed out to his mother that twenty-five dollars a week was less than he would have been earning at five bucks a day. But Nell didn't need criticism from a four-year-old smarty. So she'd made a mistake.

The Oakland job turned out to be an even worse mistake. Not only wasn't the money as good, but after a few weeks she was let go. There was nothing wrong with her dancing, the manager told her, but he was under pressure from the chamber of commerce to hire only local talent.

So Nell and Sonny retreated to Kansas City again, to regroup their forces. The setback lasted only long enough for Nell to become friendly with George Christman, a man who managed a theater at Twelfth and Walnut. Because his theater was failing, Christman decided there wasn't much of a future in Kansas City, unless you ran a meat-packing house. So one day he informed Nell that he was going to take a group of people from the theater to Hollywood—where the big money was. Actors like Charlie Chaplin and Mary Pickford and Doug Fairbanks lived in huge mansions with solid-gold bathroom fixtures, and swimming pools, and drove Rolls-Royces.

Christman asked Nell to join his expedition, which consisted of two cars and eleven people. Already bored with Kansas City, Nell jumped at the chance to take another crack at Hollywood.

Ten days later, after an exhausting automobile trip in which the members of the caravan slept under the heavens, Nell was back in Hollywood, determined to make a star of her talented Sonny. In her purse was her entire life's savings—less than a hundred dollars—which would have to last them until they got a break in movies.

They moved into a cheap hotel, and the next morning started to make the rounds of the studio casting offices and talent agencies. One look at Sonny and the casting directors would blow sky-high.

"Another kid?! Where's the dog?"

Nell was puzzled by the cold reception until she finally figured out that there were more kids and German shepherds in Southern California in the late twenties than there were orange trees—all bent on following in the steps of either Jackie Coogan or Rin-Tin-Tin.

Weeks passed, and the studio gates still did not open for Nell and her son. Patiently, day after bright day, Sonny and Nell continued to make the rounds, but there seemed to be no studio willing to hire this yellow-haired, freckle-faced moppet, or his mother. Hollywood was filled with talented, good-looking boys and girls, and with young women, like Nell, who'd been dancers on the stage, all hoping for the opportunity that would shoot them into the limelight. No one remembered Baby Sonny Yule or Nell Carter of questionable vaudeville fame.

Gradually, Nell's small hoard of money dwindled away. Rather than admit failure and return to frying chickens in Kansas City, Nell opted for getting a job. According to the "help wanted" section of the *Los Angeles Times,* the owners of a third-rate bungalow court were looking for a "hard-working, earnest and competent woman, resident manager." Nell knew nothing about running a bungalow court, but neither did the owners. She talked her way into the job, which paid no salary, but gave Sonny and her a roof over their heads. To get her hands on some meal and clothes money, Nell took a daytime job as a telephone operator with the Bell Telephone Company.

In her off hours, Nell continued to make the rounds of the casting offices with Sonny. On Sunday afternoons, when the studios were closed, Nell and Sonny would hop on a bus and go for long rides out to Beverly Hills, which was blossoming into a glittering oasis of the filthy rich.

As the two of them gazed in awe at the huge mansions, Joe Junior promised Nell that someday he'd buy her a house just like them and a great big car, "where you sit inside and the chauffeur sits outside and gets rained on."

Finally, when Sonny had reached the ripe old age of five-and-a-half, he got a break. Nell was tipped off that a man named Will Morrissey, a small-time entrepreneur, was planning to produce a small musical revue at the Orange Grove Theater in Los Angeles, and that he was auditioning children for one of the parts. Although he wanted "experienced" children, Nell was able to wangle a tryout for her little performer.

Sonny made the rest of the kids at the tryout look like the amateurs they were. Dressed in a white sailor suit, he sang "Sweet Rosie O'Grady" in a clear, sweet voice, and repeated several of his old vaudeville routines, including his imitation of the Two Black Crows.

Morrissey loved what he did and signed Sonny for a featured spot in the revue at $50 a week.

At the opening, Sonny was virtually the only one in the cast not

29

bothered by first-night jitters. Just before the overture he went around assuring the various adult performers in the show that they would be great and that there wasn't a thing in the world to be nervous about. When he heard his cue, he strutted out on the stage and went into his first number with the poise and sureness of a veteran actor. Nell, standing anxiously in the wings, beamed as the enthusiastic audience burst into applause at the conclusion of his number and demanded an encore.

When Sonny's performance was singled out by the newspaper reviewers the next morning as being especially entertaining ("Marvelous for a five-year-old," Edwin Schallert of the *Los Angeles Times* wrote), Nell was certain Sonny had taken his first important step on his way to stardom. She felt that after a few weeks of exposure in Will Morrissey's hit review, every studio in town would be after Sonny. Besides the morale boost, it was comforting to have a steady income again.

Unfortunately, the halcyon period lasted only a few weeks—just long enough for the child labor authorities to get wind of the fact that a youngster not yet six years old was working on the boards every night. This time there was no pretending Sonny was a midget, or applying for a special permit. Their judgment that the work would be injurious to his health was final. Regretfully, Sonny bid a temporary adieu to his career on the musical comedy stage.

More weeks of insecurity and of vainly making the rounds of the casting offices. Then, just when life looked bleakest, Nell received a call from a talent scout at Fox Studios. He'd been in the audience one night when Sonny was appearing in Morrissey's revue and, impressed by Sonny's talent and looks, had jotted down Sonny's name—Joe Yule, Jr.—and address in his notebook for future reference. Now the future had arrived: He had a part for a boy just like Sonny in a movie called *Not to Be Trusted*.

"Would you be interested in putting your boy in pictures?" the scout asked.

Nell told the man that she and Sonny would be at his office within the hour. She dragged Sonny off the vacant lot next door, where he'd been playing football with a group of friends, cleaned the mud off his face, dressed him in his best clothes, and took a bus to Fox, which wasn't far from where Nell and Sonny lived.

A little while later, Sonny bounded into the casting director's office at Fox Studios and did his shtick for him, with Nell watching nervously from the sidelines. The casting director was as impressed with Sonny's talent as the scout had been. Sonny nailed down the part of a midget in *Not to Be Trusted*.

So on a morning in 1926, Sonny, dressed in a miniature business suit and tiny derby, and smoking a chocolate cigar, made his first appearance before a movie camera. Nell was nervous, but Sonny was as cool as an Eskimo Pie. What was there to worry about? There were no lines to be learned, for it was a silent picture. All he had to do was listen to the director as the camera rolled. Sonny's only difficulty was with the chocolate cigar. One minute it was in his mouth, the next minute it was gone. Could Sonny help it if the cigar tasted so good it melted in his mouth?

Sonny received two hundred dollars for his first film role, which he had stepped into as easily as he had into vaudeville when he was a toddler.

With the additional money and the prospect of more movie roles to come, Nell moved out of the bungalow court and into a small house on Burns Street, near a public school in a modest Hollywood neighborhood. Because Sonny was six now, she enrolled him in the first grade—the beginning of a school life destined to be filled with constant interruptions.

The first interruption came when Sonny was signed by Warner Bros. to play another midget in a picture called *Orchids and Ermine*. As in his first movie role, Sonny was expected to smoke a cigar. Because of the problems he'd encountered with the chocolate stogie, this time Sonny was given a rubber one to chew on. A different cigar, a different problem. One day, when Sonny was puffing vigorously on the rubber stogie during a take, one of his baby incisors fell out. The director, Al Santell, looked in dismay at the tiny tooth in Sonny's chubby hand and the yawning gap in his small mouth, and yelled "Cut!"

"What the hell kind of a forty-year-old are you with your baby teeth coming out?" he ranted at Sonny.

This was a real crisis. The picture was half-finished shooting, and in all the other scenes Sonny had a complete set of teeth. The shots would have to match. And unfortunately, they were shooting on location that day—miles from a dentist.

"So what are you going to do, Mrs. Yule?" the director asked.

"No problem," she said, as she pulled a piece of gum from her own mouth, embedded the tooth in it, then stuck the gum and tooth into the hole in Sonny's smile. Cast, crew, and director breathed a communal sigh of relief.

In compliance with the law, Nell had to be on the set every day. Another section of the child labor law stipulated that minor actors be given adequate schooling by the studio. So every day, between takes, Sonny would be tutored by the studio schoolmarm.

Although Sonny performed satisfactorily in *Orchids and Ermine*, the film did not make motion-picture history, nor a star out of Joe Yule, Jr. (How many midget roles were there?)

After he picked up his last paycheck, Sonny returned to his neighborhood public school, while Nell resumed her work at the Bell Telephone Company.

Shortly after Sonny was six, a talent scout tipped off Nell that Darmour Studios was looking for a "tough kid" to play Mickey McGuire, a character out of the then-famous newspaper comic strip "Toonerville Trolley" by Fontaine Fox. The scout thought that Sonny was sufficiently tough and homely to qualify for the role.

Nell agreed, and when Sonny came home from school that afternoon, more eager to play with the kids than study, she was waiting for him with several funny papers containing the "Toonerville Trolley" strip. "We've got some studying to do," she told Sonny, pulling him down next to her on the worn couch and showing him the comic and the character she hoped he would get to play. For the rest of the day, Nell read and reread the strip to Sonny while he sat patiently by her side, absorbing every detail. By bedtime, Sonny knew the Mickey McGuire character as well as his own—because it was so much like his own.

The following morning, Nell and Sonny arrived early at Darmour Studios, only to find the outer office already jammed with other mothers and boys, all eagerly waiting their turn to be tested for Mickey McGuire. After studying the competition, Nell felt her heart sink. Not that she wasn't confident of Sonny's ability, but she suddenly realized that all the other boys had dark hair—just like Mickey McGuire did in the comic strip. For a long time, she stared with concern at towheaded Sonny. Did she dare leave him a blond for the test and hope that the studio moguls had the imagination to visualize him as a brunet?

In a moment of great decision, she jumped up from her seat, grasped Sonny's hand and dragged him out of the office and down to the shoe-shine stand on the studio lot, where she explained her plight to the bootblack.

When Sonny returned to the audition, he was no longer a blond. Patiently, Sonny and Nell waited for their turn to be tested. One by one the other boys and their mothers were called into the inner office. Each time, Nell said a silent prayer putting the hex on the unsuspecting moppet. Someone upstairs must have been listening. Each boy came out, having failed to satisfy Darmour and Al Herman, the director, in the preliminary interview.

Nell was heartsick, not out of compassion for the losers, but because Sonny might be rejected, too. She said another silent prayer.

Finally, late in the afternoon, Sonny was summoned. If Nell entered the room with trepidation, Sonny was bursting with his usual confidence. Al Herman seemed to be impressed with the freckle-faced youngster from the first and, after a short interview, led him and Nell to a stage where there was a brightly lit barnyard setting. Quickly, Herman explained to Sonny the action of the test scene. Sonny nodded his dark-thatched head.

When Herman called, "Camera!" Sonny sneaked around the corner of the make-believe barn, his small impish face wrinkled in a rough, tough scowl. Then he sat down on a box and, crossing his short legs, pulled a rubber cigar out of his pocket and started to chew on it, like an inveterate smoker.

"Good!" Herman exclaimed, after the camera had stopped rolling. "Let's try him again in costume, tomorrow."

Early the next morning, Sonny was outfitted in the derby, checkered shirt, and ragged trousers associated with the Mickey McGuire character. He returned to the stage and repeated the scene of the previous day, swaggering, scowling, and chewing on his rubber stogie with a confidence and toughness that *were* Mickey McGuire.

The next morning, when Darmour and Al Herman viewed Sonny's screen test, they knew they had the Mickey McGuire they'd hunted high and low for, the one that millions of followers of the comic strip would instantly recognize and fall in love with. Hardly able to contain their joy, they phoned Nell and asked her to bring her son back to the studio. Out came the shoe polish.

"Your boy was great in the test," Al Herman said.

"Yeah, we want to sign him to a five-year contract," Darmour said.

"How much will it pay?" Nell asked, playing her hard-to-get scene.

"Fifty bucks a week," Darmour said.

Nell wisely decided this was too important to handle herself. She sent for Mickey's agent, Harry Weber, who, after some brief haggling, got the offer raised to two hundred fifty dollars per short.

"Of course, there's one thing," Herman said, "before we can actually finalize a deal."

Nell looked worried. "What's that?"

33

"Sonny'll have to have his hair dyed black," Herman grinned. "That shoe polish isn't going to fool anyone."

3

THE FIRST MICKEY McGuire two-reeler reached Main Street USA in 1926; the last in 1932—fifty shorts in all. Al Herman ground them out at the approximate rate of thirteen a year. The first eight were silent, the rest talkies; though even in the latter, the comedy bits relied mostly on funny chases and sight gags, not the spoken word.

Still, making the transition from silent to sound pictures posed no particular problem for a kid who'd been talking on the stage since he was eleven months old. Mickey had always been rather glib for his age—whatever his age—and what is known in show business as a "quick study," able to take a page of dialogue, glance at it for a few seconds, and then spew it out in a scene with very few variations from the printed text. He survived a schedule that would have given a nervous breakdown to the average, well-adjusted, grown-up actor (if such an animal exists). What with rehearsals, wardrobe, and makeup tests, acting in the shorts, and going to school on the set between takes, he was lucky if he had a minute of the day to himself.

During his McGuire years, Mickey's education was divided between public school and the studio classroom, which he attended whenever he was making a picture. Mickey wasn't much of a scholar, either place—too restless to sit with his nose in a book very long. He didn't mind geography and history, but math wasn't for him—which became obvious in later years from the way he handled his finances.

In addition to the fact that Mickey was too restless a personality to be happy within the confines of the average public schoolroom, he had a language problem. He'couldn't help using four-letter words. Not only around the other kids, but his teacher as well. During his short career in public school, he had to be warned constantly to watch his language or face expulsion. Mickey had picked up some pretty colorful words and phrases during his training in the burlesque houses. They came so naturally to his tongue that half the time he wasn't even aware he was using unacceptable language.

But after he started working in the McGuire series, he was encouraged by his employers to talk his very worst. "The tougher he gets to be in real life," Larry Darmour told the surprised Nell, "the easier it'll be for him to play Mickey McGuire."

In the tug-of-war over who should have custody of the movie moppet's soul, the tough Mickey emerged victorious over the well-behaved one. To make the transformation thorough, Larry Darmour insisted that Nell Carter have her son's name changed legally from Joe Yule, Jr., to Mickey McGuire. No big hassle as far as Mickey and his Mom were concerned. "After the first few Mickey McGuire pictures had been released, everybody called me Mickey, anyway," Rooney recalled after he became famous. "Even Mom gradually stopped calling me Sonny and began to call me Mickey. And so did my friends and the teachers at school."

The evolution of his name from Joe Yule, Jr., to Mickey McGuire seemed so natural that after he assumed the new name, Nell changed her's to Nell McGuire. "I thought it might look better if I had the same name as my son," Nell told a friend.

It might have looked better to Nell, but it didn't sit too well with Fontaine Fox, the creator of "Toonerville Trolley." In a court action, Fontaine Fox claimed that the name of Mickey McGuire belonged to him, and that the only reason the studio changed Joe Yule, Jr., to Mickey McGuire was to avoid paying him his royalty of a thousand dollars per short that they had agreed to contractually when they started producing the two-reelers.*

Fontaine Fox may have had a point, for it wasn't long after the name change that his thousand-dollar checks stopped arriving in the mail. As soon as Fox was sure that the delay in receiving his royalty checks had nothing to do with the normal incompetence of the U.S.

---

*Information in Mickey's autobiography, *i.e.*, leads one to believe that Darmour changed the youngster's name to McGuire to beat Fontaine Fox out of his royalties. The theory behind such a tack would be that if Rooney's name were legally Mickey McGuire, Darmour could claim the shorts were based on the real kid, and not the McGuire of the cartoon strip.

Mail, the irate cartoonist brought suit against Darmour Studios, Larry Darmour, Al Herman, and Joe Yule, Jr., for purloining his name.

As suits are wont to do, this one dragged on—in fact, a couple of years passed without either side getting a definitive judgment. Meanwhile, Mickey continued to lead the double life of reluctant student and family breadwinner, appearing in a new Mickey McGuire comedy every three weeks.

Oddly enough, all that exposure on the nation's movie screens didn't propel Mickey into the kind of instant stardom that Jackie Coogan enjoyed after appearing in *The Kid* with Charlie Chaplin, or Shirley Temple following *Little Miss Marker*. The bubble-gum set who attended the kiddie matinees knew Mickey, and he was something of a hero to them, but his recognizability was nothing compared with the fame he was to enjoy later as Andy Hardy.

However, the weekly paycheck that Mickey brought home enabled him and Nell to live very comfortably in a middle-class section of Hollywood, without having to worry about coming up with the rent money the first of every month. A steady income also made it possible for Nell to pull Mickey out of public elementary school and enroll him in Ma Lawlor's professional school. Ma Lawlor's was a school for working children, certified to teach all grades from first through twelfth. Ma Lawlor herself was a tall, no-nonsense school-teacher type who wore her hair in a severe bun, and had very conservative ways. At the same time, she was aware of the needs of working children, and kept the curriculum relatively light and manageable.

Though Ma Lawlor will never be credited for turning Mickey into Phi Beta Kappa material, he'll always be grateful to her school for the opportunity it gave him to meet Frances Gumm, who was also enrolled there. (After Frances, the youngest of the Singing Gumm Sisters, made her film debut with Deanna Durbin in a musical short named *Every Sunday* in 1936, MGM signed her and changed her name to Judy Garland.) Other students at Ma Lawlor's with whom Mickey formed lasting friendships were Dick Quine, who later became an important film director; and Sidney Miller, the parrot-beaked kid from Brooklyn who had been brought out to the Coast by Warner Bros. in 1931 to play the part of Sam in *Penrod and Sam*, the Booth Tarkington classic. When Miller had time off, Warners would let him go over to Darmour Studios and do the Mickey McGuire comedies.

"Mickey was starring in them, of course, and I was just a support-

37

ing player," Miller remembers. "But I got to know Mickey very well. From that a friendship developed that's lasted ever since. Also a professional relationship. I was with him in all those great Garland and Rooney musicals. I was with him in *Boys Town,* and we've even written some songs together—one that wound up on the 'Hit Parade.'[*]

"My first impression of Mickey was that he was very tough—just like the kid he was playing—but really talented. He did his lines well, always knew them, and he was one of the few actors I've ever known who could cry on cue without any artificial means. He had tremendous concentration when he was in front of the camera. If you didn't know anything else about Mickey, you could sense that he was going to be a big star someday.

"His mother was always on the set with him, just as my mother was. Nell wanted to make sure that Mickey was up there in front, doing what he was supposed to be doing—stealing the scenes from the older actors. Her boy was the best. He got his drive from her. Not that he needed to be pushed. It was built in."

Mickey thrived on his heavy work load. His appetite was excellent, his health perfect, and his ego overbearing. Nothing fazed him; nothing worried him, except that he was not growing much. Despite his mother's nourishing meals, at twelve he was four inches shorter than the average boy of eight. He tried all sorts of stretching exercises to induce growth. He slept on a hard bed, and he answered scores and scores of advertisements that guaranteed "at least an inch per month." But the measuring tape refused to be impressed. He made up in toughness what he lacked in height. He could—and did—lick a great many boys who topped him by a head. But his pride was suffering. Moreover, he was beginning to resent the various cracks made about his stature by the smart alecks at the studio, including Al Herman who persisted in calling him "Shorty" or "Runt." He felt like quitting and taking his talent somewhere else.

But that turned out to be unnecessary.

While Mickey was burning under the collar, the fickle public, which only yesterday was clamoring for more Mickey McGuire comedies, stopped coming to see him. Exhibitors reported that men, women, and even children were growing tired of the tough boy in the derby hat, who, though he was short for his age, was getting too large to be "cute," like the Mickey McGuire of old. The

---

[*]Mickey is now a member of the American Society of Composers, Authors, and Publishers (ASCAP), with a half-dozen songs to his credit.

grosses of the comedies dropped with a resounding thud, and the losses to the studio mounted. Theater owners squawked and refused to run any more of the comedies; the bankers shuddered; and Larry Darmour began looking around for another property.

So ended Joe Yule, Jr.'s second career.

One morning, the unsuspecting Nell Carter McGuire received a legal letter from Larry Darmour's attorneys, Loeb and Loeb. Stripped of its legal verbiage, it said two things: The services of Mickey McGuire, Esq., were no longer required; and, the very name of Mickey McGuire would have to be returned to its copyright owner, Fontaine Fox. It seemed that Fox had finally emerged victorious in the battle of who owned the name of Mickey McGuire.

There was nothing that Nell could do about the demise of the Mickey McGuire series. That was show business. But fighting Irish-woman that she was, she refused to take the loss of the Mickey McGuire name lying down—at least the entire name. She conceded that Loeb and Loeb might have a point about "Mickey McGuire" not belonging to her son, but insisted that there was no way anyone could copyright the first name, Mickey. The attorneys acquiesced, and Joe Yule, Jr., finally had a first name that he liked and could call his own.

Mickey was still out of work, and not exactly a hot property in fickle Tinseltown. Six years before, he had been turned down by the casting offices because he was just another kid. Now he was being given the brush because he was "too well known"—as Mickey McGuire, of whom the public was tired.

Nell decided to let Mickey's hair grow out to its natural color. With a new look, he might fool people into thinking he was someone else, and get another movie role. Especially if he'd grow a little.

In the meantime, Mickey was offered a vaudeville contract, which he and his mother jumped at. He opened in Chicago in an updated rehash of his baby performance in vaudeville and in the *Will Morrissey Revue* in Hollywood. He sang a few songs, told a few old jokes, and did imitations of Clark Gable, Spencer Tracy, and Mae West—doing her "Come up and see me" routine in a floor-length evening gown, wide-brimmed hat, boa, and a string of phony pearls around his neck.

In spite of the fact that he was performing better than he had as a child prodigy, audiences were dissatisfied. They'd bought tickets expecting to see their old friend Mickey McGuire from the two-reelers in the flesh, not a tired vaudeville act reminiscent of Major Bowes. Fear of action by Loeb and Loeb prevented Mickey from

39

delivering what the audiences wanted—until he thought of a way to capitalize on the name and still remain within the law. Each night he would step to the footlights and explain to his "friends" in the audience that while he had no legal right to call himself Mickey McGuire any longer, "still and all, I am Mickey McGuire." Then he'd go into a bit from one of the comedy shorts.

The down-home folks roared at Mickey's clever way of skirting the law, and after that were so much on his side that he was able to get away with his songs, dances, and imitations. No matter how corny, they laughed and applauded for more. Playing Mickey McGuire to Chicago and other Midwestern cities, Mickey started to pack them in.

When Fontaine Fox got wind of how Mickey was again capitalizing on his copyrighted character, his lawyers caught up with Mickey and forced him to eliminate the Mickey McGuire bit from his act.

Audiences began staying away. The act was canceled. The fact that 1932 was one of the worst years of the Great Depression, and most vaudeville acts weren't doing business, was no great consolation. The bottom line was that Mickey was out of work again.

Saddened and chastened, the two old troupers retreated to Hollywood. A producer at Universal Studios needed a child actor for a sound film he was making called *Information Kid*. It wasn't a large or particularly demanding role, but one thing that was important, according to the studio, was that the actor who played it not be Mickey McGuire of two-reeler fame. The part wouldn't be believable with Mickey McGuire in it.

With his hair yellow, Mickey was no longer a Mickey McGuire look-alike, and the producer wanted him for the part. But there was still the matter of the name. The publicity man on the picture didn't like the sound of Joe Yule, Jr., and Mickey Yule wasn't much of an improvement. The rhythm was wrong. He liked "Mickey," but what sounded good with it? Preferably something with a Y on the end of it.

After discarding several names suggested by the publicity man, including "Maloney," "Downey," and even "Looney," Nell remembered a friend in vaudeville, Pat Rooney. Would Rooney do?

"Not bad, lady," the publicity man said. "Let me run it by my bosses and see how they like it."

Returning a few minutes later, with a pleased expression, the publicity man said, "Well, kid, that's your new name—Mickey Rooney."

Over the next year and a half, Mickey Rooney appeared in several forgettable films at Universal—a studio that at the time more or less specialized in churning out "B" pictures for the second half of double bills—such as the ones Mickey appeared in: *Fast Companions, The Big Cage, Beloved, I Like It That Way, Lost Jungle* (a serial), and *My Pal the King*, a Western fantasy starring the cowboy superstar, Tom Mix.

The New York Times of October 4, 1932, gave the Mix picture a favorable review, and for the first time "Mickey Rooney" was mentioned in the theatrical section of a major daily newspaper. "Little Mickey Rooney appears as Charles and he does quite well," was the entire mention. Hardly a rave, but, as the show business cliché goes, at least they spelled his name right.

In 1933, he had small roles in *Broadway to Hollywood* and *The Chief*, two MGM cheapies. But by the time Mickey was thirteen and a half, the offers stopped coming in. Casting directors considered him just another kid actor. They were a dime a dozen in Hollywood.

While he was waiting for his agent, Harry Weber, to call, Mickey divided his time between Ma Lawlor's and improving his proficiency as an athlete. He spent his idle hours swimming, boxing, bowling, and playing tennis and Ping-Pong. He may not have been tall, but he was good at all these sports—especially tennis and Ping-Pong.

It was Ping-Pong, of all things, that finally rescued him from obscurity. Mickey was playing in a Ping-Pong tournament at the Ambassador Hotel in Los Angeles one Sunday afternoon. The affair had been staged as part of a campaign to raise funds for unemployed screen actors. David O. Selznick, who was producing independently under the MGM banner and who was Louis B. Mayer's son-in-law, agreed to act as referee.

The moment he spotted Selznick in the audience, Mickey braced himself for an all-out effort to get himself noticed. It took Selznick just a few seconds to realize that the short towheaded boy playing such a splendid game of Ping-Pong in the finals of the tournament was the most magnetic and refreshing personality he'd seen among the younger generation in a long time. Turning to Irene, his wife, Selznick exclaimed, "Take a look at that Rooney kid! He's a better showman than most of our wooden-faced stars at the studio."

He urged his wife to take note of Mickey's pantomime and to listen to some of his ad-lib remarks. Mickey's pantomime, while not quite on a par with Chaplin's or Keaton's, had the spectators in hysterics. Every time he missed an easy shot, his face took on the melancholy expression of an actor watching one of his peers win an

Oscar. If Mickey made an impossible get, he shrugged his shoulders and dismissed the salvo of applause with the nonchalance of a Bill Tilden winning his seventh U.S. Tennis championship. Mickey's patter was equally amazing. He never stopped talking and making jokes, which probably contributed as much to his victory in the finals as his strokes.

Selznick could hardly sleep that night. The more he thought of Rooney's performance, the more excited he became. "Metro's got to sign that kid before someone else grabs him," he told his wife at the breakfast table the following morning. When he arrived at MGM, Selznick went straight to his father-in-law's office and announced, "L.B., I've found a gold mine—the most sensational kid I've ever seen. He had the audience at the Ambassador in stitches yesterday. You have to sign him."

"What's his name?" Mayer asked.

"Mickey Rooney. He used to play in the Mickey McGuire pictures."

"Oh, him." Mayer's face turned sourer than usual. "David, you ought to have your head examined. Mickey McGuire's a has-been."

Selznick exploded and spent the rest of the day composing one of his famous memos. It consumed eleven single-spaced pages and explained in minute detail sixty-odd reasons why Mickey Rooney should be signed by MGM.

As passionate as Selznick's memo was, it didn't impress the MGM brass. Eddie Mannix, the burly, tough-talking head of production, said, "Look, David, if that McGuire kid is as terrific as you claim, why should you try to unload him on us? Why don't you put him in one of your own pictures?"

"Okay. I will," Selznick exclaimed. "I'll put him in my new Gable picture."

"There's no part for him in there," Mayer pointed out.

Mayer was right. The Clark Gable vehicle on Selznick's schedule was called *Manhattan Melodrama*. It dealt with the lives, loves, and bloody end of a gangster-gambler. There was no part in the script for a child. But Selznick was undeterred by a minor detail like that. He was so high on his discovery that he called in his writers and ordered them to create a part for Mickey—Clark Gable as a young boy.

Mayer et al thought Selznick was crazy to slow down a perfectly good, fast-moving script with a sequence of the gambler as a child, which was probably the last thing a fan of gangster films wanted to see.

Initially, Mayer seemed to be right.

When *Manhattan Melodrama* was released, people weren't knocking down the turnstiles to get in to see it. The reviews of the film in both *Variety* and *The New York Times* of May 5, 1934, were anything but ecstatic. The *Times* dismissed the picture as a "routine melodrama," and to Nell's and her son's disappointment, there was no mention in the review at all of Mickey Rooney's contribution.

Obviously not an Academy Award contender, *Manhattan Melodrama* probably would have achieved only a modest degree of success, despite King Gable's drawing power, had it not been for an event that even Selznick could not have anticipated. Two months after its New York premiere, on a hot, sweltering night, John Dillinger, America's Public Enemy Number One, was shot dead coming out of a second-rate motion picture theater in Chicago. The picture he'd just seen was *Manhattan Melodrama*.

Dillinger's death helped America discover the fourteen-year-old Brooklyn boy by the name of Mickey Rooney. The following night, and for many nights to come, motion picture theaters from Maine to California were flooded with customers who came to take a look at the picture that John Dillinger had seen in his last two hours on earth—and went home having seen a fourteen-year-old named Mickey Rooney.

One month later, Mickey signed (cosigned, actually, with his mother, Nell) a long-term contract with MGM, at a starting salary of $150 a week. If his option was picked up at the end of six months, he'd be paid $200 a week until the end of the year. After that, the options would be on a yearly basis, beginning with $300 a week, all the way to $1,000 a week by 1941, if all the options were exercised. As in most long-term studio contracts of that era, he'd be guaranteed forty weeks' employment a year, and MGM had the right to loan Mickey out to other studios without his consent.

Although that was good money for a fourteen-year-old in this country's worst depression, it wouldn't be very long before Mickey's agent, Harry Weber, would realize that MGM had got the better of the deal by far.

4

ALTHOUGH HIS DIMINUTIVE face and figure had been seen fleet-ingly by millions of picturegoers in *Manhattan Melodrama*, as well as in three other MGM releases that year—*Chained, Hide-Out,* and *Death on a Diamond*—Mickey Rooney might never have separated himself from the rest of the moppet scene-stealers had it not been for the terrifying events that were beginning to unfold in Nazi Germany in the thirties. Because of Hitler's persecution of the Jews, Max Reinhardt, the Austrian stage director who was founder of the Salzburg Festival and who was celebrated for having directed such spectacles as *Faust, Oedipus Rex, The Miracle,* and *A Midsummer Night's Dream,* in both Europe and New York City, was forced to seek permanent asylum in the United States in the summer of 1934.

Aside from Hitler, what brought Reinhardt to Hollywood was an invitation from the Southern California Chamber of Commerce to put on a production of *A Midsummer Night's Dream* at the Holly-wood Bowl. The $125,000 extravaganza was to be underwritten by Hollywood's film moguls who had yielded to the pressure of Harry Chandler, publisher of the *Los Angeles Times,* to unzip their pock-etbooks to bring some culture to Southern California.

Reinhardt was no more eager to stage another production of the Shakespeare classic than the studio moguls were to risk their money. What he was interested in was becoming a film director, but none of the studio bosses had confidence in his ability to make the crossover from stage to films. Reinhardt hoped that if the production was brilliant and successful enough, one of the studios might give him a job in films. Consequently, he decided to put his all into the production and give it irresistible box-office draw by casting it with the biggest names in Hollywood.

ACCORDING TO REINHARDT's son, Gottfried, who had arrived in Hollywood ahead of his father to make advance arrangements, he received a telegram from Max urging him to get the following cast: Charlie Chaplin for Bottom, Greta Garbo for Titania, Clark Gable for Demetrius, Garry Cooper for Lysander, John Barrymore for Oberon, W. C. Fields for Thisbe, Wallace Beery for Lion, Walter Huston for Theseus, Joan Crawford for Hermia, Myrna Loy for Helena, and Fred Astaire for Puck. It was obvious that Reinhardt didn't know much about movie stars.

None of these people was available, or at any rate interested in working under the stars for a tenth of his or her accustomed salary. But for those who weren't so well-known, there was a great deal to be gained from being connected with a Reinhardt production. So when the announcement hit the trades, talent agencies, and various casting offices that Reinhardt was searching for actors to play in *A Midsummer Night's Dream* at the renowned Hollywood Bowl and that he'd be holding open auditions for all the parts, actors and actresses dropped their tennis rackets, picked up their Shakespeare anthologies, and started practicing their elocution.

Mickey wasn't doing anything spectacular at MGM that summer. He'd just finished a couple of loan-out chores for Universal and Columbia, where he'd made nonmonumental appearances in *Half a Winner* and *Blind Date*, respectively, but Metro had nothing for him. So Mickey was as eager to play Puck as Mary Pickford was. Not realizing what a boon to themselves this bit of generosity would prove to be, but eager to lay off his salary on someone else for a few weeks, Metro allowed Mickey to try out for the role.

Consequently, Mickey and Nell wound up one morning in a suite at the Hollywood Roosevelt Hotel where the auditions were to be held. Reinhardt wasn't there for the preliminary audition. That was conducted by his associate Felix Weissberger who, unlike Reinhardt, had a fairly good command of the English language.

Weissberger was delighted with Mickey's looks. Physically, this thirteen-and-a-half-old was just right for the role. He was small for his age, slightly built, and had an impish—in fact, puckish—face. When Weissberger handed Mickey a script and asked him to read a bit of Puck's dialogue, Mickey wrinkled his forehead, took a deep breath, and stumbled through Puck's opening lines as best he could.

"Not bad, not bad," Weissberger said. "Now I vant you should go home and memorize all this and come back tomorrow for another audition."

At home, Nell was pleased that Mickey hadn't flunked the preliminary test. But Mickey was bereft of his usual cockiness. "I can never learn to say those words and make them sound right," he exploded, throwing the script on the floor.

"Sure you can, Mickey," Nell encouraged him. "You just have to be familiar with them."

With a sigh, Mickey dropped into an armchair and started memorizing Puck's speeches. After he knew them by heart, he did Puck's scenes aloud, with Nell feeding him his cue lines. Gradually he began to understand the character of Puck and to get the feel of the rhythm of Shakespeare's free verse.

At the second audition, Mickey was letter perfect. He may not have understood all of Shakespeare's nuances, and he was still slightly puzzled by the phrasing and archaic language, but he recited the lines just as they were printed on the page. And, as he did, the merry impish spirit of Shakespeare's Puck danced in his eyes, and he seemed to become Puck right before Weissberger's eyes. Mickey even had Puck's laugh—partly the mocking braying of a donkey and partly the impish giggle of a child.

Weissberger nodded his approval. "Yah, goot!" Now there was only one more hurdle to get over, Dr. Reinhardt himself.

A short time later the imposing figure of Max Reinhardt strode majestically into the room, nodded curt greetings to Mickey and Nell, and dropped into a chair. Reinhardt was a squarely built man with piercing black eyes, which he fixed on Mickey momentarily. Then, through Weissberger, he ordered Mickey to begin.

An ordinary child might have quaked in his shoes, but not Mickey, who had wowed them in burlesque when he was a year and a half. By now he had Puck down pat. He not only rattled off the lines with remarkable ease, but he added little facial expressions and bits of comedy business that brought a reluctant smile to Reinhardt's thick lips. When Mickey emitted Puck's famous laugh, that clinched it. He was hired on the spot and joined a gifted cast that included Walter Connolly as Bottom, Sterling Hayden as Flute, Evelyn Venable as Helena, and Olivia de Havilland as Hermia.

Rehearsals began early in September, but only a few days before the actual premiere were Mickey and the rest of the company able to rehearse in the Bowl itself. That was because Reinhardt's team of set designers was constructing an enormous hill on the stage of the

Bowl. The hill was covered with real grass, and set into it were live oak trees and shrubbery. Even the shell of the Bowl had to be torn down to accommodate Reinhardt's ambitious ideas.

Since Reinhardt could speak only German, Weissberger had to act as his interpreter when he was communicating with the cast. It was painstaking work, but, according to Mickey, what he learned about acting technique from Reinhardt was worth every drop of sweat. Although he'd been on the stage or in front of movie cameras nearly all his life, he'd never before been directed by anyone so conscious of every little detail, or so faithful to the author's wishes, as Reinhardt. In rehearsals there was no putting in his own shtick; it was stick to the script and don't improve on Shakespeare. Reinhardt, through his interpreter, taught Mickey about body language. At one point, Puck says:

> Up and down, up and down;
> I will lead them up and down;
> I am fear'd in field and town;
> Goblin, lead them up and down.

"No, no," Reinhardt exclaimed. "Don't just read them! Use your whole body. Bounce up and down when you say up and down!"

THERE WERE VERY few laughs when you were working for Reinhardt, very few opportunities for Mickey's renowned ad-libs. But there was one occasion, after rehearsals had moved to the pastoral hillside on the stage of the Bowl, that Mickey ad libbed and got away with it—to the amazement of the entire cast. He even succeeded in breaking up the dour-looking Reinhardt.

Mickey's costume in the play was a small loincloth over an athletic supporter. At a point early in the second act when Oberon commanded him, "My gentle Puck, come hither," Puck was to drop out of the branches of a tree and land lightly on the stage in front of Oberon. Mickey tried to drop, but to no avail. His loin cloth was stuck on a branch.

"My gentle Puck, come hither," Oberon commanded Mickey a second time.

Still Mickey didn't appear. Irately, Oberon repeated his line, more commandingly and more fiercely this time, as the unseen Mickey worked frantically to free himself.

Finally, in complete frustration, Mickey replied, "I can't come hither. My leotard is hooked around a branch!"

The laugh he got was not entirely unexpected. But when the cast and director continued to guffaw, Mickey was a little mystified—

until he realized that his bare bottom was exposed to the group below.

Little more than a babe herself, Olivia de Havilland often acted as Mickey's surrogate mother during the exhausting thirteen-hour rehearsals at the Bowl. In a recent letter to me from her home in Paris, Miss de Havilland recalled: "Mickey was a very hard little worker (he looked nine years of age, was reported to be 11, and just might have been 13); in any case, I thought he was nine or eleven and when, during the exhausting thirteen-hour rehearsals, he could not keep his eyes open between scenes, he would curl up beside me, put his head in my lap and go off to sleep, having asked in advance to please waken him five lines before his cue."

Considering the magnitude of the production, it was a miracle that Reinhardt was able to get the entire play on its feet and ready for the opening in the thirteen days allotted to him for rehearsals.

In a biography of his late father, Gottfried Reinhardt writes that Max had worked out a torch parade for the last act. Stepping to Mendelssohn's "Wedding March," the parade was supposed to descend from the heights of the Hollywood Hills surrounding the Hollywood Bowl, to the bottom of the valley, and then across a specially built bridge onto the stage. But at the dress rehearsal the torchbearers reached their destination two hours after the play had ended. In the dark, they couldn't find their way through the pathless brush to the stage. After that calamity, everyone connected with the show begged Reinhardt to forget the torch parade. But Reinhardt was adamant. He wanted it, and he would get it.

The show opened on September 17, 1934, and was one of the great thrills of Mickey's young life. "It was a wonderful experience," he recalled. "Working outdoors, under the stars, with the hills all around us, and all of us dressed in those old costumes.

"I felt kind of funny when I was waiting in the wings for my first cue. I wasn't exactly scared, but I was kind of shaky. But after I was on stage, everything was all right."

Not only did Mickey perform like a veteran of the Bard, but even the parade of torchbearers arrived on time on the terrace of Theseus's palace and, with the final bar of the march, assumed their prescribed stance.

Despite the smoothness and lavishness of the performance, fear was rampant backstage that the show had bombed with the audience of fifteen thousand, who had not only filled the seats but had made themselves at home on the grassy slopes above the amphitheater. The applause was so thin that the great Max Reinhardt was not even called upon to take a bow.

49

Gloom filled the opening-night party, which saw Columbia Pictures' president Harry Cohn needling Reinhardt with: "Next time we're going to play it in Latin so the audience will understand it."

But most of their fears were unwarranted.

As Mickey and the cast later learned, the light applause opening night had nothing to do with the audience's enthusiasm for what they had seen. The problem was that with no curtain coming down after the epilogue, hardly anyone in the audience knew that the show was over. By the time the lights were turned on, the actors had left the stage and the people in the audience were scurrying for their cars in order to beat the Highland Avenue traffic.

The reviews, while not ecstatic in their praise of Max Reinhardt, were good enough to insure a hit.

The *Los Angeles Times* wrote, *A Midsummer Night's Dream,* as staged by Max Reinhardt under the Southern California stars was elaborately and beautifully staged, as well as acted." Moreover, the critic singled out Mickey Rooney's Puck as "being one of the brighter moments of the performance."

And so it happened that the rough, tough-talking, and uneducated Mickey Rooney scored his biggest success so far as a Shakespearean actor.

After the engagement ended at the Bowl, Reinhardt took the production to San Francisco, Chicago, and New York for limited engagements. It was a huge success in America's two largest cities, and so was Mickey. However, what he enjoyed the most about being a star on Broadway at the age of thirteen-and-a-half was that it gave him the opportunity to take his first coast-to-coast airplane ride.

When he returned to the Coast, Mickey had another surprise in store. Warner Bros. had decided to make *A Midsummer Night's Dream* into a major movie, with Reinhardt directing an all-star cast that included James Cagney, Dick Powell, Olivia de Havilland, Joe E. Brown, Hugh Herbert, Arthur Treacher, Victor Jory, Anita Louise, and, of course, Mickey Rooney as Puck.

Landing an important part in a major movie was just the opportunity Mickey needed to turn him into a star. It hardly seemed possible now that anything could go wrong, playing a part he knew so well and for which he'd already received considerable acclaim.

But if there's a way of screwing up an opportunity, Mickey's always had an uncanny knack for finding it. What happened to him during the filming of *A Midsummer Night's Dream* was the first of a life-long series of misfortunes for which he could blame no one but himself.

5

I N THE BOILER-PLATE language of most studio contracts there is what's known as a "morals clause." This gives the employer the right to terminate the contract if the employee behaves in such a scandalous way that it is an embarrassment to the studio—to the extent that such "immoral behavior" will cause potential customers to stay away from the box office. Today, it's difficult to invoke the clause for any reason short of murder. But in the thirties, forties and even the fifties, actors as important as Charlie Chaplin and Ingrid Bergman could run afoul of the morals clause and wind up on the sidelines.

When Mickey signed to play Puck in *A Midsummer Night's Dream* for Warner Bros., there was little need for the standard morals clause in his contract. At thirteen-and-a-half, what trouble could he get into?

However, Jack Warner was concerned about Mickey's only known "vice"—his addiction to sports, the kinds of sports in which a kid could get seriously injured and hold up production. Specifically, Jack Warner forbade him to play football, where he could hurt a knee; baseball, where he could get his brains knocked out by a wild pitch or a line drive; and to engage in high diving, where he could hit his skull on the pool bottom and break his neck.

Since *A Midsummer Night's Dream* was to be Warner Bros.'s most ambitious production to date and was intended to show the world, particularly the Eastern snobs, that Hollywood had class and could provide entertainment more worthwhile than gangster films and Westerns, the studio couldn't afford to lose an actor through a

51

mishap during production. The film was going to cost Warners at least a million dollars; any work stoppage would cost the studio at least ten thousand dollars a day. No accidents would be tolerated.

As a result, there was a special clause in Mickey Rooney's contract specifically forbidding him to engage in any contact sports.

Being the kind of fellow who has always rebelled at restrictions on his personal freedom, the mere thought of not being able to participate in the sports he loved grated on the youngster. Every day off, he would pester his mother to let him go out and play with the other kids. He promised her he wouldn't get hurt. But Nell turned a deaf ear to his pleas. Mickey was making $500 a week by then. That was a pretty healthy salary in the middle of the Great Depression, and Nell wasn't going to jeopardize that just so Mickey could have a few thrills playing sandlot baseball or football.

In addition to being rebellious Mickey has always been tenacious. And in the end, Nell wound up making a concession to Mickey's indomitable athletic spirit. The more dangerous contact sports were still verboten, but one Sunday, about a third into the filming of *Midsummer Night's Dream*, Nell had an idea how to get Mickey off her back and at the same time allow him to release some of that bottled-up energy.

"Let's drive up to Big Bear," she suggested. "You can play in the snow. Snow is soft. You can't get hurt."

A few hours later, the two of them were up at Big Bear Lake, a picture-postcard setting in the majestic San Gabriel Mountains. Snow-capped mountains all around; a frozen lake for ice skaters; snow-covered fir trees; and little kids pulling their sleighs and belly flopping on Big Bear's ice-covered main street in front of the lodge.

The weather was frigid. This was no place for the thin-blooded Nell to enjoy herself. So she took refuge in the lobby of the lodge and curled up on a sofa in front of a blazing fire. "You go out and play with the other kids," she told him.

In no time Mickey had become friendly with a number of children and was having a great time frolicking with them in the deep white powder. They built snowmen and had snowball battles. But Mickey soon grew tired of that and set out for other excitement.

He found it in a sign that read, TOBOGGANS FOR HIRE: *$2.00 an hour, $10.00 security deposit*. Since Mickey was a successful actor with money of his own, he didn't have to go to his mother for cash to rent the toboggan. He simply dug down into his jeans and pulled out twelve dollars, which he plunked on the counter. Then Mickey and his friends piled onto the toboggan and set off down the steep mountainside through a forest of pine trees.

Since Mickey was financing the ride, he took the most desirable seat—front. With its passengers whooping and hollering, the toboggan went careening down the ski slope faster and faster until finally it was completely out of control and heading straight for the trunk of a large evergreen. There are no brakes or steering device on a toboggan, and the riders must maneuver the vehicle by leaning their bodies in one direction or another. But Mickey and his friends weren't experienced enough to know about weight-shifting. In a desperate effort to slow down, Mickey extended his right leg, catching it in the snow. That was the beginning of the end. The next thing he knew, the toboggan crashed into the tree, scattering Mickey and his friends all over the area. Mickey, the only one really hurt, wound up on his back in the snow, with a leg twisted on top of his chest so it almost touched his chin. For a moment he thought it had to be someone else's leg, from the way it was positioned. Then he felt the excruciating pain and realized it was his own leg that was twisted pretzel-like on his chest.

It had to be broken. In disgust, and unable to stand the grotesque sight, Mickey grabbed his leg and pushed it back into a more normal position. After that he blacked out.

Fortunately, the sound of the toboggan as it splintered against the tree trunk, and the cries of the wounded, brought instant help from the other thrill-seekers on the powder-white ski slope. When Mickey opened his eyes, a crowd had gathered. After he was made comfortable, he was lifted onto another sled and taken to a first-aid station at the bottom of the mountain.

The large bone between the knee and the thigh was broken. That was the bad news. The good news was that the doctor told Mickey that, in pushing his broken leg away from his face, he had put the bone fragments in excellent position for resetting. "Congratulations, young man. You'd make an excellent doctor." After the leg was set and put in temporary splints, Mickey was strapped to a small toboggan and laid out in the backseat of his mother's car and driven to the Children's Hospital in Los Angeles. During the long ride, both Nell and Mickey were morosely silent, wondering what was going to happen to his part in A Midsummer Night's Dream. "Mom was sick about it," Mickey later recalled. "She'd always been so careful of me."

What would happen? Would he be kicked off the picture and

replaced? But how could the studio afford to do that? Mickey had already appeared in several important scenes. To start the film over would cost the studio an enormous sum. One thing was certain: Mickey was in plenty of hot water. How would he get out? And would he do it with his job intact?

When they reached the Children's Hospital, he was checked into a room, and his leg with the fractured femur was put in a cast and then in traction.

It doesn't take much imagination to guess what Jack Warner's reaction was when he was awakened Monday morning with the news that his Puck wouldn't be acting very Puckish for the next four to six weeks. As any veteran of the Hollywood wars will tell you, hell hath no fury like a production chief whose shooting schedule has been derailed by a careless actor.

Jack Warner, whose whole reputation as a movie genius was resting on the outcome of *A Midsummer Night's Dream*, didn't lose his temper. He just became livid.

Fortunately for future Andy Hardy fans, Reinhardt and his assistant director were able to persuade their apoplectic boss not to do anything drastic. They put their heads together to devise a solution to their problem.

One thing Warner knew: He was not going to permit Max Reinhardt to start the picture over with a new Puck at an estimated cost of a quarter of a million. That left only one avenue of escape: Revise the shooting schedule. So for four weeks, while Mickey lay in the hospital with his leg encased in a heavy cast, Reinhardt concentrated on the scenes in which Puck didn't appear or else had no dialogue and was just seen in long shots. In the latter, Georgie Breakstone, a boy of Mickey's size and build, stood in for him.

Meanwhile, the restless Mickey was on the lookout for some kind of action to break the monotony of being immobilized in a hospital bed with one leg in a sling. Not being much of a reader, Mickey exhausted that diversion after the first-few issues of *Daily Variety*. But one morning his doctor—an avid horse player—unwittingly left a copy of the *Racing Form* on Mickey's bed. Riffling through its pages, Mickey discovered a new hobby—doping the horses and wagering on them. Not through a bookie—he was too young for that yet—but mentally, he kept track of his winners and losers. After a few days of picking several winners, Mickey considered himself not just lucky but an expert on what was going on at the various tracks in the country, from Saratoga to Bay Meadows.

Soon, Mickey was expounding his knowledge of the turf garnered in the *Racing Form* to the various doctors and nurses who passed through his room. Deciding that Mickey's selections made sense, several of the more adventurous MDs evinced an interest in putting a couple of dollars on Mickey's selections but admitted they didn't know a bookie.

"You know one now," the enterprising Mickey exclaimed. "I'll book your bets."

So, to the amusement of the hospital staff, cute, little, feisty Mickey Rooney of the movies wound up running a bookmaking service from his hospital bed.

Being on the side with the favored odds, Mickey, of course, made a few bucks during his stay in the hospital. But the important thing about that period is not whether he won or lost but that, by the time he checked out of the hospital four weeks later, he was infected with an incurable case of the gambling virus. Since then Mickey has lost more money at the races than the average man earns in a lifetime.

A psychiatrist may tell you that a gambling addict has a death wish. But Mickey will tell you that he simply enjoys betting on the ponies. It's a form of relaxation that's kept him from going off his rocker when his troubles start piling up. What he forgets, of course, is that many of those troubles originated from a lack of immediate cash due to his gambling addiction. When I produced and wrote his television series in 1964, he had a phone in his dressing room on the set and between takes was either talking to his bookie on it or studying the *Racing Form*. He rarely glanced at his script until a couple of minutes before the director summoned him to the set.

Unlike a number of performers who began life in near-poverty and wound up pinching pennies, Mickey never had much regard for money. At any rate, in saving it or amassing a great deal of it. By his own admission, he's only interested in the things money can buy. As a child actor, earning from four to five hundred dollars a week, he felt rich. Not that he was allowed to keep much of his salary for himself. Most of it went into savings or to pay the bills.

Even so there was always plenty of spending money to take care of his juvenile needs. After it was gone or squandered, he could always make more. Since acting was fun for him, it was never a chore to go out and earn money. When he finished one picture, he could hardly wait for the next one to begin. Or in the case of *A Midsummer Night's Dream*, he could hardly wait for his leg to heal enough for him to continue his role in the film.

But when he was released from the hospital four weeks after the accident, his leg was still in a cast—though a smaller one—and he couldn't navigate without crutches. He played the rest of the film on one leg, the bad one always concealed from the camera. As a result, Mickey's performance was rather subdued. For the scene, for example, where the role called for him to move up and down as he spoke Puck's up-and-down speech, a special platform with a hole in it had to be constructed. During the scene, Mickey stuck the cast into the hole and rose up and down with a maneuver something like a knee bend. The scene was shot so artfully that most moviegoers never noticed it. But Mickey did and for that reason has always been dissatisfied with his performance in the movie version of *A Midsummer Night's Dream*.

Not so the nation's critics.

Variety felt that Mickey overacted slightly playing Puck, but "where he is restrained from grimacing and shouting, he is all right." *The New York Times* of October 12, 1935, gave Rooney's performance an absolute rave:

> Mickey Rooney's remarkable performance as Puck is one of the major delights of the work. As the merry wanderer of the night, he is a mischievous and joyous sprite, a snub-nosed elf who laughs in shrill delight as the foolish mortals blunder through Oberon's fairy domain.

Following Mickey's triumph in *A Midsummer Night's Dream*, it was back to MGM and mundane tiny parts in which his work was overshadowed by the stars of the films: Eugene O'Neill's *Ah, Wilderness* (1935), starring Wallace Beery, Lionel Barrymore, Spring Byington, Cecilia Parker, and Bonita Granville; *Riffraff* (1935), produced by Irving Thalberg, starring Jean Harlow, Spencer Tracy, and Una Merkel; *Reckless* (1935), starring Jean Harlow and William Powell; and *Little Lord Fauntleroy* (1936), starring Freddie Bartholomew and Dolores Costello.

None of the roles he played in these pictures was exactly a star-maker. In fact, in most of them his parts were hardly more than walk-ons, and he was virtually ignored by the critics. For example, all Frank Nugent of *The New York Times* had to say about him in *Little Lord Fauntleroy* was, ". . . and Dick Tipton, the bootblack, who lives in Mickey Rooney." But according to actress Ann Rutherford, who was also a stock contract player at MGM, and who was to make a name for herself playing Polly Benedict, Andy Hardy's girlfriend, "If somebody gave him a bit part, he would somehow make it so memorable that the producer or director would think of him again."

Many of the other insiders at MGM in those days felt the same way about Rooney. Producer David Selznick predicted he would "go far." Several of Metro's important directors whom Mickey worked with praised his versatility as an actor, and Robert Montgomery, who played with him in *Hide-Out*, considered Rooney the greatest "scene-stealer in Hollywood." But as far as 130 million Americans were concerned, the name Mickey Rooney still meant very little by the end of 1936.

Then, as frequently happens, stardom arrived from a very unusual quarter. In 1928, Sam Marx, later to become executive story editor at MGM, saw a play in New York called *Skidding*, by Aurania Rouverol. "It was a play about a small town judge and his family, and very charming," Marx recalls today. "I remembered it when I moved to Metro in 1936 and decided I wanted it for the B unit at Metro, which was under the supervision of Lucien Hubbard. But I practically had to get him down on the floor with my knees in his neck to make him buy the play. . . Anyway, . . . we picked up the property for something like five thousand dollars. Maybe less. But Hubbard had so little confidence in the project that he wound up letting me produce it for him under his supervision. And, quite frankly, I had no feelings about it turning into a blockbuster either. I figured it was going to be a nice little picture."

Which is about how most people at MGM thought about it, if they gave it any thought at all. The boys in Howard Strickling's publicity department, for example, referred to A *Family Affair*, the name it was eventually changed to, as "that potboiler with Lionel Barrymore that the B-picture guys are working on."

The other players in the first Hardy picture were Spring Byington as Andy's mother and Margaret Marquis as Polly Benedict, a different cast from the subsequent films in the series. For a while, according to Ann Rutherford, it wasn't even absolutely certain that Mickey Rooney would get the part of Andy Hardy. MGM had under contract a young actor named Frankie Thomas, Jr., and Lucien Hubbard was considering him. However, by the time the picture was ready for production, Frankie Thomas had grown too tall. He was more a leading man type, so Metro culled the ranks of its stock players and finally poked the finger of destiny at Mickey Rooney. "They thought that having a short Andy Hardy would be a little more amusing and more touching," Rutherford remembers.

A *Family Affair* was not ballyhooed like important MGM pictures. No film was considered important in those days unless it cost the studio at least a million dollars. A *Family Affair* was produced for less than two hundred thousand, and no one expected it to gross

57

more than three hundred thousand. How could it? Aside from Barrymore, there wasn't a soul in the cast who rated a line on the marquee.

This was reflected in both the *Variety* and *New York Times* reviews.

Wrote Frank Nugent of the *Times* on April 20, 1937:

> Lionel Barrymore wears the mantle of justice and the crown of thorns with his usual patience . . . as the dutiful Judge Hardy whose restraining order has checked the construction of the Carvel (Idaho) aqueduct, turned the town against him and even has begun to alienate the affections of his family . . .
>
> Mr. Barrymore knows how to handle those things, and so do the other members of the cast. Spring Byington invariably is a model of wifely and motherly understanding. Mickey Rooney is the epitome of all 14-year-olds who hate girls until they see a pretty one in a party dress. Julie Haydon, who can do better things, weeps convincingly as the troubled married daughter. Cecelia Parker and Eric Linden are Young Love in its usual form. They all have taken their "Family Affair" rather seriously and, although it was not that important, we rather enjoyed our eavesdropping at Judge Hardy's home."

The *Daily Variety* of April 21 thought so little of MGM's offering that they consigned their—favorable—criticism to their "Miniature Review" department, and gave no mention at all to Mickey Rooney. A film critic on the *Chicago Tribune,* whose views on the film reflected that of most newspaper dailies, called *A Family Affair* a "boob trap" that failed to work.

The public was the last to speak up, making its voice heard at the nation's box offices. City after city and town after town reported that the cash customers were going "wild over that Hardy picture." So much so that fans were refusing to leave the theater after the lights went up, insisting on seeing the feature a second time.

"For God's sakes," an exhibitor from Rochester wired, "let's have more of that Rooney kid. He really wowed them. The way he tripped over that doormat and looked into the eyes of that Polly Benedict girl—that was really something. The kid's a gold mine. And so is the rest of the cast. Please make another Hardy picture right away."

Completely flabbergasted, MGM officials sat up and rubbed their eyes in disbelief as *A Family Affair* went on to rack up huge grosses. Louis B. Mayer bowed to no one in his passion for hitting the box-office jackpot, but being a simple man, he loathed riddles. And *A Family Affair* was both a jackpot and a riddle. If the movie fans were turned on by little Andy Hardy and his puppy romance with Polly Benedict, that could portend a dangerous trend. Possibly the public was sick of MGM's serious romantic leading men such as Clark Gable and Spencer Tracy.

During the spring of 1937, many conferences were held in Louis B.'s office on the top floor of the Thalberg Building, and the best minds on the lot were mobilized to grapple with the Hardy problem. Finally someone came up with what struck everybody as a brilliant idea. "Let's make another Hardy family picture," Eddie Mannix exclaimed. "If it flops we will be well rid of the headache. And if it clicks, then we'll damn well know that the thing is a trend and that they want more of this Hardy family crap."

And so word came down from "The Mount" that there would be a second Hardy-family picture.

Today, deciding to make a sequel to a film that's a proven success is almost automatic, the theory being that if a picture clicks once, it may just click many more times. But in 1937 it was a major decision for an important studio like Metro to make a sequel to a B picture.

Except for Rooney, director, George B. Seitz, and writer, Kay Van Riper, most of the people involved in the success of *A Family Affair* weren't even available by the time the decision was made. Sam Marx had left MGM after overseeing the rough cut to take a loftier job as Sam Goldwyn's executive story editor; Lucien Hubbard had opened a dude ranch in Palm Springs; and Lionel Barrymore was refusing to play Judge Hardy a second time, because: (1) he was too fine an actor to accept being stuck in a B picture series; (2) it was reported he had been annoyed with Mickey's scene-stealing and, in fact, admitted having developed homicidal tendencies toward the youngster during the shooting of *A Family Affair*; and (3) he couldn't get the salary he demanded for again suffering the indignities he'd incur as a consequence of numbers 1 and 2.

Louis B. Mayer, never one to throw money around wildly, replaced Barrymore with his close friend, the courtly New Englander, Lewis Stone. The other pivotal parts, Mrs. Hardy and Polly Benedict, were recast with Fay Holden and Ann Rutherford, respectively.

When the pert, dark-haired, and vivacious teenager discovered that she was to play Andy Hardy's sweetheart, Ann Rutherford's blood pressure leaped—not because she was such a fan of Rooney's, but because she knew him a bit too well. In the previous two years, she had seen more than she wanted of Mickey while a student with him in Metro's Little Red Schoolhouse on the studio lot. There were eight other pupils in the class, including Freddie Bartholomew, Jackie Cooper, Judy Garland, and Lana Turner. But to Ann Rutherford it seemed as if there were at least eighty—all of them Mickey Rooney. No matter what part of the schoolroom she would move to, Rooney would follow her, pull her hair, or shoot spitballs in her face. In vain, she pleaded with their teacher, a young lady named Mary MacDonald, to protect her from the incorrigible Rooney's incessant teasing. But Mary MacDonald herself was badly in need of protection from the freckle-faced youngster. Who but a storm trooper could control an exuberant young man of the world like the Mighty Mite—as he was getting to be known around the lot after his first major success. Rooney's behavior notwithstanding, Rutherford wasn't stupid enough to turn down a role in a hit film-series.

That straightened out, the sequel went forward under the guidance of veteran-producer Carey Wilson. George Seitz directed again, and Kay Van Riper came up with another workable family yarn that saw Andy falling desperately in love with Polly Benedict, a baby-voiced, eyelash-batting sexpot he meets while vacationing with his family on Catalina Island.

The sequel, appropriately called *You're Only Young Once* was released on November 22, 1937. To everyone's surprise, the reviews were good, even in the staid old *New York Times*, whose sophisticated critic didn't ordinarily go for "family" pictures.

> The average American family (if, indeed, there is such a thing) has been so frequently libeled by the average program film it is a surprising experience and occasion for relief to come upon . . . *You're Only Young Once*, now playing the Rialto.
>
> Here, at least, is a "series" family (for that is what MGM intends it to be) in which the individual members react like human beings instead of like third-rate vaudevillians. The explanation obviously is that Lewis Stone plays the tolerant father, Cecelia Parker the budding daughter, Fay Holden the sweet-tempered mother, and best of all, Mickey Rooney the gosling son.

The public response was even more enthusiastic. In fact, the grosses were so gratifying to the bosses at MGM that opus number 3, soon to be known as *Judge Hardy's Children*, was put into production immediately.

In addition to Mickey's starring roles in two Hardy films in 1937, he was also in *Captains Courageous* with Spencer Tracy and Freddie Bartholomew, *The Hoosier Schoolboy, Thoroughbreds Don't Cry, Live, Love, and Dream,* and *Slave Ship.*

Judging by what MGM was paying Mickey at the time, *Slave Ship* could have been the studio's other name. In 1936, Mickey had starred in two big money-makers for MGM, *The Devil Is a Sissy* with Jackie Cooper, in which he got rave reviews, and *Little Lord Fauntletoy.* Together with the seven he made in 1937, that's nine major films. For all that work, Mickey was still earning only $400 a week, less an agent's 10 percent commission.

Nell wasn't happy about the situation and was starting to blame Mickey's agent. Harry Weber had been Mickey's agent since he had "discovered" him at Daddy Mac's Dancing School on Hollywood Boulevard in the late twenties. And he hadn't done badly by him, considering that Mickey was an unknown before the Mickey McGuire series. However, by the time Mickey had developed into a full-fledged star in 1937, Weber was critically ill and had been forced to retire from the business. When he did, he left Mickey's career in the hands of his assistant, David Todd.

At Nell's insistence, Todd went to Nickey Nafack, head of MGM's business affairs, and tried to renegotiate Mickey's 1934 contract, which he had signed when he was virtually a nobody. With Hollywood attorney Martin Gang advising Todd, Nafack reluctantly admitted that Mickey was underpaid and agreed to reward him with a new salary that would give him $250 per week above the figures contained in the contract they were terminating.

Two hundred and fifty dollars a week more was not exactly a king's ransom, but it was the best Todd could do. Nell wasn't satisfied, and in 1938 she persuaded Mickey to leave the Weber Agency and put his career into the able hands of William Morris's Abe Lastfogel, who'd been wooing the two of them for the previous year.

Lastfogel, powerful as he was, couldn't better Mickey's latest contract immediately, but he and his band of ten-percenters started a campaign that gave Mickey Rooney a brand new deal. Harry Friedman, one of Lastfogel's subalterns, could take credit for much of that. On July 20, 1939, Friedman had written Lastfogel a memo that contained a rather revealing breakdown, picture by picture, of how MGM was taking advantage of Mickey Rooney under his present contract.

For the pictures *You're Only Young Once, Love Is a Headache,*

Judge Hardy's Children, Lord Jeff, Hold That Kiss, Love Finds Andy Hardy, Boys Town, Stablemates, and *Out West with the Hardys,* Mickey Rooney received a total compensation of $30,000— or $3,333.33 a picture. He also received a bonus of $15,000; added to his compensation that first year of his new contract, he made a total of $45,000, $5,000 per picture!

Armed with that kind of ammunition, Lastfogel was able to get Mickey a brand-new, three-year contract at the end of 1939. Under the new set-up, Mickey would get $1,000 a week for forty weeks the first year; $1,250 the second year; and $1,500 the third year. Moreover, MGM had an option on his services for four more years, beginning with $1,750 per week and raised incrementally to $3,000 by the fourth year. In addition, during the first three years of the contract, Mickey was to get a bonus of $25,000 per picture, with MGM guaranteeing him no fewer than two bonuses per year.

Of course, eighteen-year-old Mickey, under the "Coogan Law" wasn't allowed to keep all that loot himself, to put in his piggy bank or to play the races with. The terms of his contract, which had to be approved by a judge of the Superior Court of Los Angeles, specified that two-thirds of Mickey's salary had to be put into an "irrevocable trust fund" in the California Bank, not to be touched until he was sixty years old. The other third of his income went into a separate trust for Mickey's mother. In addition, Nell was allowed $800 a month for living expenses for herself and Mickey, and Mickey was given $100 a week for his own use.

BECAUSE OF MGM's bonus system, in the fall of 1938 Mickey and Nell had been able to buy a rambling, two-story, Spanish-style house in the San Fernando Valley for seventy-five thousand.

Mickey's and Nell's new house was on Densmore Drive in Encino, not far from Clark Gable's and Carole Lombard's ranch. It had a red-tile roof, twelve rooms, silver fixtures in the bathrooms, and the customary swimming pool. It stood on five rolling acres, which were planted with English walnut, lemon, and orange trees. It was a lot more house than one could buy for $75,000 in Beverly Hills or Bel Air in those days, but its interior, the way Nell had decorated it, with contemporary Barker Brothers furniture, was rather ordinary. By the time Mickey became Number One at the box office two years later, the house on Densmore had turned into a real tourist attraction with a constant stream of sightseers's cars and tour buses driving slowly by its front yard. Eventually MGM had postcards printed with a picture of the Encino place on them, with the caption, MICKEY ROONEY'S HOUSE.

Though there was no doubt that Mickey had finally achieved star status, a hint of his future financial troubles could be detected in a memo from attorney Martin Gang to MGM that requested that "all taxes on moneys paid into Mickey's trust fund and on Mickey's contract salary should be paid from the trust; also all commissions payable on the moneys payable into the trust should be deducted."

The reason for this, as given by Gang, was that "it's impossible for Mickey and his mother to get along on his $40,000 a year salary under their present setup, for under present existing conditions they are in the red approximately $6,500 after taking into consideration all their necessary expenditures."

Who would have dreamed that there'd come a time when being only $6,500 in the red would look pretty good to Mickey?

6

THE WERE FOURTEEN more Hardy-family pictures in the next nine years. No one knows for sure just how much they cost to produce or how much they earned. MGM wisely chose to keep their net profits a secret, feeling that if the exact figures ever leaked out, Mickey Rooney or his mother or his stepfather, and, of course, his agents might start acquiring fancy ideas as to how much money the Mighty Mite was worth. However, a conservative estimate is that the Hardy pictures grossed around $80 million dollars, and by the time they had run their course with the public around 1946, earned back something in the neighborhood of ten times what it cost to make them.

By 1940, Mickey was the nation's Number-One movie attraction at the box office, beating out the former champ Shirley Temple, by a lot more than a nose. The Hardy pictures were outgrossing even such critical hits as *The Informer* and *The Grapes of Wrath*.

No one has ever been able to explain satisfactorily the phenomenal success of the Hardy pictures. There is a school that believes that the American public was fed up with message pictures like *The Informer, The Grapes of Wrath*, and *Of Mice and Men*, and was looking for pure escapism to take its mind off its own troubles. But there is another school that leans toward a simpler explanation: audiences were identifying with the life-style and problems of a typical American family, who lived in a typical American two-story clapboard house, in a typical American town known as Carvel, Idaho. That the Hardy family was "typical" had to be a form of wishful thinking, for few American families can have been quite so "goody two-shoes" as the Hardy bunch.

65

An example of just how *clean* a youngster Andy Hardy had to be in the eyes of the public was once touched upon in a *Reader's Digest* article by novelist Katherine Brush, who worked on one of the Hardy-family scripts:

> Infinite pains are taken to keep the family precisely average, lest parents protest that Andy is setting a bad example. Once the script had him say about a meal cooked by his mother, 'This dinner's no good, Mom.' The watchdogs over Andy's character hit the ceiling when they heard that in the dailies. A retake of the scene was immediately ordered by the MGM hierarchy. In the new version, Andy's lines were revised to read, 'It was a fine dinner, Mom. A lovely dinner. But I just wasn't hungry.'

This *Alice-in-Wonderland* approach to reality was a little more than George Oppenheimer, a Broadway playwright noted for his rapier-sharp wit, could stomach. When Eddie Knopf, head of the story department, offered him the opportunity to write one of the Hardy-family scripts, Oppenheimer retorted swiftly, "Sure, I'd love to write one, provided you let me have every member of the fucking family killed in a railroad accident in the last reel!"

Though the basic cast remained the same, there were plenty of gorgeous starlets on the Metro lot to give the pubescent Andy a new heartthrob every time he went before the cameras.

The formula was fairly simple. Polly Benedict was Andy's steady girl, but often a new face on top of a smashing figure would turn up in Carvel, and Andy would fall for her. She, being older and more sophisticated, would then fall for an older guy, and in the end a much-chastened Andy would return to Polly, who, of course, would forgive him. There was always at least one man-to-man talk between Andy and Judge Hardy, whose sage advice would set Andy straight about his life and loves. There was a whole string of these pulchritudinous young ladies: Lana Turner, Donna Reed, Esther Williams, Judy Garland, and Kathryn Grayson.

In pre-World War II America, sixty million movie fans took their Hardy pictures seriously. That was attested by the mountains of fan mail that poured into MGM every day. As a shining example of young American manhood, Mickey was asked by the parents of unruly kids to try to "contaminate" them with his goodness.

Anyone actually acquainted with Mickey knew, of course, that there was a fairly wide gulf between Andy Hardy and the real Rooney. Street-shrewd and as seemingly sophisticated as the

Mighty Mite was, it was no mean task for him to reconcile the impulses of a healthy and horny teenager with the preposterous code of behavior created for Andy Hardy by Kay Van Riper, Aurania Rouverol, and Louis B. Mayer. But Mickey had to be Andy Hardy twenty-four hours a day. Mickey wasn't even allowed to show up at a premiere of one of his pictures in his brand-new, blue Ford convertible. When Mickey attended an opening he had to drive the beat-up Model-A convertible with the torn roof that he drove through the streets of Carvel. Moreover, no glamorous starlet would be seen hanging on his arm as he went up the red carpet and into the lobby of Grauman's Chinese Theater. Usually Mickey's date on these occasions was a boy's best friend—his gray-haired mother, Nell.

7

ONE OF THE things that contributed to the success of the Judge Hardy/Andy man-to-man talks was the fact that Mickey and Lewis Stone played them with complete sincerity. Mickey, particularly. These scenes were so genuine because this was actually the first time in his life that Mickey had a father like other boys had— even if he was a fictional father. Artificial as the Hardy family was, Mickey liked it.

Lewis Stone was one of the few men in Hollywood who understood and was willing to take the time to talk about Mickey's problems and complexes—and he had many, in spite of the fact that he was one of Hollywood's most successful citizens.

Mickey wasn't totally fatherless. In 1937, Nell had married Fred Pankey, a large, handsome, genial fellow about her age who had been the proprietor of a bar on Western Avenue that wasn't doing too well. After they married and Mickey was becoming one of MGM's brightest satellites with considerable clout, Pankey sold the bar, and Nell was able to get him a job as an accountant in MGM's payroll department. According to Mickey, Pankey was a graduate of Knox College, a business school, and had a pretty good background in accounting.

Mickey was fond of Fred Pankey and in later life wished he had taken his stepfather's advice to take better care of his money, which wouldn't be rolling in forever. But what teenager knocking down a hundred thousand or more a year is ever concerned about the future? To Mickey, Pankey was a spoilsport even to suggest he was spending more than his income. As a result, they weren't as close as they might have been. They were moderately good friends, but it wasn't a father-and-son, or Judge Hardy-and-son, relationship. And Joe Yule, though he had moved West and was a featured "banana" for seventy-five dollars a week at the Follies Burlesque in downtown Los Angeles, had little time for his son. He was married again—this time to a stripper named Leato Hullinger.

Lewis Stone, on the other hand, was able to help Mickey get over some of his problems. One thing that really bothered Mickey was his size. If Mickey would become depressed about this, Stone would take him aside and point out that some of the great men of the world hadn't stood any taller than five-foot-three: Napoleon Bonaparte, General Sheridan, and Fiorello LaGuardia. Mickey took Stone's advice so to heart that after he moved into his new home in Encino he placed large, framed photographs of Napoleon, Sheridan, and LaGuardia in strategic spots around his playroom to remind him that size wasn't important.

To give you an idea of just how solid his relationship with Lewis Stone was, when Mickey became engaged to Ava Gardner the first thing he did was take her on the set and introduce her to Judge Hardy, just as if he were his real father.

Like for most Hollywood actors, much of Mickey's social life revolved around the people he knew professionally. Two of Mickey's closest male friends over the years have been Sig Frolich and Sidney Miller, both of whom he had worked with before he was fourteen years old.

He had met Frolich, a poor boy from New York's Lower East Side, on the set of *Riffraff*. Blond, slightly taller than Mickey, and several years older, Frolich had drifted to Hollywood for the usual reason—to become a star—but like so many others before him, he'd had to settle for less. When Mickey met him, Frolich was a combination extra, bit player, and sometime-stunt man. Since he posed no threat to Mickey professionally, as Jackie Cooper and Freddie Bartholomew did, the two hit it off from the start. Both had similar interests—girls and sports. In fact, it was while playing on the touch-football team Mickey organized on the lot that the two cemented their friendship. Mickey's football team was known as the MGM Lions. The Lions, with Mickey quarterbacking, became so good that during the football season Mickey and his teammates were invited by the people running Gilmore Stadium, on Fairfax Avenue, to play another team of equal caliber and size between the halves of the pro game every Sunday. Because of his film popularity, Mickey's squad was probably a bigger draw than the Hollywood pro team whose home ground Gilmore Stadium was. Mickey was turning out to have a strong appeal to sports followers as well as movie fans. People around Los Angeles thought nothing of getting up at the crack of dawn and driving a hundred miles to Palm Springs or Coronado to watch Mickey play in an exhibition tennis match. Even as a spectator, he was worth his weight in gold to the management. When he attended the Nebraska-Missouri game in Kansas City one year, all eyes in the stadium were riveted on his box. He returned the compliment by leading the cheering sections of both Missouri and Nebraska.

MICKEY HAD KNOWN Sidney Miller since their "Mickey McGuire" days. As Mickey climbed up the Hollywood ladder to stardom, Sidney became one of the regular character-actor teenagers in his buddy's pictures—*Boys Town, Young Tom Edison, Strike Up the Band, Babes in Arms, Babes on Broadway,* and *Men of Boys Town.*

According to Miller, the two of them would have a ball when they were working together. Between takes, Mickey and Sidney would find a piano somewhere on the lot and compose songs. Neither of them could read music, but by the time they were twenty they'd already had two songs on the "Hit Parade"—"Have a Heart" and "Oceans Apart," which Judy Garland recorded and made a hit.

Mickey and Sidney became such close friends and collaborators that you rarely saw one on the studio lot without the other. Even in their late teens, they enjoyed spending the night at one another's house. At Mickey's El Ranchita, as he kiddingly labeled it, they'd write songs or practice the piano and play the drums. Mickey had a whole arsenal of musical instruments—a guitar, a saxophone, two pianos, a trumpet, and a professional set of trap drums. Mickey learned to play each by ear; if not actually play, "fake it" well enough to be asked to sit in with the Big Bands—like Dorsey and Glenn Miller—when they played the Palladium.

"Mickey used to love to come to my house for the night, too," Sidney Miller recalls. "My mother and father had a little house in Beverly Hills by then. Mickey especially liked to be at our house during Jewish holidays and would come to our Seder. Mickey didn't care much for the religious aspect of it, but he loved Jewish cooking and was very fond of my mom and pop."

Actually, by the time Mickey was eighteen he was interested in less family-oriented pursuits. Like every other red-blooded American boy (except Andy Hardy), the main thing on his mind was sex. Having spent many of his formative years in backstage burlesque, he was decidedly more worldly about the birds and the bees than the average boy his age. He shocked people around the studio with the candid way he discussed the first stirrings of his libido.

Having a father who was actively employed in a striptease joint, Mickey was no stranger to the seamier side of life. He didn't get to see his father often, but since Yule and Nell were on friendly terms, Mickey's father and stepmother would occasionally be invited to have Sunday dinner with the Pankeys and Mickey at El Ranchita.

In return, Yule would invite his son and Sidney Miller or Dick Quine, or perhaps all three, to a ball game at Wrigley Field or a prizefight at the Hollywood Legion Stadium. If he wanted to give them a real treat, he'd invite them to the Follies Burlesque and let the boys view the show from a stage box. "It was a great treat for us horny teenagers to see all those bare tits and asses as they paraded on and off the runway within touching and smelling distance," Miller recalls. "Not that we were allowed to touch, but we were given a pretty good lesson in female anatomy."

Dick Quine also remembers those days with affection. "We used to sit in a stage box and pick up all the shtick from the comics," he remembers with a grin. "But after a while we got pretty blasé about all the nudity. We got to know the girls pretty well—right down to their navels. To bug them, when the girls came out and started taking off their clothes right in front of us on the stage, Mickey and I would put our feet on the railing, pick up a newspaper and pretend to be reading. It used to drive the girls crazy."

Blasé or not, Mickey had a healthy interest in sex probably dating back to his days as a performing toddler in the burlesque houses of the early twenties. According to what Mickey told his sixth wife some years later, sometimes the chorus girls would put him on their laps backstage and hug him.

"I'm not sure if Mickey started *schtupping* that early," says Sidney Miller, "but I'm sure he wasn't a virgin by the time we were eighteen." Close as they were, Mickey never confided in Sidney who the lucky girl was who made off with his virginity. "He was very discreet about those things," Miller reports. And in Jackie Cooper's memoirs, *Please Don't Shoot My Dog*, Cooper remembers an experience that he, Mickey, Sidney Miller, and comedian Phil Silvers had one evening after the four of them had had dinner together and were sitting around Silvers's apartment, keeping themselves entertained in the usual way—Mickey sang songs and did imitations, Silvers told stories about his burlesque days, Sidney Miller played the piano, and Cooper listened to a ball game on the radio. To fill in the dead spots, they talked about girls and compared notes, names, and their sexual fantasies.

Bored with just talking about girls, Silvers had the bright idea to call in a hooker. The three younger men were all for that, so Silvers called a little lady he knew and haggled with her over the phone about the financial arrangements. She wanted twenty dollars apiece, but after Silvers pointed out to her that she only had to make one trip to get four customers, thereby cutting her transportation costs, she agreed to a group rate, or five bucks apiece.

After the girl arrived and was getting down to her work clothes in the bedroom, the four men started to boast about their respective staying power in the saddle. This led to a wager: the one who lasted the longest with her didn't have to pay. Then they drew straws for position. Sid Miller was first, followed by Silvers, Cooper, and Rooney. Each man who took on the girl before Mickey was in and out of the bedroom in about three minutes flat. But when it was Mickey's turn, the door didn't open again for twenty minutes, and in the interim, there'd been some wild noises coming from inside.

When at last Mickey appeared, he was wearing a broad grin as well as his clothes.

"Did I tell you guys, or did I tell you guys?" he boasted, his chest swelling with manly pride.

While the girl was getting dressed, Mickey thanked the other three for the free "treat," and hastily slipped out. Finally the girl came out to pick up her money, and Phil Silvers cornered her. "Hey, little lady, you gotta tell us the truth. Was Mickey really in the saddle twenty minutes?"

"Are you kidding?" she exclaimed. "Four minutes of fucking and sixteen minutes of imitations."

ONE THING MICKEY is quick to admit: he never scored with any of the sexy young actresses who played with him in the Andy Hardy films. That doesn't mean he wasn't interested, however.

His favorite fantasy sex object was Lana Turner who had a small role in *Love Finds Andy Hardy*. Mickey had had a crush on Lana before she'd come to Metro; in fact, he knew her when she was only sixteen and still going by her real name, Judy Turner. Mickey caught his first glimpse of her flawless face and bountiful figure in the Malt Shop across the street from Hollywood High, both of which he, too, attended for a while. Lana was the featured attraction at the Malt Shop every day after school.

In Mickey's 1965 autobiography he boasts that he dated Lana for

73

"three or four months. Movies. Dancing. And dinners." He also described what a heady feeling it was to be driving his first car along an open road with the top down, the gas pedal pressed to the floor, and a dish like Lana Turner sitting beside him.

However, in Lana Turner's autobiography she writes, "I never dated Mickey, that adorable nut."

So as Groucho Marx once said to Margaret Dumont in *A Day at the Races*, after she questioned his belief that she needed an operation, "Who are you going to believe—me or those crooked X rays?"

Despite his bravado and cocksure ways, Mickey remained self-conscious with girls about his height. Two of the young ladies he dated back in his high-school days remember how touchy he could be.

In 1939, Lois Gilbert, a tall, ravishing, chestnut-haired beauty, once double-dated with Rooney and Dan Dailey and his girl. "Because I knew he was short, I deliberately wore low heels so that our height difference wouldn't be so noticeable," recalls the former Miss Gilbert, who today is Mrs. Arthur Marx. "Mickey realized I was wearing low heels the moment he picked me up at my folks's front door. He didn't say anything about it at the time, but later in the evening, after we'd gone to dinner and a movie and he was dropping me off again, he asked me for a second date. But he had one stipulation: 'Never wear those blankety-blank low-heeled shoes again! I don't like it.'"

Aside from that, Lois reports, Mickey was "a very nice, very polite date, and he never once tried to make a pass at me. There was only one thing I didn't like about him. In the movie he laughed so loud that everyone around thought the two of us were nuts, and I was embarrassed."

A similar experience was related to me by Eylene Sugarman, who dated Mickey when she was a student at Beverly High.

Blonde, tall, and large-busted, Elyene also thought she was doing the proper thing when she slipped on her shoes with the lowest heels before Mickey picked her up in his convertible one rainy night in February of 1940. As she stood on the threshold of her father's house, all dressed up and looking very glamorous, Mickey surveyed her from top to bottom, and then snapped imperiously, "Don't wear low heels again. I like tall girls."

The girl with whom Mickey Rooney was probably the most compatible during those years was Judy Garland. They enjoyed one another's company and admired one another's talent. As their professional relationship developed, their admiration for each other increased. Mickey had fun working with Judy, as he could with no other actress. With her, he could ad-lib in a scene or fool around without flustering her. Her timing was perfect, and she could ad lib as well as Mickey could. Each would try to rattle the other during a take. That was part of the fun of working together.

Their friendship grew stronger over the years, but it never ripened into love. This was a disappointment to Mickey's mother, Nell. After a couple of his marriages had turned sour, Nell once asked Mickey why he hadn't married Judy. His reply was, "Because it would be like marrying my sister."

That doesn't mean Mickey and Judy never went out together. For laughs, and simply to get away from the Hollywood hubbub, they used to drive to the amusement parks down at the beach and ride the roller coasters or wander through the fun house. But going out in public got to be a "drag." They were such celebrities by the time he'd become Andy Hardy and she'd become Dorothy in *The Wizard of Oz* that they were constantly being mobbed by autograph seekers or people who just wanted to touch them. "In the beginning it was flattering," Judy remarked, "but pretty soon it became hard to deal with."

To escape his fans and the danger of being bullied by some beach tough trying to show off for his girlfriend, Mickey frequently entertained his friends at his rambling ranch house in Encino. Most of his friends were young actors and actresses, with his regular group consisting of Dick Quine, Sig Frolich, and Dick Paxton, a young man Mickey met at a roller-skating rink and decided to make his stand-in (he also let him live in the Encino place), Sidney Miller, and Judy Garland.

The guests at Mickey's parties did what most entertainers do on their days off: they performed for each other. Sidney Miller would play the piano, Mickey and Judy would sing duets, and Mickey would do impersonations and play the drums. With some of his musical friends, he'd also formed a little jazz band. There would often be jam sessions until the wee hours of the morning, and the band was good enough to get bookings at some of the smaller jazz joints around town.

Mickey's parties at home were nothing like the proverbial wild Hollywood parties. No one drank much or got potted on marijuana, and there were no skinny-dipping episodes or sex orgies. "We never thought of sex or getting drunk, we were so busy performing," Sidney Miller recalls. "Besides, Mickey's the kind of person who can get totally bombed on one glass of wine."

In the days of his not-so-wild Hollywood parties, Mickey wasn't old enough to legally drink any kind of liquor. If he went to a party at Chasen's, for example, and felt like having a drink in order to enjoy the festivities, he'd have to tell his sidekick Sig Frolich, "Hey, meet me in the can, Sig, and bring along a straight shot."

One would have thought that the country's number-one movie star might have rated special treatment. But that was 1940, and Mickey was only twenty years old. The drinking age was twenty-one, and anyone as short as Mickey Rooney had to produce a driver's license before a bartender would even consider serving him alcohol.

Despite the care Mickey took not to spoil his Andy Hardy image, reports of his rakish behavior were becoming widespread in the film community and were a cause of concern to his bosses at MGM. Rumors about his unquenchable libido were beginning to make the Mighty Mite look like Hollywood's leading roué. He flirted with every pretty face he saw, and because he was an international star making lots of money, it wasn't all that difficult to get a girl to go out with him and perhaps even sleep with him. As he once admitted, "They weren't dating me for myself—they were dating the entertainer."

How much entertainment they got out of him was questionable. For one thing, he wasn't the most reliable of Don Juans. He'd make a date with one girl, become interested in another, and completely forget to show up for the first date. If a young lady was fortunate enough to have her date with Mickey proceed as planned, she might find, once she was out with him, that it would be more fun to be home alone. An unsophisticated girl might get a kick out of being seen in public on the arm of a famous star such as Rooney, but many of them complained of dying of boredom when they had to spend an evening alone with him in a quiet restaurant, with the entertainment dependent on conversation. It seemed that Mickey didn't sparkle when he wasn't surrounded by a crowd. But in a celebrity-peopled nightclub like Ciro's, Mickey could dance the rhumba until closing time. Between sets, Mickey would generally leave his girl stranded at a table by herself in order to hop on the bandstand and give the crowd a demonstration of his prowess on the drums.

Mickey loved nightclubs and would usually make a very conspicuous entrance. Conspicuous by its loudness—of clothes, for one thing. Until someone set him straight, Mickey had a fondness for wearing violent checks and plaids. Also, you could hear him coming before he hove into sight. Mickey would hardly have entered a nightclub before he'd be going about slapping people on the back and exclaiming, "Hi ya, kid," or "How's it going, toots?" This kind of greeting wasn't just reserved for the younger set; dignified grown-ups like Jeanette MacDonald and Gene Raymond or Claudette Colbert and her doctor husband were accorded the same disrespectful treatment. Mickey had no fear of rejection. To him, it was unthinkable that anyone would resent a slap on the back and a "Hi ya, toots" from the top male box-office attraction in the United States.

An extrovert of the first water, Mickey was God's gift to Tinseltown party-givers. Once Mickey accepted an invitation, the hostess would breathe a sigh of relief. Now she wouldn't have to worry about how her party would go over. No matter how mediocre the food she was serving or the music of the orchestra, Mickey Rooney could be counted on to make up for the evening's deficiencies. When things got slow, he'd be sure to demonstrate his ability to play all the instruments in the band. Without being coaxed, he'd be certain to provide a show for the guests after dinner. He'd sing, dance his inimitable specialities, and would top everything off by giving his famous imitations of Charlie Chaplin, Lionel Barrymore, Mae West, Clark Gable, and Greta Garbo. If he didn't bring a girl to the party, he'd be sure to have one when he left.

ALTHOUGH THERE WAS no evidence that the public Mickey Rooney was doing any damage to the box-office take of the Hardy films, when rumors of his girl chasing started leaking out through Hedda's and Louella's syndicated gossip columns, Louis B. Mayer summoned Master Rooney to his cavernous office and gave him a man-to-man lecture. After impressing upon his young star that he loved him like his own son, Mayer said, "You know, Mickey, your name is always in the papers . . . you're running around to all the night spots . . . You're with girls . . . doing all of that . . . You're seen at the Coconut Grove, drinking and dancing the rhumba. But you're Andy Hardy. The public expects something different. You have to stop living like that."

"But Mr. Mayer," Mickey replied in a plaintive tone, "I work like a dog when I work . . . Real hard. And I put everything into it. If I were just another kid and I was going out on dates, nobody would say a word. Now I'm not supposed to do it because I'm Andy Hardy! What am I working for?"

"I appreciate all that," Mayer steamed, "but you're *supposed* to work hard. That's what we're paying you for. Now I know you're a normal young boy, full of piss and vinegar. And I don't care what you do behind closed doors. But behave in public and don't get some jailbait knocked up. Understand?"

Mickey promised to try to keep a low public profile in the future. Just to be on the safe side, Mayer assigned one of his trusted minions from the publicity department, Les Peterson, to be the watchdog of Mickey's morals.

I first met Peterson one summer in 1938 or 1939 when I was vacationing at a resort on the shores of Lake Tahoe with my mother and sister. Tall, blond, handsome, and very engaging—and about thirty-five years old—Peterson, for some reason or another, was up at the lake by himself. He took a liking to my mother, who was also blonde and good-looking, and since my father was off somewhere playing a vaudeville engagement, he volunteered to escort her—and her two children—around in the evenings.

When I learned that Les worked at Metro, I asked him what he did exactly. He replied: "I'm Mickey Rooney's keeper."

Peterson was the perfect person to ride herd on Mickey. He was the complete "company" man. He ate, drank, and slept Metro-Goldwyn-Mayer. If Mayer asked him to meet a visiting fireman at the airport at four in the morning, he'd do it. If Mayer asked him to jump into a lake with all his clothes on, he'd probably do that, too. Therefore, when Louis B. asked him to take charge of Mickey's body and soul, he was happy to help the cause.

As Mickey's keeper, it was up to him to tag along just about everywhere his charge went—"except to the john and his bedroom,"remembers Peterson with a warm chuckle.

He not only tagged along, but he handled all the arrangements, from making hotel and train reservations on publicity tours to picking up the tab at Chasen's and Romanoff's.

In a restaurant it would be up to Peterson to remind Mickey, whenever he had a sudden desire for a "belt," that Mr. Mayer didn't want him to drink in public. Or for that matter, to smoke, either. If Mickey wanted a puff or two, Peterson would see to it that he did it in the men's room.

When Mickey felt like running down to Santa Anita, which was nearly every afternoon that the track was open and he didn't have to work, "I'd drive him to the track and place his bets for him at the pari-mutuel window, because he was too young to bet." Between races, Mickey would studiously pore over the *Racing Form* and the various dope sheets at his private table in the Turf Club. Then Peterson would buy the tickets from a never-ending fund supplied by the studio—money that eventually would be deducted from Mickey's salary. According to Peterson, Mickey would usually "lose a lot of money." Though in the beginning, Mickey had chafed at the thought of having a watchdog with him everywhere he went, he soon grew to appreciate the enforced companionship. Not only was Peterson good company, but he was efficient—and husky enough to ward off unruly fans. Because of his size, Mickey was especially vulnerable to attack from some wiseacre fan who wanted to prove that Mickey wasn't as tough as the kid he often played in some of his pictures. A firm jab in the stomach by Les Peterson would generally send the pest running.

Peterson was a particularly valuable person to have along on press tours such as the one in 1939, when Mickey and Judy Garland invaded the East to play the Capitol Theater in New York City to plug Judy's latest picture, *The Wizard of Oz*. Nell Pankey and Judy's mother accompanied the kids but stayed in the background.

Not even Mickey could anticipate the enthusiastic greeting he and Judy got from New Yorkers. A crowd of three thousand—mostly the bobby-sox set—intent on getting a view of the pug-nosed, dynamic Mighty Mite congregated on the street in front of the theater, tying up traffic for hours. If they expected autographs, they were disappointed. Peterson devised ways to sneak Mickey and Judy in and out of the Capitol without having their clothes torn off.

Between shows, Les took Mickey and Judy to luncheons, dinners, broadcasts, and newspaper interviews. During this engagement, Mickey also received a call from the mayor's office requesting him to squeeze enough time out of his frantic schedule to attend a function on Fifth Avenue with Mayor LaGuardia. "It was some kind of a ribbon-cutting event," Peterson recalls, "and Mickey agreed to go, much as he detested those things. LaGuardia was one of his idols, but he would have preferred to go out to Belmont. However, he was a good sport about it, and we drove over to the ceremony in a studio limousine. Mickey and LaGuardia hit it off famously. They kidded around together, and after Mickey cut the ribbon and was given the key to the city, LaGuardia turned to the newsreel cameramen and quipped, 'Now I've found a pal my size.' The press got a big kick out of that, and it was good for Mickey's ego, too, to see someone his size as famous and powerful as Mayor LaGuardia was at the time."

In the midst of all that success, Mickey still found time to be concerned about a friend.

"Mickey and I had lost track of each other in the couple of years when he'd become the hottest thing in the country," Dick Quine recalls. "I was a song-and-dance man then, and I'd gone to New York to be in a Broadway show, *Very Warm for May*, which Jerome Kern had written. Anyway, it folded quickly, and I was between jobs when Mickey and Judy came to New York to play the Capitol that winter. Hearing they were in town, I thought I'd go over to the Capitol and say hello. But when I got there, I couldn't get near the theater, the mobs were so huge. Christ, they didn't have enough cops to keep the streets cleared for traffic. So I gave up and went back to my dingy apartment on Forty-Fifth Street. About an hour later there was a knock on the door, and when I opened it, there were Mickey and Les Peterson, their arms loaded down with bags of stuff from the Stage Delicatessen. Kind of a 'care package.' How Mickey had the time to look me up and do all that shopping with everything else he had to do I'll never know. I'd never given him my address. But he took the trouble, busy as he was doing seven shows a day with Judy."

MICKEY HAD BECOME such a celebrity that in January of 1940 he was invited to attend President Roosevelt's annual birthday ball at the White House. Peterson, of course, was right at Mickey's side as the two of them showed up in the ballroom decked out in tuxedos. Everyone was there, from the "who's who" of the Social Register— the Astors, the Whitneys, and the Rockefellers—to important government dignitaries such as Secretary of the Treasury Henry Morgenthau, Joe Kennedy, and the president's right-hand man, Harry Hopkins. Mickey wasn't frightened by the imposing lineup— they were as interested in seeing him as he was them. Under Peterson's guidance in matters of etiquette, Mickey refrained from slapping Eleanor Roosevelt on the back and greeting her with one of his renowned "Hi-ya-tootses," but he felt pretty much at home. He was so relaxed, in fact, that when the *Life* photographers asked him to strike a funny pose for them, he hopped onto Liz Whitney's lap and clowned around with the gray-haired social matriarch while the camera shutters clicked and the flashbulbs popped. The picture turned up in the following week's *Life*, with a caption reading, "Mickey takes over the White House."

As was the custom at the president's birthday-ball dinners, one empty place was left for Roosevelt at each of the many tables in the room. That way the president could wheel over and spend a little time with each group of guests. When he reached Mickey's and Peterson's table, Roosevelt said to Mickey, "Well, my boy, some day

I hope to be able to spare enough time so that you and I can have a man-to-man talk."

"Yes, sir," Mickey replied, in all seriousness, completely unaware that Roosevelt had been kidding him. "You say when. I can get time off from the studio any time for that."

Roosevelt threw back his huge head and roared with laughter.

TWO MONTHS AFTER the president's 1940 birthday ball, Mickey and Peterson were back on the road again—this time to Detroit, Michigan, for the world premiere of *Young Tom Edison,* in which Mickey was starring. During his stay in the motor capitol, Mickey was invited to meet and spend the afternoon with Edsel Ford, in his office at the Ford Motor Company in Dearborn. The two of them spent a stimulating couple of hours together discussing cars. Edsel Ford was so intrigued with Mickey's earthiness that at the end of their session he presented the Mighty Mite with a brand-new Lincoln Continental—the first of its kind ever manufactured.

YOUNG TOM EDISON was a solid box-office hit, although some of the nation's critics weren't too sure that Mickey Rooney was the proper actor to be portraying the wizard of Menlo Park. *Time,* for example, wrote that Mickey gave:

> ... his most sober and restrained performance to date. That he did not succeed entirely was partly the fault of the production, partly because the picture featured Mickey in a role so different from the usual ones that puzzled cinema-addicts did not know what bewildered them the most—seeing Mickey Rooney as Thomas Alva Edison or the future Wizard of Menlo Park as ebullient as Mickey Rooney.

With Mickey's indefatigable interest in wine, women, and the ponies, it's a wonder he had time to concentrate on his acting at all. But in spite of a multitude of those diversions, Mickey remained dedicated to the acting muse and proved it by the many varied roles he played so successfully in his peak years at MGM and the huge number of fans he acquired along the way.

After the first five Hardy pictures, Mickey became so blasé about playing Andy that he frequently would arrive on the set with only the faintest notion of his lines. But when it came to the bigger and better pictures, Mickey gave all five-foot three of himself— *Stablemates* (with Wallace Beery, who called Mickey a "brat" but a "fine actor"); *Boys Town* (with Spencer Tracy, who was too polite to call Mickey anything, though there must have been times when he was tempted to); and *Babes in Arms* (with Judy Garland, who was so enamored of Mickey that she had nothing but kind words for her costar).

Sidney Miller, who worked with Mickey not only in *Boys Town* but in *Babes in Arms* and *Strike Up the Band*, says he was always impressed by Mickey's "great ability to concentrate on a scene, no matter what else was going on. I remember one day when we were making *Boys Town* ... I played Mo Kahn, the barber. But this day I wasn't in the scene. In my spare time I was working on a song with Mickey called, 'Love's Got Nothing on Me.' That day Mick was doing a big scene with Spencer Tracy, when I walked onto the set to watch. Tracy was telling him, 'You're no good, Whitey, You're a bad boy. I've been able to handle bad boys, but you're the exception.' At that point, Mickey as Whitey pleaded with him: 'Father, let me stay in school. The guys are beginning to like me. Let me stay in Boys Town. I'll be good. I promise.' At that point, the script called for Mickey to start crying and keep it up through the remainder of the scene. Mickey ... was so touching he had everybody on the set in tears ... the grips, the cameraman, even Norman Taurog, the director.

"After the take, Mickey spotted me standing on the side and rushed over. 'Hey, Sid,' he said. 'I've got the bridge to the song. Listen to this.' And he pulled me over to the piano and started playing and singing the song we were working on. In the middle of this, Taurog came over and told Mickey that he'd have to do the scene again. 'Why? I thought I was good,' snapped Mickey with a frown. 'Mike shadow,' Taurog explained.

"Mickey scowled the way he always did when he didn't want to do something, then took a deep breath and agreed to do the scene again. It must have been a four-minute scene, and this time Mickey did it better than the first time. The tears started rolling down his cheeks in the exact same spot. It was like he'd been able to turn on a faucet. Everyone around was crying again. Then Taurog yelled, 'That's great. Cut. Print.' Without a beat, Mickey rushed right back to the piano and started singing, 'I'm not afraid of the moon, Love's got nothing on me, My heart's humming a tune, And I'm still free as can be ...'"

BOYS TOWN WAS written for the screen by Dore Schary and John Lee Mahin, and it was such a resounding success, both critically and at the box office, that Schary was made a producer right after that.

82

Eventually, he took over the reins of the studio from Louis B. Mayer.

The consensus of the nation's critics was that the story of Father Flanagan's school for delinquents was well made, perhaps a little too sentimental, but definitely a crowd-pleaser.

Frank Nugent, reviewing *Boys Town* for *The New York Times* in September of 1938 attributed most of the success of the pictures to a young man named Mickey Rooney:

> Mickey is the Dead End Gang rolled into one. He's Jimmy Cagney, Humphrey Bogart, and King Kong before they grew up, or knew a restraining hand. Mickey, as the French would understate it, is the original *enfant terrible*.

Spencer Tracy got only one mention, while Mickey was the cornerstone of the entire review. Lionel Barrymore certainly knew what he was doing when he bowed out of the Hardy pictures after making *A Family Affair* with the incorrigible scene-stealer.*

But if Mickey was what made *Boys Town*, he was even more outstanding in *Babes in Arms*. Mickey not only received top billing over Judy Garland, who by then was a pretty big name herself after scoring heavily in *The Wizard of Oz*, but according to *Variety's* reviewer, he was the whole picture.

> Mickey Rooney . . . gives out plenty and shoulders all responsibility for swinging the picture into the top classification.
>
> . . . Mickey provides one of the most extensive performances ever given on the screen. He sings, dances, gives out with a series of imitations, including Eddie Leonard, Gable, Lionel Barrymore, President Roosevelt. His piano playing (whether or not dubbed in) is terrific and he plucks the strings of a cello as if he knows how. It's Rooney all the way.

Mickey also impressed his peers. The members of the Academy of Motion Picture Arts and Sciences nominated Mickey Rooney for Best Actor in 1939, along with Robert Donat for *Goodbye Mr. Chips*; Clark Gable for *Gone with the Wind*; Laurence Olivier for

---

*In the end, Tracy had his last laugh, for his portrayal of Father Flanagan won him an Oscar for Best Actor, while Mickey had to be satisfied with a "special" miniature Oscar for his "contribution in bringing to the screen the spirit and personification of youth, and as a juvenile player setting a high standard of ability and achievement."

Wuthering Heights; and James Stewart for *Mr. Smith Goes to Washington*. It was no small tribute to Rooney even to be nominated that year when you consider the actors who weren't: John Wayne and Thomas Mitchell in *Stagecoach*, Melvyn Douglas in *Ninotchka*, and Burgess Meredith in *Of Mice and Men*. No actor—no matter how young or short or how many years he has ahead of him to win —likes to come away from the awards night empty-handed; but losing out to the British star Robert Donat whose brilliant portrayal of a scholarly schoolmaster in England made *Goodbye Mr. Chips* one of Hollywood's classics, couldn't have been too bitter a pill for Mickey to swallow.

OSCAR WINNER OR not, there was no doubt by the summer of 1939 that Mickey Rooney was MGM's most important property, not excluding its majestic trademark lion. Mickey had a value that couldn't be estimated in dollars alone and an image that had to be guarded as closely as Shirley Temple's purity.

So when Joe Yule, anxious to capitalize on his son's success, changed his billings on the marquee of the bump-and-grind emporium on Los Angeles's Main Street to SEE MICKEY ROONEY'S FATHER, Louis B. Mayer had a fit.

The mere thought that Mickey's fans, who were then only vaguely aware of his sleazy heritage, would not know for sure that his father was holding forth in a lewd strip joint (which Mickey frequently visited), was something the straight-laced Mayer was unwilling to tolerate.

Knowing Mickey's independent nature, however, Mayer decided not to make too much of an issue of it. He simply called Mickey in and suggested that he say something to his father about the impropriety of his billing—not only in front of the theater but in the Follies's newspaper ads. Perhaps he could even talk Yule into retiring. After all, he'd been working hard all his life, and Mickey certainly could afford to support him.

But Mickey refused to interfere. He told Mayer that his father was a grown man and pointed out that burlesque was considered a noble profession in their family. Furthermore, he was proud of his old man.

That failing, Mayer had his legal department dispatch a letter to the Follies theater management, mentioning Metro's displeasure. That resulted in a phone call from the Follies manager, claiming he had a perfect right to bill Yule as Mickey's father since he *was* his father.

Consequently, Louis B. hastily convened a gathering of his top executives, where it was decided to offer Yule a three-year contract at Metro for $100 a week.

Since he was only earning $75 at the Follies, Yule accepted MGM's offer and on August 10, 1939, signed on as a member of the MGM stock company. The day he left The Follies, a picture of Yule appeared in the *Hollywood Citizen*, kissing all his stripper friends, including "Rosita Royce and her pigeons" goodbye.

There was no mention of his last job in MGM's press releases, however. Most of their newspaper handouts attributed Yule's retirement from the "legitimate" theater to Mickey's great love for his father and his desire to work on the same lot with him.

Yule, on the other hand, denied that nepotism had played a role in getting him the job at Metro, though, when pressed, he did admit to a reporter that "Mickey might have had something to do with it." He was able to maintain his sense of humor about it, however. When asked if he had an ambition to play a particular role in the movies, he cracked, in a W. C. Fieldsian deadpan, "My ambition is to be as much of a success in the movies as I was on the stage."

According to Sidney Miller, MGM hardly used Yule after they signed him: "They just wanted him out of the burlesque show. But whenever they did give him a small part, Mickey would go down on the set and laugh it up. 'That's my pop,' he'd exclaim loudly and proudly after Joe did his stuff in front of the cameras. Then he'd clap like a madman."

Yule never doubted who the real star of the family was. In 1939, when Mickey departed from Los Angeles's Union Station on one of his publicity tours East, a huge crowd of fans arrived to see him off and get his autograph. Among them was Yule, who went completely unrecognized until he threw his arms around Mickey and started to kiss him goodbye. At that moment, the family resemblance was so striking that it couldn't be ignored, and the fans started asking for Yule's autograph, too.

"You know," Yule later recalled to a friend in a voice filled with sadness, "it was the first time in my life anyone's ever asked for *my* autograph."

8

B ABES IN ARMS was such a huge success that MGM decided to make a sequel in 1941 and call it *Babes on Broadway.*

Again Mickey and Judy were the main marquee attractions, although there were other talented performers in the cast, including Ray MacDonald, Virginia Weidler, and Mickey's friend Dick Quine, who had scored an acting success on Broadway in *My Sister Eileen,* and had been signed to a long-term contract by MGM.

Despite all the talent in it, *Babes on Broadway* wasn't as effective as the original. Dick Quine remembers it for only one thing: his friend Mickey's amazing rehearsal habits. "In the plot, Mickey, Ray MacDonald and I were supposed to be a dance team in vaudeville," Quine says. "And we had a lot of intricate tough numbers to learn. So Ray and I would rehearse and rehearse, but Mickey never showed up until just before we were ready to shoot. Then he'd say to us, 'Let me see it.' And we'd do it for him, all those intricate tap routines and complicated Busby Berkeley moves. Then he'd get up and say, 'Okay,' and do it with us, but he'd really be faking the whole thing, while we were actually doing the hard stuff. But when it got on the screen, nobody looked at Ray or me—everyone was watching Mickey, and not even realizing he was faking the steps."

Babes on Broadway was one of the few pictures Mickey made in that period that wasn't a smashing success. The reviews were lukewarm and the grosses disappointing. But Mickey will never forget *Babes on Broadway* for another reason: it was while filming it that he first set eyes on Ava Gardner.

Matrimony was about the furthest thing from Mickey Rooney's

mind when he reported for work on the set of *Babes on Broadway* one hot July morning in 1941, dressed for his Carmen Miranda number. Clad in a long slit skirt, bolero blouse with phony breasts underneath, huge platform-soled shoes, and a fruit hat larger than he was, Mickey looked more like a vaudeville comic than a Don Juan. And comic he remained—until he finished the number, walked off the set, and saw Ava standing behind the cameras with Milton Weiss, one of Metro's press agents. It was her first day at the studio, and Weiss had been assigned to take the young starlet on a tour.

The sight of her literally took Mickey's breath away. He'd seen, and had, plenty of pretty girls, but there was something different about this one. She had chestnut-colored hair with a reddish glow to it, skin the color of white jade, greenish eyes, and a sulky smile. Her figure was beyond hyperbole—high, firm breasts with prominent nipples, a slender waist, and long beautiful legs. She was wearing a cheap summer dress, because she could afford no better, having arrived from the North Carolina boondocks only the week before with little money. But she couldn't have been more attractive if she'd been wearing an Edith Head gown. Without really trying, her every move exuded raw sex, but this was tempered by a certain degree of reserve that served notice on any interested males that she was not going to be an easy target.

Whether Mickey sensed this unattainability and it only deepened his interest, or he was simply blinded by her radiant beauty, one will never know for sure. But we do know—Mickey has admitted this openly—he made up his mind to marry Ava Gardner the moment he laid eyes on her. Whoever the hell she was.

IT MUST HAVE been fate.

Several months earlier, the tall, sensuous brunette from North Carolina had made a screen test for MGM in New York. The test proved three things: that she couldn't act; that it was almost impossible to understand her lazy North Carolina drawl; and that she was enormously photogenic and about the sexiest creature to walk the Earth.

On the basis of the latter, George Sidney, who was in charge of selecting new starlets for MGM, recommended to his bosses that she be given a contract for $75 a week.

While she was waiting to make the move West, Ava Gardner was sitting around MGM's publicity office in Manhattan one afternoon, talking about her future in Hollywood. "Well, if I make it big there,

I'll tell you what I'll do," she told the publicity staff grouped around her. "I'll marry the biggest movie star in the world."

Winking at the other press agents, one of the staff ducked into an adjoining office and returned with a photograph behind his back.

"Would you like to see the biggest star in the world?" he asked Ava.

"Sure." She thought she was going to see a picture of Clark Gable, her idol, so when the press agent unveiled a full-length shot of Mickey Rooney, "Ava nearly died," one of the other men present recalled, who was in on the gag.

MICKEY LOOKED LIKE even less of a catch dressed in South American drag. But he wasn't going to let an opportunity to meet the studio's latest femme fatale slip through his fingers. Without so much as a pause to remove his makeup, Mickey walked right over to Milton Weiss and the new girl in town, extended his hand and said cheerfully, "Hello, I'm Mickey Rooney."

"This is Miss Ava Gardner," Weiss said.

"Hello," drawled Ava indifferently. Although by now she knew she was in the presence of the world's number-one movie star, she didn't seem bowled over by it. There wasn't a trace of a smile on her beautiful lips.

Ava's indifference to his boyish charisma was ignored by Mickey. Without further preliminaries, he asked her out to dinner that night.

"No, I'm busy," Ava replied dryly.

Actually she was, but not with another man. She didn't want to leave her older sister, Beatrice, informally known as Bappie, who had come West to chaperone Ava and with whom she shared an unimposing little apartment on Franklin Avenue. Never mind her initial opinion of Mickey, which was anything but flattering.

Rejection was an experience Mickey rarely had. When the unusual girl came along who didn't want any part of him, Mickey would shrug it off and go on to the next conquest. But with Ava, he had to have her, no matter what.

DURING THE LUNCH break, Mickey removed his platform shoes and fruit hat for the walk to the studio commissary with his coterie of cronies: his stand-in, Dick Paxton, his friend Sidney Miller, and his "keeper," Les Peterson. While they were having lunch at their regular table, Ava Gardner came in with Milt Weiss. The sight of her dazzled Mickey again and immediately took his mind off the bowl of "Chicken and Matzo-Ball Soup à la Louis B. Mayer" that was on the table in front of him. With his soup spoon halted in midair, Mickey dispatched Les Peterson over to Weiss's and Gardner's table to ask them to join him. Flattered by the continuing attention, Ava glanced in Mickey's direction, raised one eyebrow, and executed her enigmatic smile. But she made no move to join Mickey and his companions. Then Mickey made a tactical error: he stood up and waved to her. Recalling that moment to a friend later in her life, Ava said, "Jesus, I thought. He seems to have shrunk since this morning. But then I remembered: of course—the platform shoes! He didn't have them on in the commissary."

In spite of getting the cold shoulder, Mickey couldn't take his eyes off Ava, couldn't stop talking about her to his friends at the table, and couldn't stop showing off for her whenever he thought she was glancing in his direction. The others at the table—particularly Sidney Miller—tried to humor Mickey out of his rapture. They pointed out that from the way the young lady ignored his attempts to attract her attention or make her laugh, she obviously wasn't interested. Mickey found that impossible to believe. Wasn't he the greatest star in the world, the idol of the bobby-soxers, friend of the president? No girl in her right mind would turn down a chance to go out with him. When his friends continued to ride him about this almost childlike infatuation, Mickey boosted, "Okay, you guys, you can laugh. But someday I'm going to marry her."

Against the advice of well-meaning friends and business associates who warned him that Ava wasn't his type and that she would be bad medicine for him, Mickey set off in relentless pursuit of her. For days he pressed Ava with notes, gifts and telephone calls, but she remained as cold to his overtures as a marble statue. Whenever he phoned to ask her for a date, her reply was the same: "I can't tonight, Mickey. I'm busy."

In truth, she had nothing more exciting to do than spend another night in her cheap apartment with Bappie, listening to the radio, looking through movie fan magazines, or writing letters home to the folks in North Carolina.

A number of theories have been advanced about why Ava preferred to stay home in her little apartment instead of going out on the town with the world's number-one movie star. Some Ava watchers say it wasn't coyness or coquettishness; she simply wasn't attracted to Mickey and was waiting for someone tall, dark, and handsome to ask her out. Others believe that she simply wasn't very interested in dating any man, because her mother, a rather conservative church-going Baptist, had instilled in Ava a real fear of the consequences of sex. A third hypothesis suggests that Ava's technique of "studied indifference" was a deliberate scheme to entrap Mickey. She *wanted* to make good her boast that she would "marry the biggest star in Hollywood." She might have been ambivalent about Mickey's size, but there was a lot of clear-cut ambition among her motives when she finally agreed to date him. After all, for an unknown from North Carolina to be seen with the world's biggest star could be a tremendous boost to her career—particularly when they were both at the same studio. She just had too much class to be obvious about it.

Whatever its genesis, her coolness toward Mickey made him all the more determined to win her. And with his kind of determination, it was inevitable that the two of them would wind up on a date sooner or later. It happened sooner than Mickey had dared to hope—about a week after their first encounter on the set.

That day, while Mickey was shooting, he sent one of his gofers down to MGM's still-picture studio, known on the lot as the Shooting Gallery, where Ava was posing for some cheesecake stills. Mickey's emissary relayed another dinner invitation to Ava from the "king of the lot." When Ava yawned and declined for the umpteenth time, the gofer exclaimed, "You're crazy, Miss. Don't you realize how good it would be for your career to have Mickey Rooney in your corner?"

Concerned that she might be overplaying her hand, Ava consulted Milt Weiss after she'd finished posing. "Will it really help my career, Milt, if I'm seen with Mickey Rooney?"

"You'd better believe it," Weiss replied.

When Mickey phoned Ava that evening, he found her attitude had softened. She was warmer and friendlier, but she still turned down his invitation to take her to Chasen's because she didn't want to leave Bappie by herself. Seizing the opportunity, Mickey invited Bappie, too. Surprisingly, Ava said okay and they set a time.

Overjoyed, Mickey picked up the two sisters at their modest apartment around eight and drove them to Chasen's in his Lincoln Continental. There he plied them with champagne and caviar and introduced Ava to crepes suzette, which was to become her favorite dessert. Mickey was "on" for the entire time, full of jokes, imitations, and Hollywood anecdotes, most of which passed way over Ava's and Bappie's heads. After they'd eaten their fill, Mickey grabbed Ava by the hand and took her table-hopping in the celebrity-filled room, to show her off. Ava must have met more stars that evening than she had in the entire month she'd been in Hollywood.

91

Later, Mickey dropped Bappie off at the apartment and took Ava dancing at Ciro's. Dancing presented a bit of a problem; Mickey's tousled head barely reached Ava's shoulders.

At first it was difficult for Ava to become accustomed to their disparity in size, but, gradually, as the good life started to grow on her, she found herself accepting it. What if her escort was the shortest male star in the movies? What better way for a young starlet to get her picture in the fan magazines or her name in the gossip columns? When they were on the dance floor, flashbulbs were constantly popping at them from every corner of the room.

In spite of the fact that Ava was beginning to find Mickey tolerable as a companion, she remained indifferent to him as a potential lover.

Which didn't discourage Mickey in the least. In fact, when he was dropping her off at her apartment after their very first date—without their having so much as kissed—Mickey suddenly said, "Ava, will you marry me?"

She dismissed his question the way a mother would the prattling of a little child. "You must be crazy!" she exclaimed. Then, with a condescending smile, she added "Good night" and ducked into her apartment.

From that moment on, Mickey's pursuit of Ava moved into high gear. He awakened her early the next morning to tell her how much he'd enjoyed the evening. She, in turn, thanked him in a sleepy voice. Mickey played the rest of the scene almost the way Andy Hardy would.

"You don't have a car, do you?" he said.

"You know I don't."

"It must be hard for you to get to the studio."

"Oh, it's not too bad," Ava said.

"Well, it's too far to walk, isn't it? Why don't I stop by and pick you up?"

"All right," Ava said, not overly enthusiastic.

Driving Ava to the studio became a regular part of Mickey's life.

Sidney Miller remembers how Mickey acted when Mickey and Ava would arrive at the studio in his convertible with the top down. "Mickey would drive her all over the lot, shouting to everybody he knew on the studio streets, 'Hey, this is my new girl. She's going to be a big star. Isn't she gorgeous?' And then he'd stop the car, stand up on the seat behind the steering wheel and point her out to everybody, embarrassing hell out of her."

Since Ava was a novice who wasn't ready yet for a part in films, all this exposure with Mickey did wonders for her self-confidence. It also made her realize that there was more than one way to become famous in Tinseltown. Before many weeks had passed, they were seen going everywhere together. Daytimes, to baseball games, auto races, the track. Evenings, to the Tropics, Romanoff's, the Mocambo, and Chasen's. Everywhere there were fans, photographers, and the welcoming smiles of headwaiters to remind Ava that her escort, no matter how much more he resembled the king's jester than the king himself, was a powerful star who could open many doors for her.

Like many celebrities, Mickey hated those moments when he had to be alone. He hated them to such a degree, in fact, that sometimes when he had a date with Ava he'd send one of his lackeys to pick her up in his Lincoln and bring her back to his home in Encino. That way he wouldn't have to spend any time alone in the car on his way over the mountain to Franklin Avenue.

Since Ava was the only girl Mickey was taking out in 1941, his sexual frustration was beginning to get the better of him. Often there'd be frantic wrestling bouts between him and Ava. There'd be plenty of heavy petting in the back seat of his Lincoln, but Ava had no intention of going all the way with Mickey. This infuriated him. After dropping Ava off at her apartment, he'd depart in a huff. The following day, however, he'd make amends for his aggressiveness and send her roses by the dozen or sprays of orchids.

When her resistance continued, he started proposing marriage seriously and quite often. According to Ava's recollection of those days, "Mickey proposed marriage to me twenty-five times in as many dates." Each time she would brush him off with the same reply: "You're crazy, Mick. We hardly know each other."

But no girl, no matter how aloof, could go out with a man nearly every day without beginning to soften, without beginning to feel something more than just friendship for him. Soon her negative replies softened to: "Marriage is a serious thing, Mick." Or, "I don't want to marry anyone until I'm positive that it'll work out."

Finally there was stage three, which showed signs that she was, at long last, beginning to regard him seriously as a suitor. Instead of a flat turndown, she'd ask, "What'll our life be like, Mick?" Mickey would then outline in glowing terms his idea of a healthy marriage: They'd be big stars together; they'd go everywhere together; he'd buy her mansions and jewelry and fancy cars. Life would be one big jamboree.

Ironically, Ava wasn't interested in the glitzy part of marriage.

She wanted to know what life together at *home* would be like. In his desperation to make love to her, Mickey couldn't think much beyond the bedroom: Vine-covered cottage for two; idyllic hours between the sheets; and laughs, lots of laughs. It was Andy Hardy's fantasy. Naive as she was, Ava wasn't sure if that was enough to make the two of them happy, though she was beginning to waver as 1941 neared its end. Looking back on that period, Ava once confided to a friend, "Occasionally a shrill voice would sound in my brain, warning that maybe life with Mickey would be like living on a sound stage. He'd always be 'on.' But whenever the warning sounded, Mickey would drown it out with a joke."

Despite her doubts about Mickey, she was beginning to like the new deference she was accorded at Metro as his girlfriend. She was aware that once her picture at his side attending premieres and fancy parties stopped appearing in the newspapers and fan magazines, along with the constant linkage of their names in the gossip columns, she would fall back into the relative obscurity of being just another MGM starlet who had yet to appear in a picture.

In addition, life at the top was beginning to appeal to her. Mickey was awakening in her hedonistic tendencies she hadn't known existed. She discovered that she enjoyed staying out late nights and that she had a tremendous capacity for liquor.

After the bombs fell on Pearl Harbor on Sunday, December 7 and the United States became embroiled in World War II, people's attitudes about life, love, and the pursuit of happiness underwent tremendous changes. Couples with no intention of getting married were suddenly and impetuously rushing down to City Hall to apply for wedding licenses. Not to escape the army—that gambit wouldn't work—but simply to enjoy a little wedded bliss before rushing off to war and possible death.

BECAUSE OF HIS draft number, Mickey was in no immediate danger of having to exchange his custom-made clothes for army khaki. But who's to say that the possibility of going into service didn't hasten his decision to pop the question to Ava again, on Christmas Eve, 1941? It was Ava's nineteenth birthday, and Mickey had thrown a party for her at Mike Romanoff's. On the drive home, long after midnight, he asked her the same old question, but this time he got the reply he wanted.

"All right, Mickey," she replied. "I'll marry you."

Christmas morning he showed up at her apartment with a diamond ring, which he had confidently bought two weeks earlier. No girl, not even one with North Carolina gumption, could have fought Mickey Rooney off forever.

They sealed it with a kiss, but no more. Mickey didn't know if she was still a virgin—he suspected she might be—but he wasn't to find out for sure until their wedding night. Which had yet to be decided. Mickey pressed her to have the wedding on the following day, but Ava was less eager. She told him that she wanted time for a nice honeymoon and that he should find out from the studio when there would be a break in his shooting schedule.

Mickey was on cloud nine as he drove back over Coldwater Canyon to his home in Encino. There he awakened his mother and stepfather and broke the news to them. Nell was about as enthusiastic as any normal mother would be after being awakened at three in the morning, to learn that she would soon have to start sharing her meal ticket with an ambitious young actress.

At the studio the following day, Mickey proudly told the members of his clan, who weren't wildly ecstatic, either. "Oh, I know you think she's not the girl for me, but you're wrong," Mickey insisted to Carey Wilson producer of the Hardy series. "We're in love and she's going to be a great wife."

Next, Mickey phoned Hedda Hopper, the *Los Angeles Times* syndicated gossip columnist. She was aware, of course, that Mickey had been dating Ava Gardner, but she didn't believe the news of their engagement, even coming directly from the Mighty Mite's mouth. She decided that if it was the real thing, the announcement would have come from Metro's publicity department. Deciding to check out the item before publishing it, Hedda phoned Howard Strickling, who promptly denied there was any truth to it. "Sure he's gaga for her," Strickling admitted, "but as far as an engagement's concerned, it's just wishful thinking. She's Charlie Feldman's girl."*

Strickling assured Hedda that *if* the couple became engaged, she'd be the first to know. Consequently, Hedda killed the story. Big as she was, she dared not cross the Metro lion.

Just to be sure, Strickling hunted Mickey down. He found most of Mickey in his dressing room—his head was up in the clouds somewhere. Mickey giddily confirmed the truth of his and Ava's engagement.

---

*Feldman was her agent, and almost everyone just assumed they were having an affair.

"Mr. Mayer isn't going to like you marrying Ava," Strickling said. "You're the biggest star in the business. You can't just throw your career away on anybody. Don't get me wrong. Ava's a very sweet girl, and she's certainly built. But you have obligations to the public, and to Mr. Mayer who believed in you enough to hand you the Hardy series on a silver platter."

Mickey didn't understand what his private life had to do with Mayer, the studio, or the public.

Strickling wasted no time explaining Mayer's point of view. "L.B.'s protecting his investment in you, Mickey. Fans lose interest in stars who get married. They want them single and available. You see, in their fantasies, young girls see themselves married to you. Andy Hardy, in particular, ought to remain single and celibate. In the public's eye he's still a kid, and innocent. How can they think you're innocent when you're banging the hottest broad in town?"

Mickey protested that he wasn't "banging" her. Their relationship was cleaner than Andy's and Polly Benedict's. Marrying a girl you loved was the honorable thing to do, he insisted, and it ought to please his public as well as Mr. Mayer.

The only concession Strickling could get the star to make was that he promised to keep the engagement a secret until Strickling arranged a meeting between Mickey and L.B.

Mickey had had plenty of conferences with Mayer in the past and had always managed to come out of them without his wings being clipped too short. But this time he insisted that Ava come along as his back-up. Mayer would have preferred it otherwise, so after Mickey and Ava were ushered into his vast office, hand and hand, Mayer gave his young star a frigid greeting and ignored Ava altogether. Benny Thau, the solidly built head of talent, sat behind his boss, looking like his number-one hit man. And Howard Strickling was ensconced on a window seat, his arms folded across his chest.

Mayer was famous for getting what he wanted in these show-downs in his second-floor corral. He'd rave, wheedle, cajole, plead, and shout until his victim surrendered from exhaustion. Although he gave Ava the fish eye occasionally, he ignored her most of the time, concentrating his biggest artillery on Mickey. At one point he simply forbade Mickey to marry Ava.

Calmly, his chin jutting out the way it did when he defied Judge Hardy, Mickey told Mayer he had no right to talk to him that way. It was his life! Mayer shouted that it wasn't just his life so long as he was working for him. Frightened by all that bombast, Ava cowered in a corner, looking demure and awfully frightened. This was her first encounter with the tyrannical boss of the Culver City lot. Whether she knew it or not, her future at Metro hung in the balance. If Mickey backed down, she could expect to feel the full force of Mayer's vindictiveness. How dare a nobody try to sabotage the career of his hottest star!

When bombast failed, Mayer tried to embarrass Mickey: "Why do you want to marry this girl? You know all you want to do is get inside her pants?" Even Benny Thau, no stranger to foul language, was shocked to hear his boss talking that way in front of the quiet Southern beauty.

Mickey, the romantic, stuck to his guns. He put his arm around Ava's waist, drawing her close to him. At this demonstration of love, crocodile tears welled up in Mayer's ratlike pale eyes. He was the father figure again. "It would break my heart to see you unhappy. Please believe me, Mickey," he pleaded. "I've always been like a father to you. Believe me, this is not the girl for you." Moreover, he continued, there was a war on. How could Mickey contemplate marriage knowing that he could be drafted any minute, leaving his wife pregnant and alone.

Mickey refused to be swayed by Mayer's insincere rhetoric. Squeezing Ava's hand, he said, "Mr. Mayer, I love this girl and she loves me. And if you don't want to give us your blessings, I'll be glad to go to another studio. I think I know a couple of places that would like to have me."

Mickey had been around Hollywood long enough to know Mayer's vulnerable points. Mayer gnashed his teeth a little more, but when he realized his sharp words couldn't puncture their romantic balloon, he took a deep breath and said what they wanted to hear: "Okay, congratulations, Mickey. Go get married. Just don't expect me to support her if you go off to war."

SINCE HE COULDN'T destroy the relationship, Mayer did the next best thing. He took control of it. He ordered Strickling to make certain that the wedding was arranged as discreetly as possible, to take place in a small town where publicity could be held to a minimum.

Mickey was so happy to be marrying Ava that he didn't even object to the fact that the wedding arrangements were being taken out of his hands, from buying the ring to choosing a wedding site to finding a place for Mickey and Ava to live after the honeymoon.

All these details landed in the capable hands of Les Peterson.

Strickling couldn't have found a man more qualified for the job. Not only had Peterson proved himself by keeping Mickey out of hot water for the four years he'd been assigned to him, but the San Jose native loved to motor around the state during his vacations and was familiar with every small city and hamlet between San Francisco and Los Angeles. A few days of exploration, and he'd be able to come up with the ideal setting for an elopement.

An elopement wasn't exactly what Ava had in mind. She'd always wanted a big church wedding, with all the trimmings. Not wishing to cause his employers any further displeasure, Mickey talked Ava into doing it Mayer's way.

After selecting a platinum wedding band, which Mickey approved, Peterson found a small apartment for him and Ava in the Wilshire Palms, a deluxe apartment complex near Westwood. Their apartment consisted of a kitchen, two bedrooms, and a living room, with white walls, white carpets, lots of mirrors, and beige leatherette furniture. It looked more like a fancy motel than the retreat of an important movie star, and was a bit of a comedown from Mickey's ranch in Encino, where he would have preferred to go on living. However, there were his mother and stepfather to consider. He wouldn't feel right about evicting them. Neither did he want to live there with them and his bride. Aside from personal considerations, Mayer deemed it advisable for Mickey and Ava to live somewhere that wasn't already a regular stop for sightseers and tour buses, which El Ranchita was. Publicity was to be avoided at all costs. After taking all these things into account, Mickey resigned himself to living in the Wilshire Palms, which MGM was paying for.

BY EARLY JANUARY of 1942, Peterson had finished scouring the sticks of California for the ideal wedding location and had come up with the town of Ballard, which was tucked away in the foothills of the Santa Ynez Mountains, a few miles up the coast from Santa Barbara, the county seat. Peterson's first foray into Santa Barbara was for the purpose of swearing the local newspapers to secrecy. In return for keeping mum until afterward, he promised them exclusive pictures of the wedding, which would be taken by MGM's best still photographer. Then, after ascertaining that Mickey and Ava would be able to obtain a wedding license on the spot, he drove up to Ballard and completed arrangements for the wedding. It was to take place in a little white Presbyterian church presided over by the Reverend Glen H. Lutz. In selecting the setting, Peterson completely ignored the fact that Ava had been raised a Southern Baptist and Mickey was a Christian Scientist.

ONCE HE'D RESIGNED himself to the inevitability of the marriage, Mayer tried to be a good sport about it. In addition to giving Mickey a race horse from his own stable as a wedding present, he hosted a massive stag party for Mickey in his private dining room at MGM the day before the wedding. Many of Metro's most important male stars were there, and after the meal each rose individually to offer ribald marital advice to the young groom—everything from how to prevent a bad back to how to explain lipstick marks on his fly when he came home from a busy day at the studio.

For the finale, Spencer Tracy told the story of the pebbles in the sink. "During the first year, every time you make love to your wife, Mickey, you put a pebble in the sink. Beginning the second year, every time you love your wife you take a pebble out of the sink. You know what, Mickey? You'll never empty the sink."

No strangers to the marriage-go-round, most of the stars roared with laughter and kidded the groom even more when he naively protested that his life with Ava would be different.

At the end of the roast, which Mickey remembers as being closer to a "barbecue in which I spun on a spit," the Mighty Mite rose to his full height and told the gathering: "Thanks, you horny bastards. And the first guy I see looking hard at Mrs. Rooney gets a right hand to the teeth!"

9

THE WEDDING WAS set to take place on Saturday, January 10, 1942. Like something out of a cloak-and-dagger movie, the wedding party surreptitiously left Hollywood early in the morning, hoping to avoid attention, and headed up the Pacific Coast Highway for Santa Barbara in two cars. Ava, Mickey, and Les Peterson led the small procession in the Lincoln. Bappie, Joe Yule, Sr., Nell, Fred Pankey, and a studio photographer were all squeezed into the second car, a studio limousine. In Carpinteria, a few miles south of Santa Barbara, Mickey got out of the car to phone ahead to the county clerk, J. E. Lewis, and asked him to prepare a wedding license for him and Ava. Then Peterson drove them to Lewis's house in Montecito, where they picked up the license, the usual three-day waiting period having been waived because they were celebrities.

From Santa Barbara, the wedding caravan snaked its way through the mountains to Ballard and the church, where they were met by the Reverend Glen H. Lutz, a tall, heavyset fellow whose haircut was so short and high over the ears it looked as if it had been done by a Marine barber.

Ava's sister Bappie was the maid of honor, and Lutz's wife supplied the wedding music on a tinny-sounding upright piano.

Mickey, in a new charcoal-gray, double-breasted suit with a green polka-dotted tie, was visibly nervous as he stood between Ava and Les Peterson, who not only acted as best man but wrote the press releases. Mickey stumbled through most of the ceremony and almost dropped the ring while trying to slide it onto Ava's finger. On the ring was engraved the inscription, "Love forever." As Mickey

101

quipped some years later, the ring should have read, "Number One."

Ava was wearing a dark-blue, tailored suit, which she'd been able to buy with the wedding bonus she'd received from MGM. She appeared radiant, concealing her disappointment over the small wedding like the good sport MGM expected her to be.

Once Mickey and Ava were pronounced man and wife, the Metro photographer took the official photographs. Standing on a stool Peterson had brought along, but which the photographer carefully cropped from the shot, Mickey appeared as tall as Ava in the pictures that appeared in the next morning's press.

After the photo session, Peterson found a telephone and called Metro to release the announcement that the couple was married. By then Louis B. Mayer had realized the futility of trying to keep such a monumental event a secret. For days now, MGM had been deluged with phone calls from the press. Strickling, keeping his promise to Hedda Hopper that she'd be the first to know, had to keep denying the rumors. But Mayer knew that sooner or later it would leak out. As a result, he had ordered the studio to rush into release Mickey's latest picture, *Life Begins for Andy Hardy,* so that they could capitalize on the publicity that was bound to hit the country.

It hit big. After Strickling handed Hedda the scoop, the wedding of the Mighty Mite to MGM's sexiest starlet became the lead item in her column in the *Los Angeles Times* on Sunday morning. Not only that, but a huge photo of Mickey smiling admiringly at Ava took up three full columns at the top of the front page. The photo was accompanied by a long story, which covered every detail of the wedding day, from the clandestine drive north to what music the minister's wife played during the ceremony.

FOLLOWING THE CEREMONY, Mickey kissed his relatives goodbye and watched with relief as everybody but Ava and Peterson took off in the second car for Los Angeles. Then he hopped behind the wheel of the Lincoln and drove Ava and Peterson to the place Peterson had chosen for their honeymoon: The Del Monte Hotel on 17 Mile Drive in Monterey—today, the Lodge at Pebble Beach, home of the Bing Crosby National Pro-Am Golf Tournament. The rustic beauty of the place, with a view of the rugged Monterey shoreline, made it the ideal spot for honeymooners. And if the groom had thought to bring his set of matched golf clubs, all the better.

But that wasn't Les Peterson's main concern when he chose this spot for the honeymoon. Monterey wasn't far from San Francisco, which would be the opening city on a long promotional tour for *Life Begins for Andy Hardy,* set to open the following week.

The combination of golf clubs and Les Peterson didn't augur too well for a smooth honeymoon, thought Ava during the four-hour drive north through some of California's prettiest countryside. Years later, whenever Peterson would bump into Ava around Hollywood, he would always say to her, kiddingly, "Remember me, Ava—three on a honeymoon." And then he'd laugh.

How could she have forgotten him? "When you came down to breakfast he was there," she said in recalling the honeymoon for a friend. "When you had dinner he was there. And when you went to bed, he was damn near there."

In all fairness to Peterson, it wasn't quite as Ava remembered it. Once he'd checked the dazed couple into the hotel and supervised a short session with newsreel photographers who'd dropped down from San Francisco, Peterson got back into the car and headed north for San Jose, for a family visit. "I told Mickey and Ava I was going to drive up there and spend the night," Peterson says today, "and that I wouldn't be back until morning."

Alone at last. Now that they were, the nervous couple wondered if they didn't still need Peterson. When they'd finally had their fill of champagne and moonlight, and the moment of truth was at hand, terror apparently filled both their hearts. In spite of her outward sophistication, Ava felt all of her mother's horror of sex welling up in her as she slipped into a floor-length, white nightgown and stretched out on the bed to wait for Mickey to come out of the bathroom.

And Mickey, even though he'd had plenty of women, was as apprehensive as if this were the first time. In the bathroom where he was changing into his pajamas, he was as nervous as the bridegroom in a latter-day TV sitcom. He put his pajama top on backward and became entangled in the arms and legs. It could have been a scene right out of *Andy Hardy Loses His Virginity.*

Suffice it to say, before the night was over they had consummated the marriage, and much to Mickey's delight—or should we say astonishment?—he discovered that Ava had been a virgin.

Although she proved more than a match for Mickey in bed, the exhilaration of knowing he'd been the first to have her kept him awake long after she dropped off to sleep. He filled in the time writing letters home to his folks. Of all of Mickey's varied accomplishments in life, before and after Ava, he has counted among his proudest the fact that he was the first man ever to possess that gorgeous body.

Les Peterson showed up again early the next morning and stuck as close to them for the rest of the honeymoon and publicity tour as a Secret Service man to the president. At first Ava resented this intrusion on their privacy, but once she realized what kind of a husband Mickey was going to be, she became almost grateful for the presence of a third party. Mickey may have had joie de vivre, fame, and money, but he had no idea of the role a husband was supposed to play once he was out of the sack.

Charged with that Andy Hardy-ish energy, he couldn't be confined to four walls, whispering sweet nothings in Ava's pretty ears the morning after. Besides, what was there to talk to Ava about? She'd come from a small town in North Carolina and wasn't too hep to show-business talk. Neither was she interested in sports. Her idea of a good time was to stay in the suite and "laze around" all day. But that wasn't for Mickey. He was there to play golf on the most beautiful, difficult course in the world.

"Golf?"

Of course. What did she think he'd brought his clubs along for?

"But I don't play golf," she protested.

"That's okay, Hun. I'll play. You watch."

Even though she didn't know a sand trap from a putting green, Mickey was eager to show off his golfing prowess for her. Though he'd only been hacking away for a couple of years, he was already shooting in the low eighties at Lakeside. If that didn't make up for his lack of height, nothing would.

After following him around for eighteen holes, Ava opted to stay in their suite, playing gin with Les Peterson, for the rest of their stay. If Mickey wasn't indulging his passion for golf, he was on the phone talking to his cronies in Los Angeles. During Mickey's long absences, Peterson kept Ava company by playing cards with her, entertaining her with stories of the studio, and treating her to ice cream and chocolate sodas because she had no money of her own. He was pleasant enough company but no substitute for a real husband.

Mickey was oblivious to Ava's unhappiness on the honeymoon. From his chauvinistic upbringing on the burlesque circuit, it was his opinion that a wife was supposed to do what her husband wanted her to do: Look pretty, keep him company at dinner, not complain when he was out with the boys, and be ready to hop into bed whenever the mood hit him.

Ava was too shy to complain openly to Mickey and angry with herself for having gotten into this mess. But as far as Mickey was concerned, the honeymoon was a success. He shot a 79 one day, and indulged his other need at least as frequently as any amorous groom.

As for Ava, she was relieved when Peterson advised them, four days into the honeymoon, to pack their bags and prepare for the long promotional tour for the Hardy picture.

"We drove to San Francisco," Peterson recalls, "and checked into the Palace Hotel, where we got the presidential suite—the same suite where President Harding died."

While her husband spent the day being interviewed, photographed, fawned over, and talking to his friends back home, Ava sat in a corner looking pretty and feeling thoroughly bored. When Mickey wasn't working, he, Peterson, and Ava went sightseeing and rode the cable cars. On their second day in the City by the Bay, their names were temporarily pushed off the front pages by the shocking news of the death of Carole Lombard. Her United Airlines plane had crashed on the way to Indianapolis, where she was to make a War-Bond tour appearance.

"My wife arrived by train, after Mickey finished his business in San Francisco," Peterson recalls, "and drove his car back to Encino for us. Then Mickey, Ava, and I proceeded to Chicago by Union Pacific. We spent the night at the Ambassador East, did some more promotion for the picture, then took the Twentieth Century for New York. We checked into the New Yorker Hotel, because Mickey and I were old friends of the proprietor."

During a press conference at the hotel, Ava sat in a deep chair while Mickey perched on the arm. In that way, the difference in their height was not too apparent. Soon after their arrival in New York, Bappie trained in from Los Angeles. Now Ava had a companion to go shopping with. Like a couple of schoolgirls, the two of them embarked on a tour of Fifth Avenue's most elegant stores to hunt for new outfits to wear to President Roosevelt's birthday ball on January 30, to which Mickey—and of course his wife and traveling companions—had again been invited.

Before going to Washington, D.C., however, the four of them took a side jaunt to Boston, where Mickey entertained at a Red Feather Community Chest function. The Cabots and the Lodges were also there, but it was Mickey who was stage center most of the time, while Ava hung back in corners looking beautiful but dumb. Pretty as she was, Ava did not share her husband's natural talent for dealing with the fans and the press. Much as he claimed he dreaded

105

interviews, the moment Mickey was in a reporter's presence he felt compelled to prove himself a man of intelligence and knowledge by talking rapidly and loudly on every subject under the sun, and gesturing with his hands. As someone once remarked about him, if you asked him for the time he'd end up telling you how a watch was made. He considered himself an authority on everything.

From Boston, Mickey and Peterson journeyed to Fort Bragg, North Carolina, to entertain the soldiers. Ava would have been a better bet to entertain the sex-starved GIs, but she, shunning the publicity, elected to take a side trip to her hometown of Smithfield to see her mother and family. Ava's mother, Molly, was bedridden with cancer, and Ava was deeply if silently disappointed that Mickey refused to accompany her there to meet her family. This could be Mickey's last opportunity to meet Ava's mother, but he was uninterested.

The dying Molly greeted Ava with stoicism and uttered not a word of complaint about her illness. Moreover, when Ava continued to grouse about the mistake she believed she had made in marrying Mickey, Molly summoned the strength to lecture her on the "duties" of a good wife.

Meanwhile, at Fort Bragg, Mickey Rooney was doing what every able-bodied movie star not yet in his country's service was expected to be doing—lifting the morale of those boys in uniform unfortunate enough to have been drafted first.

Or was he? E. J. Kahn, the *New Yorker* writer, happened to have been stationed at Fort Bragg and chronicled Mickey's visit in an amusing article for his magazine.

Kahn wrote that the local press was reluctantly allowed a picture-taking series:

> ... a General and another Colonel rushed in and we proceeded to take some photographs. Although Mickey didn't seem to relish having his picture taken, he always managed expertly, the moment before the camera clicked, to break into his broad, trade-marked grin. The only untoward incident involved one of the Colonels, who, evidently figuring that he would never again have a chance to be photographed with so luminous a character, almost sprained his back as he posed, bending from the waist toward Rooney in a desperate effort not to be caught with his head out of the shot.
>
> While all this was going on, a few soldiers had gathered outside the building, waiting for Mickey to emerge and to get to work on their

morale. As soon as we had finished taking pictures, Rooney strode out onto the balcony and waved to the boys below. He then bounded off into the night.

According to Kahn, Rooney returned two days later.

He arrived in the morning and was taken on a sightseeing tour by the Commanding General. He then rode in the General's car to a small body of water where some soldiers were climbing up and down rope nets draped over a floating wooden platform, practicing landing operations. The General and his abbreviated guest got into a large barge and were ferried out to the float. Rooney stood up in the boat and put one foot on the net, holding the post long enough for pictures to be taken of what looked like the start of a daring ascent. As soon as the photographer was satisfied, the actor's manager grabbed Mickey's arm and pulled him back down. Then some soldiers climbed all the way up and Mickey applauded like an apathetic seal. It didn't seem quite right, however; the gifted actor, sitting in a shallow boat and patting his hands together limply, looked amateurish playing the part of the audience.

Mickey also visited various ranges where soldiers had been tidying things up in anticipation of the visit. He seemed only moderately interested in the activities of the enlisted men. His manager spent most of his time looking at his watch. The only weapon the actor fired was a light machine gun. He was astonished by the noise he created with the pressure of his autograph finger and yelled, 'Wow!' After he had fired the gun, however, he didn't seem to care about inspecting the target. It is the only instance I've ever encountered of anyone's shooting at something and not wanting to know how close he came to hitting it.

That seemed to be the extent of Mickey's "morale lifting" at Fort Bragg before he and Peterson rejoined Ava and Bappie in Charleston, and the four of them proceeded by train to Washington, D.C., and President Roosevelt's birthday festivities.

"Ava, Bappie, Mickey and I all sat at one table," Peterson recalls. "And there was the usual empty place for Roosevelt. After we were there a while, Roosevelt wheeled over in his wheelchair and had one course with us. He had a hard time taking his eye off Ava, then duty called and he said goodbye, thanked us for coming and wheeled over to another table."

The next day, after Mickey made a few War Bond appearances in the nation's capital, the four of them went back to Hollywood by train.

The honeymoon was over, in more ways than one.

10

MICKEY AND AVA hadn't been settled in the Wilshire Palms very long before both came to the realization, independently, that their marriage was sick.

Mickey may have been over twenty-one and a huge success, but emotionally he was too young to accept the obligations of marriage. Once Mickey had satisfied himself sexually, he wanted to go on living as he had before, racing around in fast automobiles with his gang of friends, nightclubbing, playing golf, and gambling at the racetrack. Ava, on the other hand, was too shy for the fast lane. She wanted to cook Southern dishes for Mickey, listen to phonograph records, and write letters to the folks in North Carolina. Or maybe just sit around and talk to her husband.

According to Mickey, Ava wasn't a bad cook, and she was a pretty good housekeeper. She even liked to do the shopping and was always adding little wifely touches to the decor. Mickey, however, was bored with that aspect of marriage.

Sidney Miller believes he was the first guest to have dinner with them in their apartment after they returned from their honeymoon. Having observed their relationship firsthand, he reports: "Mickey was crazy about her. But Ava always impressed me with being kind of cool, and that her career was the most important thing. She loved Mickey, I guess, but in a condescending way. Like to her, he was a darling little kid. She was a kid, too, younger than Mickey actually. But she acted more grown up—at least she was taller."

Another friend who dined with them in the apartment reports a different relationship. He found the two of them behaving "like

109

school kids, giggling, smooching, and even wrestling on the floor the entire evening."

There had to have been some of that, otherwise the marriage wouldn't have lasted as long as it did. But it was doomed from the start, according to Ava who, several marriages later, told her agent, Charlie Feldman, "I think I knew long before Mickey and I were married that we weren't meant for each other. I was stupid enough to think marriage changes a man. I know better now . . . I did everything humanly possible to make my marriage to Mickey work. He was 'onstage' all the time, and I was careful not to offer him any competition. I was his greatest audience at home or out. I cooked for him, and I cleaned for him. I puffed up his ego at the expense of mine many times. I was a devoted, loyal and good wife in every sense of the word. But, I was demanding. I didn't expect more than I wanted to give, but I did expect that much in return. Also, I think I'm enough companionship for my husband. I didn't like being on the go every minute of the day, with parties, clubs and dinners nightly."

On the other hand, Ava wasn't the kind of a wife who enjoyed sitting home alone, either. So on those occasions when Mickey left her to go out with "the boys," she sat in the apartment and "burned." No young bride, even one not as beautiful as Ava Gardner, could be expected to do otherwise.

For most of Ava's young life she had been subject to severe stomach cramps. Aside from menstrual problems, they were brought on by worry and tension, according to Ava's doctor. Although he felt sorry for her, Mickey eventually grew inured to her physical complaints. As a result, he hardly looked up from his *Racing Form* one night, about five weeks after their honeymoon trip, when Ava started to complain about the severity of her cramps.

Mickey's attitude was like that of many doctors: take two aspirins and go to bed. Meanwhile, should he bet on the seven horse in the third race, or the three horse in the seventh race?

But this time the cramps didn't go away, and Mickey finally had to summon the doctor. It turned out Ava had an inflamed appendix and had to be rushed to Hollywood Hospital for emergency surgery.

Frightened by the experience, Mickey reformed temporarily. He was at Ava's bedside when she regained consciousness, and during her convalescence he brought her flowers and candy and spent as much time as he could with her.

For a while after Ava returned home to complete her recovery,

110

their married life was fairly serene. Mickey was full of concern for Ava and couldn't do enough for her. He didn't even put up much of a squawk when the surgeon who performed her appendectomy sent him a bill for ten thousand dollars—about nine thousand dollars more than the going price. When you were a movie star of Mickey Rooney's importance, you accepted being overcharged with a shrug.

Forced to stay home nights while Ava was convalescing, Mickey fought hard to overcome his boredom. To keep her entertained, he would talk about football and baseball and gossip about things he'd seen and heard at the studio. Most of this was over Ava's head, or else she just wasn't interested, and her lack of repartee exasperated him. Had he been less self-involved, he might have noticed a slight change in her attitude. She no longer insisted on cooking dinner for him as she had when they were first married. In fact, she asked for a live-in cook/housekeeper. This was all right with Mickey, but since there was no room for a live-in servant in their apartment, it meant they'd have to move to a larger place. Possibly a house.

That, too, suited Ava, so they turned the problem of finding one over to Les Peterson. In no time he came up with an attractive bungalow for them to rent at 1120 Stone Canyon Drive in Bel Air.

Now that he'd given Ava a luxurious home, plus a housekeeper to cook and clean for them, Mickey happily turned his energies to his busy schedule at the studio. He was about to go into *The Courtship of Andy Hardy*, which was full of exploitable parallels with his real-life romance and marriage, and that film was to be followed by *A Yank at Eton*, in which he would costar with Freddie Bartholomew.

Ava, on the other hand, was still a nonentity at the studio except for being Mickey Rooney's wife. She was getting a walk-on in a movie every now and then, as a hatcheck girl or a model, and she was sought-after for cheesecake layouts down in Metro's Shooting Gallery. Nevertheless, it was beginning to bother her that her husband was such a huge star and she was still a nobody. Ava didn't display too much unhappiness, just so long as when they returned home together from the studio in the evenings, she could kick off her shoes, tie up her hair, and relax in a skirt and sweater. But this was no cure for Mickey's growing restlessness after work. He dreaded the long nights when Ava would sit silently writing letters home to North Carolina or chatting about small-town gossip she'd heard from her mother. Moreover, her ability to converse with her loquacious husband didn't seem to be improving. "Talking to her was like talking to a brick wall," he once confided to a friend. "She would agree with what I said, and then sink into a silence again."

Thinking that perhaps her sullenness stemmed from her stalled career, Mickey decided to use his clout to help Ava land some decent parts. He placed her in the hands of his agent, Johnny Hyde, but it was actually his own hustling at the studio that got her started.

Soon she was working regularly. Bigger and better walk-ons at first: she played a fashion model in Joan Crawford's *Reunion in France* and a Czech resistance fighter in *Hitler's Madman*. Early in the spring of 1942, Ava landed her first talking role, in *Kid Glove Killer*, which starred Joan Crawford, Marsha Hunt, and Lee Bowman.

Now, Mickey and Ava had something to do in the evenings besides going to bed or not talking to one another. Because her acting was still pretty amateurish, Mickey coached her. He gave her practical tips on how to stand, how to walk, what to do with her hands. He even showed up on her set in the mornings with last-minute instructions. "Keep your chin up, Ava," he said. "Don't look hang-dog. Remember, you're a gorgeous creature. Don't slump." Or, "Keep your eyes on the person you're talking to."

Despite Mickey's acting lessons, Ava's screen appearances evoked little emotion among studio heads and the audience except boredom, or annoyance at the fact that her hillbilly accent was still a little too thick to understand. Had she not been Mickey Rooney's wife, her future at the studio would have been uncertain when her contract came up for renewal. No dummy, Ava was well aware of her shortcomings, and this put her into a depression that didn't make her any easier to live with.

It was no wonder Mickey jumped at every opportunity to go to a party or a nightspot—with or without Ava. Not that she was any asset at social events. According to Mickey, Ava would sit in a corner and look beautiful.

But in April she started coming out of her shell at parties. With the help of a couple of martinis she was no longer a wallflower. At one studio party, for example, she danced several dances with Tom Drake, a young, handsome contract actor she knew from the studio. Since Mickey was off in another part of the room entertaining and paying no attention to her, Ava didn't think he'd mind.

She didn't know Mickey. When he realized she was dancing with someone else, and evidently enjoying it, he flew into a jealous rage. They fought all the way home and after they got there. This time

Ava dished it out, too. Feeling absolutely no pain from the liquor she'd drunk, Ava told Mickey she'd dance with anyone she damn-well pleased, so long as Mickey was ignoring her and showing off for everybody else.

Hurt, Mickey told Ava that she ought to be a little more apprecia-tive of him. Also of his efforts to help Ava get her career started. Ava sneered at his ability to help her and threw up to him the fact that he didn't even have the clout to get her the part she wanted in *The Courtship of Andy Hardy*. She was referring to the role of the girl Andy almost falls in love with. Mickey had pitched Ava to Carey Wilson, but in the ei 1 the producer of the series decided she didn't have the experience and hired Donna Reed instead.

Ava had been quietly resentful about his lack of success on her behalf when the argument about Drake started. But when Mickey told her that he'd done his best, Ava scoffed at him and taunted him about his size. She screamed that she was tired of living with a midget! Then she walked out of the house and moved back in with Bappie on Franklin Avenue.

Mickey could take anything else, but the crack about his size was the ultimate insult. It, plus her walkout, threw him into a complete spin, which began to show up in his work in *The Courtship of Andy Hardy*. Mickey's acting seemed to have lost all its energy and verve. Worried, Carey Wilson took it up with Eddie Mannix, the burly Irishman who was head of production and all around trouble-shooter for Mayer.

After viewing the dailies, Mannix had to admit that Mickey and Ava's separation, which was known only among a select few at MGM, was taking its toll. Not only was Mickey's acting abnormally subdued, but he had dark rings under his eyes that were giving him a dissipated look.

"He's beginning to look as old as his father," Mannix cracked. "If we don't pull him out of this, we can change the title of the picture to *Andy Hardy Goes to the Poor House!*"

After enlisting Bappie's support, Mannix summoned Mickey and Ava to his office, where he lectured them on the futility of divorce. They'd merely had a lover's spat, he insisted, and as a reward for their going back together, he promised Ava a good part in a movie.

That was the clincher. Ava and Mickey kissed and made up, following which Ava moved out of Bappie's apartment and back into the house on Stone Canyon.

MGM's head shamus kept his word and got Ava a role in a movie—but not at MGM. He loaned her out to Monogram to appear in a B-minus picture with the Dead End Kids—*Ghosts on the Loose*. In it, Ava proved once again to be no Ethel Barrymore, but friends who dutifully went to see it were surprised that she showed some flair for comedy.

Together once more, Mickey and Ava were soon regulars on the nightclub circuit, which they had temporarily forsaken for the bedroom in the inchoate stages of their marriage.

Nightclubbing was no cure for what actually ailed the marriage, a complete lack of anything in common. In fact, it only exacerbated the situation. It was at the Mocambo, a new "in" nightclub on the Strip that Ava met Frank Sinatra for the first time. By now, most of the forties Big Band vocalists had been signed to movie contracts. Sinatra was not yet attached to a studio. However, the thin young man from New Jersey was still the biggest heartthrob among the girls in the bobby-sox crowd, and had been rewarded with his own coast-to-coast radio show, which emanated from NBC in Hollywood. It was during this period that he and the Rooneys first met at the Mocambo.

Ava later confessed to a friend that the moment she set eyes on Sinatra she knew "he was dangerously attractive." Sinatra felt the same way about her, which Ava intuitively sensed. But to avoid another jealous fit by Mickey in a public place, Ava feigned indifference to Sinatra's flirting. This just whetted his appetite for her, and when he was asked to sing with the orchestra he stepped to the mike and dedicated the number to Ava Rooney.

Another time, Mickey took Ava to the Palladium. They danced a few dances, after which Mickey's clowning and mugging on the dance floor attracted the attention of Tommy Dorsey, who asked Mickey to sit in with the band and play the trap drums. Mickey not only played the drums, but he also doubled on trumpet, completely ignoring Ava, who was left to entertain herself at their table.

Around midnight, Ava had had enough. Without telling Mickey, she stormed out of the place and drove back to Bel Air in the family car.

Mickey had to go home by cab. When he finally did get there, about three in the morning, he apologized to a tearful Ava, slipped into bed and, thinking it would help pacify her, started making love to her. For some reason, she didn't plead a headache, and mechanically went through the motions. Then she eased herself out of bed and started toward the bathroom. After three or four steps, she spun around in her nudity, and said slowly but clearly, "If you ever knock me up, you little son of a bitch, I'll kill you!"

She then ran for the bathroom, with Mickey following at her heels. Having longer legs, she reached there first, slammed the door, and locked it. Mickey dropped to his knees, pounding on the door with both fists, and cried out in anguish, "Why, Ava? What have I done?"

That a scene like that didn't provoke Mickey into walking out on Ava is a sign that he still loved her. Slowly, however, he was becoming disillusioned with the marriage, and that summer, for the first time, he didn't object to going to Chicago on a publicity tour without her.

Half a continent away from Ava, he could enjoy the local night-spots and racetracks without feeling guilty about leaving her at home. He also enjoyed an unexpected windfall that made him wonder what was best—to be "lucky in love" or at the track.

"I remember this Friday night at the Chez Paree in Chicago," Peterson recalled. "After Mickey's PA [publicity] appearances at the theater, we went to see Helen Morgan at the nightclub. While we were sitting at our table, this jockey came over and started talking to Mickey. He was a little bit tipsy, and he said, 'Bet on me tomorrow in the seventh race at Arlington.' He gave us his name, which we didn't recognize. We only knew that he wasn't one of the big boys. He kept pointing to himself all evening whenever he caught Mickey's eye. So the next day, Mickey insisted that we go out to Arlington Park—we didn't have a matinee to do—and bet on this guy in the big race. Now in the same race was Whirlaway, the triple-crown winner of the previous year, and Eddie Arcaro was on him. Then Mickey looked up our jockey's horse and saw that he hadn't come in in the money in twenty-five races, and that he was going off at ninety-eight to one. Anyway, Mickey put a hundred on the nose, and insisted that I, who never bet on a horse race in my life, put fifty on him, too. Well, to make a long story short, it was a muddy track and this nag astounded everybody by beating Whirlaway and Arcaro. Mickey was delirious. After we collected our money—Mickey won about twenty grand and I got ten—we went down to Marshall Field's and started buying out the store. Among other things, Mickey bought gorgeous diamond earrings for Ava, and I bought a smaller pair for my wife."

Ava appreciated the diamond earrings, and for a few days after Mickey returned home there was peace and possibly even a few moments of bliss. But then Mickey reverted to his old ways and, by August of 1942, it was obvious that the marriage was going nowhere except a divorce court. Mickey refused to change his life-style. His absences from home were becoming more and more frequent, and his boredom with Ava, except as a sex object, increased.

Ava, on the other hand, was no longer the doormat for Mickey she'd once been. From her association with some of the other, more worldly, actresses at the studio Ava had come to the realization that she was far too attractive to stay at home alone nights while her husband was out on the town. There were plenty of men around, all taller and more agreeable than Mickey, who'd be happy to spend their evenings with Ava. Because of her strict Southern Baptist upbringing, Ava wasn't about to start having affairs while she was still married to Mickey. But after hearing the other girls talk, a new spirit of independence began to emerge in her.

One night, while Mickey was out playing poker with the boys, Ava joined a group of her friends at Ciro's. When Mickey returned home, he was shocked not to find Ava in bed waiting for him. This precipitated a fight when she did finally arrive, around three A.M. and slightly tipsy. As the fight simmered down, Mickey had the nerve to suggest that a baby might save their marriage. He then put his arms around Ava and tried to kiss her. Ava recoiled, calling him every name in the book.

Mickey was hurt. Ava was hurt. For a few days, there was an uneasy truce. As always during these periods of détente, Mickey was properly contrite and deferential, promising to be a good, thoughtful husband in the future. Ava doubted if he'd ever change but was not yet ready to make the big move

They drove to Tijuana one morning for a day of fun south of the border. At lunch, while they sipped margaritas and enjoyed the music of a strolling mariachi band, they looked as happy as they did in their wedding pictures. Then Mickey took her to the races at the Agua Caliente track, where his interest in a couple of fillies that looked good to him in the *Racing Form* caused him to neglect the filly by his side. As a result, she called him a rotten bastard, and they fought the whole way back to Los Angeles in the car.

The great conciliator, Mickey assuaged her with a barrage of apologies and sweet talk in time to take her out to dinner at Chasen's. During dinner, the mood at their table was cheerful enough to make their friends who stopped by believe everything was okay again with the Rooneys. But after dinner, Mickey had to play the big shot by buying drinks for everyone at the bar. Fed up with his drinking, Ava went home by herself in a cab.

When Mickey arrived home around midnight, the living room looked as if a motorcycle gang had been turned loose in it. In her

116

fury with Mickey, Ava had taken a knife and sliced up all the upholstered furniture. That quarrel festered for several days.

One night, Ava finally announced she'd had enough. "Get the hell out!" she yelled at Mickey.

"If I get out," he answered, "I won't come back."

"Good. Don't come back. I don't want you to come back. Now get the hell out of here!"

With a shrug, he silently started for the door. He was confident that she'd lose her nerve and call him back before he reached the threshold. The silence was deafening. With manly pride, Mickey kept going right out the door.

It was just slightly over eight months since they had taken their wedding vows.

WOUNDED, BUT STILL infatuated with Ava and ever hopeful she'd have a change of heart, Mickey moved back into his mother's and step-father's house in Encino. There he explained to the concerned Nell that he and Ava had just had a little fight, really nothing more serious than a lover's spat, and it was sure to blow over. Then he trudged wearily upstairs to his old bedroom, wondering how he could have failed so miserably as a husband when he'd never failed at anything else.

AVA, MEANWHILE, DETERMINED to sever all ties with Mickey, moved out of the house in Bel Air and back to the Wilshire Palms apartment, which the studio had retained.

Mickey called constantly, pleading for Ava's forgiveness and "one more chance." He bombarded her with presents, including a lot of jewelry and a ten-thousand-dollar mink coat.

The warmth of the mink skins must have caused Ava to thaw slightly. She invited Mickey to come home again. All was forgiven, she told him. But despite both parties' good intentions, fighting erupted almost immediately, and two nights later Ava forcibly ejected Mickey from the apartment.

His pride hurt, Mickey continued to pester Ava with phone calls, sometimes waking her in the middle of the night with demands that she take him back. Terrified that Mickey might try something violent, Ava asked a close friend of hers from the studio, Leatrice Carney, daughter of the silent movie star John Gilbert, to move in with her at the Wilshire Palms.

Says Leatrice, "My chief memory of the time I spent there, maybe five months, was Ava's terror of Mickey coming to 'get her.' One

117

night her fears became a reality. He literally broke the door down when she wouldn't let him in. We had to struggle with him to get him to leave. I think he was crazy with frustration because she wouldn't sleep with him. He wanted her so badly, but she no longer would have anything to do with him."

Ava was so terrified of what Mickey might do that she phoned Howard Strickling and told him she would expose their marital mess to the media if the studio didn't do something to restrain Mickey's behavior. Strickling took up the problem with Mayer, whose solution to the crisis was, "Keep them away from each other—and keep them both busy."

The film Mickey was about to go into—*A Yank at Eton*—was to be shot almost entirely on location in Connecticut, but not for a couple of months yet. To handle the Mickey-Ava problem, Mayer ordered that *A Yank at Eton* be pushed to the front of the production schedule to get Mickey out of town as soon as possible. To keep Ava in California, Mayer saw to it that she was cast in one small role after another.

Mickey phoned Ava from Connecticut nearly every night, but Leatrice intercepted his calls and warded him off with the same answer: "Ava's not in."

Actually, Ava rarely went out, preferring to stay at home nights, entertaining and cooking for her new friends: attorney Jerry Rosenthal and his wife; Tony Owen and his wife, Donna Reed; and Minna Wallis, the agent.

A Yank at Eton completed filming in October of 1942, at which time Mickey raced back to Los Angeles to take another shot at repairing his broken marriage. His first evening at home he rushed over to the Wilshire Palms, where Ava was hosting a small dinner party. When she refused to open the door, he tried to break it down with his shoulders, screamed all kinds of uncomplimentary things at her, and wouldn't go away until she threatened to call the police.

Mickey seemed to be on the verge of cracking up. In addition to a failed marriage, he was now faced with the prospect of Army service.

The previous August, Mickey had received word from his local draft board in Westwood that he had been classified 1-A and was to report to the Army induction center in downtown Los Angeles in September for a physical. Mickey was scared to death—not of going off to war, but of losing Ava for good. He realized that once he left her for any prolonged period of time the chance of their getting back together would be slimmer than it already was.

118

It is doubtful if that is the reason Louis B. Mayer tried desperately to get an Army deferral for his biggest box-office attraction. More likely he was motivated by business and acted independently of Mickey when he interceded on his behalf. At any rate, the Metro-Goldwyn-Mayer files are bulging with correspondence between MGM and Local Draft Board 245. The full weight of the world's most important film studio was thrown behind an effort to keep Mickey Rooney out of uniform.

Mayer turned that problem over to Eddie Mannix, who, in a sworn affidavit to the draft board, on behalf of Loew's, Inc., submitted a "request for occupational deferment." Claiming that Mickey Rooney was a "necessary man, within the meaning of the selective service regulations, to an industry" Mannix pleaded that Mickey should be reclassified 2-A. To bolster his argument, Mannix even included in the affidavit a scene from an up-and-coming Andy Hardy film, *Andy Hardy's Blonde Trouble.* In the scene, Andy announced to his mother and father that he was thinking of volunteering for military service.

Mrs. Hardy was shocked that her "baby" would voluntarily risk his life when it was improbable that he would be drafted for at least a year. But Judge Hardy was of the opinion that Andy should do what his conscience dictated.

EMILY: Why, why should Andy go to war?

JUDGE HARDY: Emily, for the same reason I fought—and my father fought. Perhaps I can best explain it with the words from the first chapter of Genesis: "God created man in his own image," but those we're fighting want to create a world in their own image, a world of tyranny, cruelty and slavery. We're not fighting this war for a conquest, Emily, but to make a world that will be safe for our children. We're fighting for tolerance and decency, and for the four freedoms that the President of the United States has so simply stated. It is to make this world safe that our nation has placed it in the hands and hearts of our millions of free men and women. Your son, Andrew, is one of those millions.

The affidavit went on to state that "the 25 million Americans who will see this picture must gain a greater and fuller understanding of, and sympathy with, the American fundamentals. We plan that each succeeding Hardy picture will further this idea, carry Andy, as he grows older, closer to the war, and reveal through Andy and his parents, the actual experiences of the young American boy who has taken such a step. The morale of the Hardy family should, and will be the highest type of morale of the American family.

"Moreover, Mickey is irreplaceable and it will cost the studio millions in other films planned and ready to go with him starring in them, if he is drafted."

Mannix followed the first affidavit with a second one on August 28, 1942. In this one he stated that *The Human Comedy* starring Mickey Rooney, was to begin shooting on August 31, and that it would be a hardship on the studio to lose him."

On September 3, the appeal was turned down, but the draft board gave Mickey a three-month extension so that he could finish the picture and temporarily reclassified him 2-A.

On December 18, the day the three months elapsed, Mickey received another notice, reclassifying him 1-A and giving him another date to report for his physical. Four days later, Mickey and Irving Prinzmetal, one of MGM's most respected attorneys, appeared before Draft Board 245 on Westwood Boulevard to appeal the decision. On December 30, the draft board turned down Prinzmetal's request, and Mickey was eligible for service again.

That, however, didn't deter MGM. On January 6, 1943, Eddie Mannix dispatched another affidavit of appeal to Mickey's draft board. In this document he quoted a number of national leaders and government officials about how important the motion picture business was to the country's morale. Mannix even quoted Lieutenant General Dwight Eisenhower's statement that "Motion picture entertainment is as important to the people on the home front as butter and meat."

The document took eight double-spaced pages in all, but despite its comprehensiveness the appeal was turned down by the board in a vote of five to zero on February 6, 1943.

By now MGM's efforts to keep Mickey out of the Army were beginning to reach the public prints, and Mickey and the studio soon realized that for Mickey to be deferred while ordinary boys were being rushed off to war and possibly their deaths could only cause resentment among the movie-going public. That kind of publicity could kill off an actor's career faster than a string of bad pictures.

To try to restore some of the polish to his tarnished image, Mickey announced to the press that he was willing to serve in the Army or continue making pictures if the government decided that actors were essential. "Whatever the government decides it's okay with me," Mickey declared.

Before reporting for his physical, however, Mickey wrote a note to the local board of education* on March 3, "requesting records of physical examinations made of me in the past." Armed with his records and a recent statement from Nell saying that her son had been bothered lately with "heart flutter" and "high blood pressure," on March 15 Mickey reported to the Army induction station on Main Street for his physical. On March 16, Lieutenant Colonel Edgar H. Bailey, the commanding officer of the Los Angeles army induction station, reported that "Mickey Rooney, the film actor, has been rejected for Army service." Bailey added that the actor had been referred to the induction center by his draft board and had received a "thorough examination."

On March 18, Mickey was notified by the draft board that he had been reclassified 4-F. Mannix and Mayer were informed of this in a studio interoffice memo written by Les Peterson on the following day and were delighted. So, of course, was Mickey.

It was a bizarre series of events for Mickey, who, from all appearances, was in robust health, to go from 1-A to 4-F in so short a time. But it didn't surprise his personal physician who believed that Mickey's high blood pressure could have been caused by the tension in a failing marriage.

Whatever was responsible for his sudden poor health, Mickey was free, at least for the time being, of Army service.

He was also free of the yoke of marriage. On January 15, 1943, Mickey had formally separated from Ava. And on May 2, Ava killed any hopes Mickey might have had for a reconciliation by filing for divorce in Los Angeles, claiming half of Mickey's property and earnings. The grounds: grievous mental suffering and extreme mental cruelty, which was standard for most California divorces in those days.

Mickey didn't fight her charges, and the case went before Superior Court Judge Thurmon Clark on the twenty-first of May. Ava wore the same blue suit in which she'd been married.

---

*It was part of the board of education's policy to insist that minors under contract to studios have a yearly physical examination.

On the stand, Ava was subdued. When her attorney, Alo G. Ritter asked her what Mickey's cruelty consisted of, Ava told the court, "He wanted no home life with me. He told me so many times."

"Is it true he left you alone much of the time?" the lawyer asked.

"Yes, he did," Ava replied tearfully. "He often remained away from home. Twice he stayed away for long periods. He spent a month with his mother once, and when I protested he told me he simply didn't want to be with me."

To everyone's surprise, before the case was over, Ava suddenly waived her claim to half of Mickey's property. All she wanted, she told the court, was twenty-five thousand dollars in cash, a car, her furs, and the jewelry he'd given her.

As it turned out, her diminished demands didn't come entirely from the goodness of Ava's heart. The lords at MGM were still looking out for the welfare of their number-one son. On the eve of the courtroom proceedings, Eddie Mannix had taken Ava aside and implied that things would not go well for her at MGM if she "took Mickey to the cleaners." If she'd go easy on him, he promised her better roles in the future.

Who said there weren't some benefits to be derived from the old studio star-system?

An interlocutory decree was granted on May 21, but neither of the litigants would be free to marry until the divorce became final a year later. That was all right with Mickey. The eternal optimist, he had every confidence in his ability to win her back.

11

I F, AS SOME believe, hard work is the antidote for a broken heart, Mickey should have been well on the road to recovery by the time he eventually went into the Army in June of 1944.

Between the day he and Ava officially parted and the day Mickey exchanged his loud sports jackets for Army khaki, Mickey seemed singlehandedly to be supplying the nation's movie theaters with product.

In 1942 he starred in *The Courtship of Andy Hardy, Andy Hardy's Double Life* and *Andy Hardy Steps Out*; in 1943, *A Yank at Eton, The Human Comedy, Girl Crazy,* and *Thousands Cheer*; and in 1944, *Andy Hardy's Blonde Trouble* and *National Velvet.*

These films did all right at the box office, but in the judgment of most critics Mickey Rooney's performances were beginning to suffer from too much exposure, especially in the Hardy series, which was beginning to wear a little thin. *The Courtship of Andy Hardy* was the thirteenth of the series and, according to Bosley Crowther, "one of the less distinguished Hardy films."

Mickey's overexposure was not his fault. He was strictly an employee of MGM, and in return for his $2500 a week was expected to perform in any film the MGM hierarchy ordered him to. The results, with just a few exceptions, were the kind of picture about which Mickey's detractors could say, "Mr. Rooney cried all the way to the bank."

About *A Yank in Eton, The New York Times* wrote, "Draw a deep breath, ladies and gentlemen, and check your sensibilities at the door . . . *Andy Hardy at Eton* is a fearful thing to see."

123

Thousands Cheer, a big, gaudy MGM musical revue with an army-camp background was not strictly a "Rooney picture." In fact, if such a thing were humanly possible, Mickey almost got lost in the all-star cast. Originally planned as a schmaltzy Joe Pasternak musical love story about a soldier (Gene Kelly) and a colonel's daughter (Kathryn Grayson), it slowly developed into an all-star extravaganza of the kind only MGM could make because only MGM had so many stars under contract. In addition to Kelly and Grayson, the picture featured John Boles, Mary Astor, José Iturbi, Ben Blue, Frances Rafferty, Judy Garland, Eleanor Powell, Red Skelton, Ann Southern, Lucille Ball, Frank Morgan, Lena Horne, Margaret O'Brien, Marsha Hunt, Marilyn Maxwell, June Allyson, Gloria DeHaven, Virginia O'Brien, Donna Reed—and Mickey Rooney. Plus the bands of Kay Kyser, Bob Crosby, Benny Carter. Plus a symphony orchestra. Plus a military band.

Mickey Rooney didn't make his appearance until the film's climax when he emceed a huge, army camp show. "Mickey's stint is not exactly a show-stopper," *The New York Times* wrote, "except for his take-off on Gable and Tracy doing a scene from *Test Pilot.* But *Girl Crazy* was all Rooney and Garland, with Mickey getting unqualified raves when this picture opened in New York in December of 1943. "Hold your hat, folks. Mickey Rooney and Judy Garland are back in town, and if at this late date there are still a few die-hards who deny that they are the most incorrigibly talented pair of youngsters in the movies, then *Girl Crazy*, now at the Capitol, should serve as final rebuttal," *The New York Times* reviewer wrote.

Two of Mickey's most successful films of the war years were *The Human Comedy* and *National Velvet*—both notable for being a "first." *The Human Comedy* because it was the first story of William Saroyan's to reach the screen, the *National Velvet* because it made a star of Elizabeth Taylor.

It's a wonder *The Human Comedy* was made at all.

Strange as it seems, one of the fans of Saroyan's Pulitzer Prize comedy, *The Time of Your Life*, was Mickey's boss, Louis B. Mayer, who didn't ordinarily go for the unusual. He didn't see a movie in Saroyan's one-set play, but he thought so much of his talent that he offered the playwright $300 a week simply to come to MGM in 1942 and look around.

After getting the feel of studio life for several weeks, Saroyan wrote a story about a youngster who worked as a telegram delivery boy in a small town. He obviously had seen a number of Hardy films, for the main character in *The Human Comedy* was not unlike that of Andy Hardy, and the film's small-town background of Ithaca, California, not a great deal different from Carvel, Idaho.

Saroyan's yarn had the anticipated effect on Mayer, according to Sam Marx, who was back in his old job as MGM story editor. "L.B. made an instant deal as soon as he heard Saroyan's story," Marx recalls today. But after Mayer saw the first draft of Saroyan's screenplay, kicked him off the *Human Comedy* project. Incensed, Saroyan demanded to be permitted to buy back his story for eighty thousand dollars. But Mayer refused. Instead, he assigned Howard Estabrook to write a final and shootable screenplay, and Clarence Brown to produce and direct the film.

From the moment Mayer bought the story from Saroyan, there was never any doubt that Mickey Rooney would be chosen to play the part of Homer Macauley, the Western Union delivery boy around whom the whole "human comedy" revolved.

By the time the film was completed, there was so little of Saroyan's script remaining that the playwright was only given "original story" credit on the screen. Saroyan got the last laugh, however, for he had retained the right to turn his story into a novel, which became the country's number-one best-seller one week after its release. Not only that, Saroyan won an Oscar for Best Original Story, while the writer of the screenplay, Howard Estabrook, didn't even get a nomination.

The picture was a huge success, too, in spite of the fact that the critics couldn't make up their minds whether they liked it or not. "The dignity and simplicity of the idea shade off into cheap pretentiousness," Bosley Crowther wrote, while James Agee noted, "The best one can say of it is that it tries on the whole to be faithful to Saroyan; not invariably a good idea."

If most of the critics objected to what they referred to as the picture's "cheap sentimentality," almost to a man they liked Mickey Rooney's fine performance. "There is a tenderness and restraint in his characterization, along with a genuine youthfulness, such as he has not known for a long time," Bosley Crowther wrote.

The Motion Picture Academy nominated Mickey for Best Actor for his performance. This time, he lost out in the final balloting to Paul Lukas for *Watch on the Rhine*. But Mayer didn't care. *The Human Comedy* was a big money-maker and, incidentally, Mayer's favorite picture of all time.

Although Mickey Rooney got first billing when *National Velvet* opened at New York's Radio City Music Hall in 1944, it was sixteen-year-old Elizabeth Taylor, playing in only her second film, who drew most of the attention. Even though she had played second fiddle to a collie in *Lassie Comes Home,* her physical attributes and acting talent had impressed Sam Marx, who produced the film. In fact, he had been so impressed by her looks and ability that even while the Lassie picture was still in production, he invited producer Pan Berman, who was searching desperately for an actress to play the lead in *National Velvet,* to look at Taylor in the rushes. "Pan had a script and was ready to go into production, but he still had no girl," Marx says, "so I called Pan and told him, 'You'd better come and look at this Elizabeth Taylor—because she's your girl.'"

Berman saw on the projection room screen what Taylor had, and immediately signed her for *National Velvet.* She was so successful in the role that she stayed at MGM for nineteen years. And *The New York Times* wrote, "This fresh and delightful Metro picture based on Enid Bagnold's best-selling novel of some years back, tells by far the most touching story of youngsters and of animals since Lassie was coming home . . . Director Clarence Brown has drawn some excellent performances from his cast, especially from little Elizabeth Taylor, who plays the role of the horse-loving girl with refreshing grace . . . Mickey Rooney is also affecting, if somewhat less airily so, as the boy who helps her train her jumper and gains a new and happy outlook thereby."

MICKEY, FOR ALL his hard work and good reviews, was still carrying the torch for Ava, and so close to his heart that it's a wonder he didn't singe his soul.

Living in a town like Hollywood, where every date a starlet or pretty actress had was reported in the gossip columns, didn't make it any easier for Mickey to get through the ordeal of trying to forget Ava.

Ava wasn't looking seriously yet for another husband or steady boyfriend. She seemed content to be sharing her apartment with Bappie again. Nevertheless she kept her name in the public prints by dating a string of bachelors and unhappily married men: Jimmy McHugh, Lee McGregor, Turhan Bey, John Carroll, Robert Walker, Fernando Lamas, and Peter Lawford.

By her own admission Ava wasn't interested in any of these men. But they were big spenders, and she enjoyed the publicity she derived from being seen with them.

Determined though she was to have a good time, Ava wasn't much happier after the divorce than she was while she was battling with Mickey. (One Hollywood wag wrote, "She's lost her hobby.") In fact, by the fall of 1943 Ava was seriously considering packing her bags and moving back to North Carolina, and she might very well have if her career hadn't received an unexpected boost.

Ava was handed a script of *Three Men in White*, one of the famous Doctor Gillespie series about a lovable old curmudgeon played by Lionel Barrymore, and told she was to play the part of a seductress. It wasn't the leading female role; she was to play a girl whom Dr. Gillespie would use to tempt Van Johnson, a young intern who wanted to become Gillespie's assistant. It was the old doctor's way of testing the younger one's strength of character.

The role didn't call for great acting but was large enough to throw the inexperienced Ava into a panic. Instinctively, she turned to Mickey for acting instruction and help in interpreting the role. Mickey jumped at the opportunity to reestablish contact.

It wasn't much of a jump from acting lessons to dating again. Before long they were seen dining and dancing in all their favorite Hollywood night spots. Rumors were beginning to spread that they would soon be permanently reunited, especially after a reporter from the *Los Angeles Examiner* caught them at the Palladium one night and started pumping them about their relationship.

"I love Ava a great deal," Mickey declared, clutching Ava's hand across the table. "Maybe we will be reconciled. We're young yet. Both of us are glad we caught our domestic error in time to correct it for a long and happy life together."

Ava squeezed Mickey's hand in return. "That's right. I couldn't get along without Mickey, and I guess he couldn't get along without me."

Tender words that certainly augured a reconciliation in the near future. But whatever hopes Mickey might have nurtured about remarrying Ava were dashed as soon as the filming of *Three Men in White* was completed. Once the picture was "wrapped," Ava seemed to realize that she no longer needed Mickey.

The trade papers wrote glowingly of Ava's performance as a young siren, and the public seemed to like her, too. Ava was rushed into *Maisie Goes to Reno*. This time Ava played a rich divorcée, a part that didn't require much acting, and with the confidence born of good reviews, she didn't bother to ask Mickey for help. Perhaps she should have. Bosley Crowther used such adjectives as "abominable," "weak," and "sultry but stupid," to describe Ava's performance.

While Ava was basking in her bad reviews, Mickey and Les

Peterson embarked, in late fall of 1943, on another invasion of the Eastern seaboard to plug his latest film, *Andy Hardy's Blonde Trouble*—which needed all the help it could get from its star to keep it from bombing completely. This was the first Hardy film to be released in more than a year, and despite three writers' valiant efforts to dig for new nuggets, the series gold mine seemed to be running out. In this one Mickey was allowed to age enough to become a university student, but in the words of one critic, his "sex life remained at the gee-whiz-she-kissed-me stage."

One of Mickey's last stops on the tour was Pittsburgh. And because of what happened there, it's unlikely that Mickey will ever forget the smoky city. He'll certainly never forget Sam Stiefel. For if it hadn't been for the latter's influence, Mickey might never have left MGM—one of the worst tactical errors of his life.

"We were at the theater one Saturday afternoon," Les Peterson recalls, "when a man came to the stage door and asked the stage manager if he could meet Mickey Rooney. His name was Sam Stiefel, a name we weren't familiar with, but it turned out he had money, owned a number of movie theaters in Baltimore and Philadelphia, and also a string of race horses on the West Coast. Anyway, we agreed to see him, so the stage manager sent him back to Mickey's dressing room."

Stiefel was a short, squarely built man who wore suits with wide lapels and flashy silk ties and looked about as trustworthy as a pit boss at Las Vegas. "If there had been a Jewish Mafia, he'd have been a member," claims Hollywood attorney Greg Bautzer. But Mickey liked Stiefel because he professed to be a big Mickey Rooney fan. In fact, he admitted to Mickey that at a charity auction in Philadelphia he had bid for, and bought, a pair of drumsticks allegedly used by Mickey when he played the drums with Tommy Dorsey's orchestra at the opening of the Palladium in 1940.

"He wanted to take us to dinner, which we couldn't do that Saturday because we had a couple of more shows to do," Peterson says, "but Sunday we had the whole day off. In those days Pittsburgh was closed on the Sabbath, and that included theaters. So Stiefel took us to the Oasis Club in New Jersey, which was a long ways off. All the time he kept telling Mickey how great he was, and expressing sympathy for all the trouble he'd had with Ava Gardner. But at dinner he got down to the real reason behind his visit. After he found out from Mickey what he was making a week from MGM—I think he was getting $1,750 for forty weeks, plus bonuses—Stiefel told Mickey that he was nuts to be working for MGM on a salary.

128

'You should have your own company and make your own pictures.' When Mickey admitted that he was an actor and not much of a businessman, Stiefel offered to manage Mickey and run the company for him. What he didn't tell Mickey was that he wanted to get into movie production in the worst way and was using Mickey as a stepping-stone to that goal. You see, his former partner, a fellow named Eddie Sherman, had gone to the Coast and was managing Abbott and Costello, and Stiefel was jealous of him. He wanted to be in the more glamorous end of show business, too. Anyway, he spent the evening painting a glowing picture of what Mickey's career would be like if only he'd let Stiefel manage him. Mickey was intrigued—especially when Stiefel mentioned he owned race horses. Before the evening was over he had Mickey thoroughly convinced that they ought to go into business together and form their own production company."

Shortly after his publicity tour, Mickey returned to the Coast to begin his acting chores in *National Velvet*, which was to commence shooting on January 19, 1944, with the young and still unspoiled Elizabeth Taylor playing opposite him in the role that was to lead to her superstardom.

As soon as he wound up some business matters in Philadelphia, Stiefel followed Mickey to Hollywood. He cemented their friendship by loaning Mickey money. He also established a relationship with Mickey's mother, Nell, and his stepfather, Fred Pankey. Soon Stiefel was taking the whole Rooney family out to Hollywood's swankiest bistros and showering them with presents and helping them out financially.

In spite of Mickey's studio income, approximately $125,000 a year with bonuses, he and Nell could not get by on the forty thousand that was left them after Uncle Sam took his cut, his agents took their cut, and two-thirds of his gross went into safekeeping at the California Trust Company.

This situation, of course, played right into Sam Stiefel's hands. The fact that Mickey couldn't live on a straight salary was an eloquent selling point for his needing his own production company to shelter some of his income. Once Mickey gave him the green light, Stiefel started the wheels in motion to form a company.

While he was waiting for the secretary of state in Sacramento to approve the incorporation papers, Stiefel continued to salve Mickey's ego and to subsidize him at the racetrack. Not only didn't he mind seeing Mickey pick losers consistently, but he seemed to encourage his gambling. When Mickey had a day off from the

129

studio, for example, and he was feeling blue about losing Ava, plus the fact that he was due to take another Army physical in a few weeks, Stiefel would pat him on the shoulder and say, "Come on, kid. Forget about your troubles. Let's go to the track."

According to Les Peterson, Stiefel's pockets were always bulging with cash—which was available for a loan without collateral whenever Mickey ran into hard luck. Mickey, of course, wasn't unluckier than any of the other suckers, but having a larger income than most entitled him, he felt, to wager more than the average horse player. As a result, he was usually out of money about halfway through the afternoon. At which point Stiefel would reach into his pocket, whip out a roll of hundred dollar bills, and ask Mickey to help himself. If Mickey said five hundred would see him through the day, Stiefel would press him to take a thousand. After all, why be a piker? If there was one thing Mickey wasn't, it was a piker, especially at Santa Anita. But if there was one thing Mickey *was,* it was a schnook. It never seemed to occur to him that his new business partner might be keeping track of all the cash he laid out for Mickey.

In March, the incorporation papers came through from the state, and Rooney, Inc. was now an entity. The stockholders were Mickey Rooney (president); Samuel E. Stiefel (secretary-treasurer); and Mort Briskin, an attorney Stiefel had known for years, in charge of the company's legal affairs. As one of his first duties, Mort Briskin sent a memo to MGM's accounting department on March 21, 1944, requesting that "all checks for Mickey Rooney be made payable to the order of Mickey Rooney, and instead of sending them to the California Trust Company, as authorized by Rooney and Nell Pankey on the date of October 22, 1941, these checks be sent to the California Bank's main office in Hollywood, in care of Mr. Odell." (Mickey, having reached the age of twenty-three, was now old enough to receive his money directly, instead of having it go into trust.) Once Rooney, Inc. had money to work with, Stiefel set about trying to renegotiate Mickey's contract so that he would have the right to "make outside pictures," recalls Mort Briskin today. "And Mayer agreed to give it to us, too. But then that March Mickey had to take another Army physical, and when he was reclassified 1-A and his induction into service seemed imminent, Mayer reneged on the deal."

So for the immediate future at least, the function of Rooney, Inc. remained limited to handling Mickey's personal appearances, the merchandising of his name (Mickey Rooney comic books, for example), collecting his salary, and investing his income in a number of things, including a stable of race horses. Stiefel sweetened the pot by throwing in some of his own nags that, together with the ones he purchased with Mickey's money, became part of the company's assets.

Since Mickey's acting chores in *National Velvet* were not yet completed when Mickey was reclassified 1-A in March of 1944, MGM was thrown into a bit of a panic. Not ten minutes after the postman delivered the new classification, Eddie Mannix dispatched another letter of appeal to Draft Board 245, requesting "a six-month extension on the grounds that his entering the Army will interfere with the *National Velvet* shooting schedule."

In mid-April this latest appeal was turned down, and Mickey was notified to report for induction in thirty days. Still not giving up, Mannix wrote another letter to the draft board on May 1, requesting "a meeting to discuss the Rooney situation."

Either the manpower shortage was becoming critical, or Draft Board 245 no longer gave a damn about MGM's shooting schedule because on May 4 a very curt letter arrived at MGM advising Eddie Mannix that Mickey Rooney "will be inducted sometime in May of 1944."

Mannix immediately made another plea, asking the draft board to forget the six-month extension he had originally asked for and just give Mickey enough time to complete his work.

On May 11, a final curt note came bouncing back from the draft board, turning Mannix down flatly and informing him that Mickey Rooney would have to don khaki in thirty days.

Realizing he had done everything he could to keep his boy out of the Army, Mannix quickly got Pan Berman, the producer of *National Velvet*, on the phone and exhorted him to tell Clarence Brown, the director of the film—and a notoriously slow and meticulous director—to "shoot all remaining Rooney scenes first, no matter how it messes up the schedule."

With his days as a civilian numbered, Mickey ran headlong into the problem of his mother's finances. How would she keep El Ranchita going after her son went off salary at MGM? The only money Mickey had been able to save was tied up in irrevocable trust funds. Mickey's friend and benefactor Samuel E. Stiefel came to the rescue, assuring Nell and Mickey that there wasn't a thing to worry about. If Nell ran short of cash, all she had to do was "holler" and Stiefel would be there to bankroll her until Mickey could return from the front and start making big money again.

No sooner was Mickey relieved of those burdensome thoughts

than he started hearing disquieting rumors around the MGM lot about the fate of the Hardy pictures. Unable to get Louis B. Mayer to level with him, Mickey wandered one day into the office of scriptwriter Bill Ludwig to see what he knew. A contract writer at MGM for many years, Ludwig had scripted a number of the better Hardy pictures and was considered the studio maven by most of its employees.

Ludwig can still remember how depressed Mickey looked when he walked into his office that afternoon so many years ago.

"What's the matter, Mick?" Ludwig asked, looking up from his typewriter.

"What's going to become of me?" Mickey asked with a frown.

"Become of you? What do you mean?"

"I hear they might stop making the Hardy pictures," Mickey said. "You know anything about that?"

Ludwig shrugged. "Well, after fourteen of them that's always a possibility."

"That's what I mean. What's going to become of me?"

"You're a great talent," Ludwig reminded him. "You'll keep right on going."

Mickey shook his head. "No, no. I'll wind up playing bad jockeys, like Frankie Darrow."

"What are you talking about, Mick? Not with what you've got. You can do anything. What would you like to do?"

"I'd like to direct," Mickey replied, "but they're never going to let me direct. They'll never give a million and a half bucks to a little Irish song-and-dance man."

"You're crazy," Ludwig said.

"No, I'm not. That's what's going to become of me. I'm going to wind up like Frankie Darrow, a bad jockey," Mickey reiterated.

"Oh, come on. You know how good you are? Cary Grant told me the other day that he thinks you're the biggest talent in the business. You've got everything."

"No, I haven't," Mickey pouted.

"No? What is it you want?"

Mickey heaved a deep sigh, and said. "You know, Bill, I'd give ten years of my life if I were just six inches taller."

Faced with the permanent loss of Ava, the end of the Hardy series, and his income about to drop from $2,000 a week to the fifty-dollar-a-month buck private's pay, who could blame Mickey for feeling crestfallen during the short time he had left as a civilian?

He'd been calling Ava every now and then, just to keep in touch

132

with her on a platonic basis. But on Tuesday, the thirteenth of June—the day he officially went off the MGM payroll—he took a chance and decided to invite her out to dinner for old time's sake.

"Well, this is it," he told Ava when he finally got her on the phone.

"What's happened, Mickey?"

"I'm going into the army tomorrow."

"Oh, Mickey. How do you feel?"

"Lots of guys have gone into the service. I have no complaints."

Then he asked her to dinner at the Palladium, and she surprised him by replying that she'd go.

Later that evening the two were seen at the Big Band emporium, dining and holding hands. In the shot of them that appeared in the *Los Angeles Times* the following morning, Ava looked more radiantly beautiful than ever, but Mickey seemed less a suitor than her kid brother, clad in a dark blue "bar mitzvah" suit, white shirt, and conservative tie.

The sight of them together at the Palladium immediately started speculation that they were on the verge of marching up the aisle again. But Mickey didn't dare let himself consider such a pipe dream until he was saying goodbye to Ava at her apartment door later that night.

"Mickey?" said Ava in a breathy voice.

"Yes, darling."

"I'll wait for you, Mickey. When you come out, I'll be waiting."

Mickey couldn't believe it. "And will you come downtown tomorrow morning to see me off?"

"Maybe," replied Ava, before ducking inside her door.

Hopeful that she'd keep both promises, Mickey felt considerably better when, early the next morning with about fifty other recruits, he reported to the Army induction station at 610 South Main Street, in downtown Los Angeles. In fact, Mickey was in such high spirits that when he and the others were marched down Main Street to the Pacific Electric train depot, he posed for the press photographers shouldering a duffel bag taller than himself. His high spirits sagged, however, when he arrived at the Pacific Electric station. Eddie Mannix, Les Peterson, and a host of his cronies were there to see him off. But not Ava.

Oh, well, an ex-husband couldn't expect a gorgeous dish like Ava to get up at five in the morning just to wave goodbye to him. But that didn't mean she wouldn't still be waiting for him after the war, rationalized Mickey as he stepped aboard the Pacific Electric train bound for Fort MacArthur, and waved to his friends receding in the distance.

12

A<small>T THE FORT</small> MacArthur induction center overlooking Los Angeles harbor, Mickey went through the usual processing and a brief indoctrination speech by a tough top sergeant, who seemed to take particular delight in mentioning that they had a "movie star" in their ranks who shouldn't expect any special favors.

Before he got out of the Army, Mickey would have to take a lot more of that kind of razzing from officers and noncoms and even his buck-private peers. Inwardly, Mickey burned at the unfairness of it all. Now that he was in, he just wanted to be left alone to serve his country the best he knew how. But outwardly he learned to respond with either a broad grin or a wisecrack or both—until he was accepted by the group. After three days, Mickey and his fellow inductees were shipped off to Fort Riley, Kansas, for basic training.

Going from the comparatively easy life of America's number-one movie star to the life of an Army dogface was not the easiest thing in the world for a man as emotional and spoiled as Mickey. He didn't have time to feel sorry for himself during the day, but the nights spent with men with whom he had nothing in common except a dislike of service life were interminably long and the memories of Ava impossible to blot out.

Mickey spent the hours between evening chow and taps writing Ava long, passionate, and sometimes maudlin love letters. For a time, she answered them, if not passionately, at least cordially, and she always reiterated her promise to be waiting for him at the end of the war. But then her letters became briefer, with longer and longer intervals between them, until finally, in late summer, they stopped

135

coming altogether. When his letters went unanswered, Mickey started phoning Ava. But his attempts were unsuccessful, for Bappie kept answering. It was her job, apparently, to keep Mickey at bay.

The lack of communication between them was beginning to drive Mickey crazy. Then one night, when he was lying in his bunk recuperating from a hard day's march in the one-hundred-degree heat, Mickey was called to the telephone in the dayroom of the barracks. Since it was after taps, the dayroom was empty and dark, the only illumination one bare light bulb hanging from a wooden lamppost outside the window. The receiver on the wall pay telephone was hanging by its cord as Mickey ran excitedly to put it to his ear.

After a tentative "Hello," he was overjoyed to recognize Ava's voice on the other end—until he heard what she had to say. She wanted him to stop writing and phoning her. When Mickey broke into tears, she insisted that it was all over between them and that it would do him no good to cry. Mickey reaffirmed his undying love, and when that failed to soften her, he asked her if there was anybody else.

The phone went dead. Ava had hung up on him.

Stunned, Mickey sat alone in the dayroom, in the glare of that single naked light bulb, his chin resting forlornly in his hands. This time he didn't have to turn the tears on mechanically, the way he did in front of the cameras.

Mickey was so tormented by the loss of a girl whom he considered his private property that, in the ensuing days, he started drinking seriously for the first time in his life.

As if the loss of Ava were not traumatic enough, Mickey picked up a newspaper a few days later and read in one of the gossip columns that Ava Gardner was now the steady girlfriend of eccentric millionaire Howard Hughes. At this point, according to a biography called *Ava*, by Roland Flamini, published in 1983, Mickey came completely unglued, went AWOL, and flew to Los Angeles. "MPs were waiting at Los Angeles Airport to take him back to Kansas, and Metro had to pull strings to prevent serious trouble," writes Flamini. Strickling [Howard Strickling, head of publicity at Metro at the time] also succeeded in keeping it out of the papers."

There was no mention of that incident in Mickey's autobiography. In fact, he writes that he only left Fort Riley once while he was stationed there. According to him, this leave was officially sanctioned so that he could fly back to Los Angeles to comfort his mother, who'd received a death threat through the mail from some anonymous kook. That story turned up in the Los Angeles press and has the ring of a Howard Strickling publicity release to it. Which account is correct is anybody's guess, though it is a matter of record that Ava became Howard Hughes's regular girlfriend that summer and that Mickey was extremely upset about it. By his own admission, he became so tormented that he started to drink heavily for the first time in his life. But he could not blot out the pain as he lay awake nights in his bunk, thinking about Ava and Howard Hughes.

MICKEY WAS DRINKING pretty heavily by the time he finished basic training at Fort Riley and was shipped to Camp Seibert, Alabama, in early September. Because of who he was, Mickey was assigned to Special Services, charged with the responsibility of organizing an entertainment unit that could go overseas and entertain the GIs in the front lines. The Army was having trouble getting some USO shows to go anywhere near the fighting, so it recruited talent from its own ranks. Since there was no bigger all-around talent in show business than Private Rooney, he was the logical choice to lift the morale of our fighting forces.

While he was getting his act together at Camp Seibert, Mickey picked up a new friend: Jimmy Cook, one of the finest saxophonists ever to blow a horn in the Big Band era. Cook, a handsome, soft-spoken man, recalls that he first met Mickey one night in the day-room. "Mickey was at the piano, playing the blues, probably for Ava," Cook says, "so I got out my horn and started playing along with him. We sounded good together. Until then, I never suspected what a hell of a good musician Mickey is. I thought it was just publicity that he could play all those instruments, but he really can. Anyway, I guess we had a lot in common, and we've been friends ever since."

They have remained such good friends, in fact, that Cook was one of the select few chosen to appear on "This Is Your Life," when the NBC program was devoted to Mickey in 1983.

IF MICKEY AND Jimmy Cook had much in common, the same couldn't be said for Mickey's relationship with Betty Jane Rase, a comely local belle whom he met shortly after his arrival at Camp Seibert.

A beauty-contest winner who'd recently been crowned "Miss Alabama of 1944," not to mention having been "Fifth Runner-up" in the previous year's Miss America doings at Atlantic City, Betty Jane had all the qualities that had attracted Mickey to Ava Gardner. She was seventeen, beautiful, and as southern as black-eyed peas. The

137

only differences were that Betty Jane was a blonde and a couple of inches shorter than Ava. But what the hell? A guy on the rebound couldn't expect to have everything, especially in a town like Birmingham.

Of course, Mickey didn't set out intentionally to find another Ava, but since he was still awfully lonely and well into his cups the night he was introduced to Betty Jane, he was fairly vulnerable. As Mickey later remembered his mood that night, "I'm lucky I didn't propose to my top sergeant."

The entire courtship took place over the period of two weekend passes. On the first weekend, Mickey and Jimmy Cook were sprung from Camp Seibert to attend a special showing of his movie *Girl Crazy*, and a party to honor the film's star in the not-too-distant city of Birmingham. Mickey was standing, drink in hand, making small talk with a couple of army officers and their wives, when Lily Mae Caldwell, a reporter from the *Birmingham News*, who was a close friend of Betty Jane's and had accompanied her to the previous year's beauty contest at Atlantic City, tugged at Mickey's elbow, and introduced herself.

"Mickey, ah want you to meet mah good friend Betty Jane Rase. She's Miss Alabama."

"Well, hello there, Miss Alabama."

"Oh, Mr. Rooney! How y'all?"

From that point on, Mickey was feeling just fine. According to Jimmy Cook, "Mickey's eyes bugged out at the sight of Betty Jane's figure." Whether it was her figure, her title, or her sugary Southern accent that most appealed to him, Mickey has never been quite sure, since he admits to having had quite a glow on the night they met. It probably wasn't her mind. Some who remember Betty Jane from that period say, perhaps harshly, she was just "a naive little teenager who was impressed with being in the same room with a movie star." But Jimmy Cook believes she had more on the ball than that. He claims that in addition to her looks, "she was a very good musician. She played excellent piano, and sang very well."

How much singing she did before Mickey proposed isn't quite clear. But by Mickey's own admission he popped the question before the night was over, and Betty Jane accepted. Because she was a minor, Betty Jane needed the consent of her parents, Edward and Lena Rase, who lived in a small house in a typical Southern working-class neighborhood. Edward, in fact, was out of work, so when the Rases heard whom Betty Jane intended to marry, they were as pleased as any poor parents would be to have their daughter headed for the altar with a movie star.

A week later, on Sunday September 30, 1944, Mickey and Jimmy Cook, who was to be best man, flew into Birmingham for the wedding. The ceremony took place at the home of Mickey's commanding officer. Edward Rase gave the bride away. According to Lily Mae Caldwell, writing in the *Birmingham News,* the Rases "were as proud almost as if General Robert E. Lee had won the Battle of Appomattox."

After spending his wedding night in a Birmingham hotel room Mickey was back at Camp Seibert in time for reveille. If he was aware that Marriage Number Two was a mistake, it couldn't be detected in his sheepish grin as he fell wearily into line to answer roll call.

If there were problems, there wasn't much opportunity to work them out, for Mickey and his unit received their overseas orders a few days later. Destination: the European Theater.

Thanks to his soft-hearted commanding officer, Mickey and Betty Jane spent the following weekend together. The day after, Mickey found himself on a troop train bound for New York City.

Mickey apparently didn't feel much one way or the other about leaving his bride of only a week. They'd been together so little, and he'd been drinking much of that time. All he'd had the opportunity to learn about Betty Jane was that he now had a wife who was almost as pretty and sexy as Ava—someone to boast about to the other GIs in the barracks. Someone to come home to after the war, provided he made it home. In bed, Betty Jane was certainly an adequate replacement. In fact, Joe Yule III was conceived their first night together. Mickey had no way of knowing this, of course, as the troop train chugged north along the dimmed Eastern seaboard one crisp October night. From New York's Pennsylvania Station the debarking soldiers were bussed across town to the Hudson River and marched up the gangplank of the *Queen Mary,* which was waiting to take them to England.

"It was a miserable voyage," Cook recalls. "Four thousand GIs jampacked aboard a ship built to accommodate a thousand. Not only that, we were billeted way down in the bowels of the ship. During the trip, the latrines above us broke and all that shit was coming down on our bunks and over everything. Then when we got to England some officers, who'd never been anything as civilians, suddenly decided to take it out on Mickey and the rest of us because he was a celebrity and we were an entertainment unit and not a fighting force. So they put all of us on twenty-one days straight KP after we got to England. Mickey, of course, hated it, as we all did, but he took it like a good sport, stuck it out, until we were eventually shipped over to Le Havre and then Paris."

In Paris, Mickey's unit was billeted in an encampment on the outskirts of the city, where he and the rest of the men in that Special Services unit could finally start organizing a show to take to the front lines.

Given the ebb and flow of the fighting, troops rarely stayed in one place long enough to see a show. Supplying them with live entertainment presented an almost insurmountable problem—until Mickey, with typical ingenuity, conceived a new form of war entertainment that completely solved the mobility problem. He invented the "jeep show," and got special permission from General Eisenhower to put it into effect.

"Here's how it worked," Jimmy Cook remembers. "Instead of one large show, we broke the unit up into about twenty 'jeep shows.' A jeep show consisted of three or four men in each vehicle. Attached to the jeep would be a trailer with a little stage and public address system on it. In Mickey's show, for example, there was an accordian player, a singer, and Mickey. Mickey would emcee, sing, and tell jokes. I wasn't with him, but in my show we had a trumpet, I played sax, a guitarist, and Bobby Breen was the vocalist. These shows were so mobile we could drive anywhere with them. We'd go right up to the front lines, park, and do a show for guys who were in foxholes being shot at. Sometimes we were so close to the front that the Germans stopped their firing to listen to our music. Sometimes, after a large area had been taken by the Allies and made secure, all of us jeep shows would wind up in one town together. Then, as Ed Sullivan would say, we'd put on a "really big show" for the troops who were stationed there. One big orchestra, many different kinds of acts, men dressed up like girls. Mickey did the emceeing, in addition to doing a lot of comedy bits and musical spots."

All through the winter of 1944 and into the spring of 1945, as the American forces slogged their way toward Berlin through France and Belgium, the jeep shows were right on their muddy heels. They entertained in snow, rain, and even under enemy fire. "Sometimes we slept on the ground," Cook recalls. "Sometimes we were billeted with cooperative German families as we got closer and closer to Berlin."

According to Cook, Mickey was a "real crusader" when it came to

140

entertaining the troops. "He'd get two hours sleep, and then go out and put on three or four shows in one day, and right up front, where there was real danger of stopping a sniper's bullet." For his efforts Mickey was promoted to Technical Sergeant 3/C.

After he'd been in France about a month, Mickey received a letter from Betty Jane, who was still in Alabama, informing him that she was pregnant. Mickey was delighted. The idea of having a wife and child waiting for him at home kept his spirits high when he was up to his knees in mud or dining on Army C-rations in what remained of some bombed-out German farmhouse or barn.

The war in the European Theater ended on May 7, 1945, but the Japanese didn't surrender in the Pacific until August. Consequently, Mickey, who'd been in service less than a year and didn't have the points for immediate discharge, continued to do his thing for the Army of Occupation until early 1946, traveling, in his rough estimation, 115,000 miles.

On July 4, Mickey received word from Betty Jane that she had given birth to a healthy baby boy weighing seven pounds six ounces. As they had agreed upon previously, Mickey's firstborn was officially named Joe Yule III. But that name vanished about the same time the baby was weaned, and he's been known as Mickey Rooney, Jr., ever since. When Betty Jane and the baby were strong enough to travel, Mickey arranged for them to move into El Ranchita with his mother and stepfather. He had them flown by chartered plane from Birmingham to Los Angeles. The expense was outrageous, especially to a man on an enlisted man's pay, but wartime priorities being what they were, public transportation was out of the question.

As he waited for the war to end, Mickey continued to entertain the Army of Occupation with the same untiring showmanship that made him one of the world's favorite entertainers. But now his mind was on getting home, and mail call was the highlight of his day. If he was lucky, there'd be letters from Betty Jane and his mother, giving him reports on the latest cute things Mickey Junior was up to. When Mickey received a mailed snapshot of his son, a blue-eyed blond with a turned-up nose just like his own, he couldn't wait to show it to the other fellows in his unit.

Mickey became impatient. He was anxious not only to see his son, but to get on with his career, which, even while he was in the Army, had undergone some interesting developments.

To wit: November 4, 1944, was the date Metro-Goldwyn-Mayer, under peacetime circumstances, would have had to exercise its option on Mickey's services for another year. This pickup would have brought his salary to $2,500 a week for a minimum of forty weeks. But under the rules that major studios played by during wartime, when an actor's option came up for renewal while he was in the service of his country, his contract would automatically be extended for the same length of time that said actor had been unavailable for work.

However, Sam Stiefel, who'd been cagily waiting for the appropriate time to spring his surprise, refused to play by those rules. Two months before Mickey's option came up, on August 26, Stiefel had Mort Briskin notify MGM that there would be no automatic extension of Mickey's contract just because he was in the army. In fact, announced a story prominently featured on the front page of the *Hollywood Reporter* on August 28:

> Morton Briskin, attorney for Rooney, Inc., a corporation recently formed to handle Mickey Rooney's affairs, announced Saturday that his company will file suit in Federal court within the next two weeks, applying for a "declaratory relief action," and asking the court to uphold its contention that Rooney's entrance into the Army and not being paid his weekly salary by MGM automatically abrogates the star's contract with the studio . . .

On the same page of the *Hollywood Reporter* was a full-column editorial by its editor and publisher, Billy Wilkerson, excoriating Mickey for allowing his representatives to act as they had.

> We don't know what they have been feeding Mickey Rooney or who has been feeding him, but the announcement in a different column of your *Reporter* today is not the Mickey we have known or the boy all of you have admired so much. The whole thing looks to us as if the minority of Mickey's new corporation is about to sink the major owner of that stock—Mickey himself.
> . . . Mickey Rooney asking for a cancellation of his agreement with MGM, and the reasons for asking for such a cancellation, is a pretty weird piece of business. Pretty bad behavior.
> . . . never in our looking over the affairs of this business have we ever seen such a protective hand on the shoulder of anyone as the one L.B. always extended to Mickey. He adored that kid, fought many studio battles to bring him up to where he is; watched his scripts, ordered them rewritten to care better for the advance of Rooney, counselled him at all times, giving him more attention than most fathers would give a son, and because of it Mickey has become one of

142

the industry's great stars. Mayer . . . did EVERYTHING for the kid, and in Mayer doing it, MGM did it, and for it all, they get slapped in the face with a request for an abrogation of his contract.

Sam Stiefel's gambit to abrogate Mickey's contract, solely on the basis that MGM had failed to send Mickey a "formal notice of suspension" when he went into the Army, was pretty nervy.

By taking Mickey off the company payroll, MGM hadn't done anything unusual. There had never before been a need to send an actor who went into the service "formal" notice of suspension. He simply was removed from the company payroll until he returned.

As a result, the consensus of MGM's battery of high-priced attorneys was that the studio was legally in the clear. Nevertheless, Thau, Mannix, and Mayer panicked slightly when the same legal experts raised the possibility that "nobody can be quite sure how Briskin's claim will be interpreted by the courts. We therefore advise that the studio ought to exercise its option on Rooney to protect our interests and put him back on salary."

After getting the green light from the front office, Floyd Hendrickson, in charge of MGM's business affairs, advised Briskin and Stiefel that while what they were doing was without precedent, they would exercise Mickey's option and start paying him again.

If MGM could be intimidated so easily, Steifel apparently decided they might as well go for the whole ball of wax, and promptly asked for a meeting with Benny Thau to discuss a new contract for Mickey Rooney, and on October 11, they got it. Stiefel, Briskin, and Abe Lastfogel, the head of William Morris, sat down with Benny Thau and outlined their demands. In addition to Mickey's right to have his own radio program, they asked for $7,500 a week for him, with a forty-week guarantee, or $300,000 per year.

Benny Thau labeled those figures "preposterous" but indicated he was willing to negotiate something they could all live with. The negotiations took place over the next several months, but it wasn't until February 4, 1945, that the two sides finally arrived at an agreement.

On the following day *The New York Times* reported the details of Mickey's new contract on its theatrical page:

Mickey Rooney, now a private in the Army somewhere in Belgium or France, will resume his screen career for Metro-Goldwyn-Mayer after the war at a salary of $5,000 a week. Under his new contract, the 24-year-old star receives a number of unusual concessions in regard to

143

radio and stage personal appearances, which conceivably could double his annual film earnings . . .

In addition to the weekly salary, which runs forty weeks a year, the corporation receives a bonus of a hundred and forty thousand for signing the deal; half of this amount has been paid; the remainder is payable in two years. The contract covers seven years with yearly options, and provides that MGM must exercise the first option (for the second year) thirteen days after Rooney is discharged from the Army.

Among other concessions, the actor is allowed to do 39 weeks of radio a year plus four guest appearances. While MGM can limit these radio appearances to 26 weeks, if it is believed they are injuring his screen value, Rooney can resume broadcasting the following year, if MGM exercises its option for the succeeding forty weeks.

Radio was anathema to Louis B. Mayer. He felt, with some justification, that the broadcasting medium was the kind of unfair competition the movie industry didn't need because admission was free. If the public could be entertained by their favorite stars for nothing while sitting comfortably in their armchairs at home, why should they bother going out to the movies?

But with Mickey Rooney such a tremendous money-maker for the studio, in the end Louis B. Mayer and Benny Thau acquiesced about his right to perform on radio.

Although he had been motivated mainly by his own self-interests and desire to be a producer, Stiefel's idea that an actor should be his own boss, with a right to be selective about the films he appeared in, started a revolution in Hollywood that eventually saw much of the power taken away from the studio moguls and put in the hands of the talent. After the war, other important personalities demanded more control of their own destinies and a larger slice of the profit pie.

However, because Mickey, no matter how justified he might have been, was in the vanguard of the palace rebellion, most of the old-line Hollywood establishment considered him a traitor to the town that had nurtured him to success. It remained to be seen what reward Mickey would reap or what price he would pay for his quest for independence.

13

F OR THE SHORT-TERM outlook, however, Technical Sergeant
Mickey Rooney was pleased with the way his life was going.
Not only did he have a brand-new contract guaranteeing him $6,250
per month, even while he was in the service, his own firm, and a
brand new son, but by mid-December of 1945 there was no longer
any valid reason for Mickey's jeep-show unit to exist. The fighting
on both the European and Pacific fronts was finally over. All that
remained to be done was for the diplomats to screw up the peace—
and for Mickey to pile up enough "points" to be discharged.

As a result, Mickey was transferred to the Armed Forces Radio
Network in Frankfurt, Germany. There he was given duty as a radio
announcer and all-around entertainer until he had enough "points"
to qualify for discharge. By February 12, 1946, Mickey had fifty-
seven points, earning him the right to be a civilian again. On February 15, General Eisenhower awarded him the Bronze Star for
"exceptional courage in the performance of his duties as an entertainer." The citation stated that "His superb personal contribution to
the morale of the Armed Forces in the European Theater of Operations cannot be measured." Three days later he was on his way, by
ship, to Fort Dix, New Jersey, where he was to be processed for
discharge.

Two weeks later, after a slow and uncomfortable ocean crossing,
Mickey arrived at the Army Separation Center at Fort Dix. To the
reporters who greeted him at dockside and queried him about his
future plans, Mickey ebulliently announced that in addition to making pictures for MGM, he planned to have his own radio program.

He said that his partner, Sam Stiefel, was already negotiating with Campbell Soup, who wanted to sponsor it. Following that, Mickey left for the Big Apple on a twenty-four-hour pass.

On Wednesday, March 6, 1946, Mickey took his final physical, picked up his severance pay, an honorable discharge certificate, and his "Ruptured Duck" lapel pin and immediately boarded the Twentieth Century Ltd. for California, to rejoin Betty Jane and his eight-month-old son, Mickey Junior.

Three days later, on a beautiful sunshine-filled morning, Mickey hopped off the Super Chief in Pasadena, the usual debarking spot for celebrities who wished to avoid the crowds and confusion at Los Angeles' Union Station. Mickey was still clad in his Army uniform, his chest bedecked with service ribbons; a happy grin on his face.

Waiting on the station platform to greet him were Betty Jane and Mickey's mother, Nell Pankey. Nell, looking plump and matronly in a polka dot dress, did not appear much taller than her dimunitive movie star son, but Betty Jane, in a tailored suit and high heels, towered over her returning soldier. To Mickey's dismay, she had grown a couple of inches since they had last been together, making it necessary for him to stand on tiptoes to kiss her. That was one of the drawbacks of marrying a teenager who had not yet finished growing.

Their height difference, however, wasn't the main reason Mickey found it difficult to communicate with Betty Jane, as he quickly discovered once he was alone with her in his palatial ranch house in Encino. What irked him more was the fact that they still had nothing in common.

Once they hugged and kissed and she showed him Mickey Junior asleep in his crib, and the Mick gave his approval, they found they had nothing more to talk about. They were the same strangers they'd been on their first meeting in Alabama.

What made the situation worse was that Mickey was still in love with Ava Gardner—or Mrs. Artie Shaw as she had become since they had last spoken. With Ava unobtainable—at least for the moment—Mickey seemingly decided he might as well stay with what he had. Mickey had not yet reached the stage in his life where getting a divorce was relatively easy.

Determined to make the marriage work, Mickey contacted a real estate agent who took him and Betty Jane house-hunting. They found a house in the fifty- to seventy-five-thousand-dollar range in Encino, not far from his mother's place. Mickey had to swing another loan from the studio in order to make the down payment.

Once that was settled, the excitement of having a new home and decorating it gave Mickey and Betty Jane a topic of conversation—until they were completely settled in their San Fernando Valley love nest.

Mickey realized that his wartime marriage had been a serious blunder. He was thoroughly bored with this country girl from Alabama.

At least, during the day, he had his film work to entertain him. The studio was already making plans to shoot the "last" of the Hardy series, *Love Laughs at Andy Hardy*. According to Bill Ludwig who wrote the script, Mickey was still concerned about his future once the Hardy series ended, but he presented a cheerful front on the set.

After his day's work was finished and he had to go home and be alone with Betty Jane, Mickey often became moody and argumentative—something like he had been with Ava during the last stages of their marriage, and a pattern that was to become familiar in most of his marriages.

Betty Jane had been a teenager when she'd married Mickey, with immature expectations of what it would be like living with her movie-star husband. For some reason—perhaps it was his diminutive size and the kinds of parts he played in movies or perhaps it was his own immature nature—his peers at the studio had never accepted him socially. As a result, his friends were limited to Sig Frolich, Bill Paxton, Dick Quine, Sid Miller, Jimmy Cook, and a few others among the lesser lights in the industry. They, when Mickey did bring them around the house, didn't particularly interest Betty Jane.

Realizing she didn't like his friends, Mickey started leaving Betty alone in the evenings and going out by himself. This, of course, led to complaints that he never took her any place and relentless questioning about where he had been. Betty Jane may have been tantamount to a hillbilly, in Mickey's estimation, but she wasn't naive enough to buy his alibi that he had merely been out "with the boys."

Probably the most important thing that kept Mickey from walking out on Betty Jane for good in the first few weeks he was home from the war was Mickey Junior. He enjoyed the novelty of acting the role of father, of watching his son develop from an infant to a toddler who could say "Da da." So much so that Mickey fell into the trap of believing that more children could save an ailing marriage.

Their second baby was conceived in May, approximately two months after Mickey had arrived home, and kept the marriage from reaching the divorce court for another two years. With Betty Jane enceinte and tied down to caring for Mickey Junior, her husband felt free to roam in the evenings and—when he wasn't shooting a picture—to play golf and go to the races during the day.

UNHAPPILY, A BAD marriage wasn't all that Mickey had come home to. His new business partnership with Sam Stiefel was about to cause him all kinds of trouble. Shortly after he'd shed his uniform, Mickey learned from Stiefel that he owed the former theater operator more than one hundred thousand dollars. According to Stiefel this was cash out of pocket that he'd loaned Mickey and his mother—especially his mother—during the war years when Mickey wasn't receiving his salary from MGM. This enormous debt came as a shock to Mickey, who had no idea he had borrowed so much, if indeed he had thought of that money as a loan at all. Any money Mickey had been able to save when he was a minor was still locked up in irrevocable trust at the California Bank; and while Mickey was back on salary at the studio, he didn't have anything like one hundred thousand dollars to hand over to Stiefel.

To Mickey's relief, the big hearted Stiefel told him not to be concerned. Under their partnership agreement, he'd simply accept half of Mickey's earnings. A straight fifty-fifty split. Mickey was so delighted about not having to come up with a balloon payment for Stiefel that he bought his mentor's idea. Besides, why should he distrust him? This was the man who had successfully renegotiated his MGM contract before it had terminated, the man who promised to make him wealthy. What difference did it make if he had to give him half of his earnings?

NOW THAT ROONEY, Inc. was a going concern, Stiefel rented a plush suite of offices at 8782 Sunset Boulevard. Stiefel ran the actual day-to-day business operations. Mickey was given a desk, a secretary, but little to do except sign his name.

Stiefel had big plans for Mickey—all of which might have worked out *if* Stiefel had known what he was doing, and *if* the movie business hadn't become bogged down in the first of its many postwar depressions. As the late Sam Goldwyn put it, "People are not going to the movies in droves." Ten million ex-servicemen were so happy to be home that they didn't want to go out in the evenings. The monster television was beginning to raise its ugly head. There was a shortage of dollars because defense plants had laid off millions of workers. As a result, the public was becoming more selective about what to spend its entertainment dollars on. Movies such as *Love Laughs at Andy Hardy,* which Metro filmed after Mickey returned from the war, were no longer a box-office draw.

Being the fourteenth in the series might also have had something to do with the public's apathy toward *Love Laughs at Andy Hardy.* To most fans it just seemed a stale remake of everything that had gone on before in Carvel, Idaho. In the words of the esteemed Bosley Crowther:

". . . now that Mickey Rooney is back from the late unpleasantness, it appears that the nature of Andy is no different from what it was before, and that Mr. Rooney has grown a little broader, comically speaking, but that he certainly hasn't grown up."

Mickey was still a big enough star that he didn't have to worry about having to play jockey parts, "like Frankie Darrow," as he had once feared. The first option on his new contract was, as required, exercised thirteen days after Mickey was out of the army, so Mickey was set for at least a year—and so was Stiefel. Moreover, with the Hardy family dead and buried, Mickey was now available to play more mature roles. The first of these was the title part in *Killer McCoy,* a prizefight story that was to be the birth of a grown-up Mickey Rooney on the screen. The film augured well for Mickey as a serious actor. It grossed over two million dollars domestically, and it pleased most of the critics, including Tom Pryor of *The New York Times*: "Mickey Rooney is in there punching now . . . and whatever one may think of him as a prizefighter, he is a wonderful little actor. . . . We wouldn't compare his ring prowess with that of John Garfield in *Body and Soul,* but then these are pictures with different approaches to a common subject and, in its own way, *Killer McCoy* is quite O.K."

Not so okay was *Summer Holiday,* a musical remake of *Ah, Wilderness,* which, when it was finally released in 1948, one of the critics thought ought to have been retitled *Ah, Foolishness.*

On the home front: the child who was to keep his marriage from exploding into a thousand alimony payments turned out to be no help at all to Mickey's domestic problems. Between the time of conception and the day their second baby was born early in January of 1947, Mickey and Betty Jane's home was a scene of never-ending quarrels.

The first public hint that all was not well with the Rooneys appeared as early as August 1946, when Hedda Hopper reported in a syndicated piece in the *Los Angeles Times,* "Betty Jane Rooney, who is expecting in January, is at present visiting her mother in Birmingham, Alabama, with Mickey Junior and will return in two weeks.

"Mickey, meanwhile, will finish his current Metro picture [*Love Laughs at Andy Hardy*] in September, and will start on October 1st on an aerial tour of 43 cities with a two-hour personal appearance show. Mickey will be back in January for the birth of the baby, and to inaugurate his personal radio show." But Mickey was nowhere in evidence to pass around cigars to the good people of Birmingham.

There are two versions of why Mickey was in Hollywood when Betty Jane was giving birth in a Birmingham hospital.

In Los Angeles Superior Court in June 1947, Betty Jane charged that Mickey "deserted me and sent me back home to Alabama to have my baby."

In reply to her allegations, Mickey said, "She left against my wishes and pleading for Birmingham to have her second baby. She has never returned or offered to return, although I admit such an offer would be meaningless. I naturally wished to be available when my baby was born. There exists insurmountable barriers between us which made our separation inevitable, and further marital relations impossible."

The separate maintenance action took place in June, but as early as January 28 of that year, just two weeks after Timmy's birth, a story datelined Birmingham appeared in the *Los Angeles Times* reporting that Mickey Rooney's second marriage had hit the rocks, the source—Mickey's mother-in-law: "Nothing has been settled, and no legal action has been taken," Mrs. Rase said. "Property settlement discussions are under way."

SHORTLY AFTERWARD THE financial arrangements were settled with Mickey agreeing to give Betty Jane fifteen thousand dollars a year for ten years, a house, and to pay for all her existing medical bills, which totaled twelve thousand dollars. The lawyer representing Betty Jane, former Judge Leonard Wilson, flew into Birmingham from Los Angeles and got her signature on the papers in the presence of her parents, who acted as witnesses.

It was a fairly stiff price for Mickey to be forced to pay for the pleasure of such a miserable and short marriage. And because he had so little actual cash to spare out of his Metro salary after paying off his agents, business managers, partners, and Uncle Sam, his settlement with Betty Jane simply added to his financial woes. So

150

did frequent court appearances to answer her charges that he was remiss in his monthly payments.

A bachelor again, Mickey sold the house at a small loss and moved back into El Ranchita with his mother and stepfather. But he didn't spend much time there. During the day he was either at the studio or in his office at Rooney, Inc., playing at being an executive—or at the races. And nights he was either out with his buddies or in some lady's arms.

It was no problem for a man of Mickey's worldwide reputation, income, and ability to entertain to find a girl who was willing. Mickey seldom seemed to want much more from any woman. "He was never a good husband," Nick Sevano says, one of a long string of business managers who handled Mickey during his career. "He only married for the sex part of it. He never went home. I could tell the minute he was bored with a wife. He'd say to me, 'What are you doing tonight, Nickeroo? I thought we'd have dinner. . . .' You see, he was always on the make. A beautiful woman would drive him up a wall. But lots of times he couldn't lay the girl of his dreams unless he married her first. The man had deep insecurities because of his size. He was the Huckleberry Finn of America. Every kid wanted to be like him, but no dame wanted to be married to him. Because he wasn't handsome. To them, he was just a crazy little kid. But a lot of dames used him as a stepping stone to movie careers. That's why he had to get married so many times."

But if Mickey thought he was through with Betty Jane and could just go on living it up, he didn't know very much about ex-wives or women scorned. In June, Betty Jane's attorney, Leonard Wilson, moved in Superior Court to set aside the agreement his client, who was still in Birmingham with both children, had made with Mickey the previous January.

In that agreement they had signed a pact not to accuse the other of "moral misconduct." Now Betty Jane wanted more money than she had originally settled for, and Mickey was accused of all kinds of things, from playing around with other women to fraudulently hiding his real income and assets behind "a phony firm." Mickey was also asked to pay Betty Jane's attorney five thousand dollars; that sum was wanted so that he could continue to prosecute her fight for a larger share of his earnings.

At the end of the hearing, the judge ordered Mickey to pay Leonard Wilson five thousand dollars. At the same time Betty agreed to go on accepting $1,250-a-month temporary alimony for herself and her two children, as provided in the original property

151

settlement, until such time as future litigation might prove the agreement unfair. Somehow Mickey managed to come up with the cash to pay the lawyer and he shook off his marital worries enough to concentrate on his acting chores in *Killer McCoy*.

THAT SEPTEMBER, WHILE he was still shooting *Killer McCoy,* Mickey's marital status changed dramatically again. This time for the better. While he was on the set one day, Betty Jane showed up and announced to everyone that she and Mickey had "kissed and made up." Mickey smilingly confirmed that one of Los Angeles's Superior Court judges had been working with him and Betty Jane for the past month to effect a reconciliation. That she was there and he was hugging her warmly were ample proofs that the judge's efforts had paid off.

Most people doubted if the patch job would last, including gossip columnist Louella Parsons, but Mickey's and Betty Jane's actions belied this when they rented a house with a swimming pool on fashionable Ambassador Avenue in Beverly Hills for $750 a month. Still, for a few weeks it seemed that the marriage was as on track as it ever had been. This was the first time since Timmy had been born that Mickey had really been around his second son. There was a novelty to watching the two boys grow, and he came to love them.

But he still didn't love Betty Jane. And before long he was out girl chasing in the evenings.

One of these girls turned out to be more than just a one-night stand. Mickey thought he'd found real love this time and moved in with her. For a few weeks that fall, he was contented, even contemplating marriage with his new roommate. But she decided that a married man with two children and lots of alimony to pay was not a very good risk for a husband. So one morning she woke up and announced to Mickey that she was going to leave him. And despite her protestations that she still loved Mickey, she married someone else two days later.

Being the kind of a man who couldn't stand solitude—even a dull wife was better than eating dinner by himself—Mickey returned to Betty Jane and the kids for a brief period.

During the daylight hours Mickey didn't have time to dwell on how unhappy his home life was. At the studio he was shooting *Words and Music,* a huge, expensive musical that was allegedly the story of composers Rodgers and Hart, with Mickey playing Larry Hart to Tom Drake's Richard Rodgers.

One evening, after a hard day before the cameras, Mickey came home to find that Betty Jane was not alone. She had invited a male friend to have dinner with them. Mickey had no objection to the man's presence—he thought theirs was just a platonic relationship. After dinner and a few hours of conversation, fatigue caught up with Mickey, and he excused himself and went to bed, leaving Betty Jane and her guest in the living room.

Upstairs in his bed, Mickey couldn't sleep. He was worried about his career, marriage, and money if he and Betty Jane split up again, which seemed inevitable the way things were going. He didn't know what to do. He didn't want to leave the children, for he'd grown to love them and enjoyed their company. But at the same time he knew he couldn't go on living with Betty Jane. They were just kidding each other that they could make it work.

Finally, after Mickey heard Betty Jane letting her guest out the front door, he went back downstairs to get a drink of water. Somehow the final conflagration started and, when the fireworks were finally over, Mickey packed his bags and moved out of Betty Jane's life for the last time.

Once again, El Ranchita became his official residence. When he completed work on *Words and Music* in early December, he and Stiefel took off for London where Mickey had been booked for a four-week engagement at the Palladium, starting January 5, 1948, at $15,000 per week.

Mickey was a huge success doing the same vaudeville routines he had done on his American publicity tours for years. British audiences brought him back for eight and ten encores and usually wound up giving him a standing ovation.

Mickey and Stiefel arrived in Hollywood from their London triumph in early February. "Mickey packed them in every night," Stiefel announced to the local press. "The grosses were huge and the Londoners couldn't get enough of The Mick."

Betty Jane had had enough of him, however. Their divorce hearing was in Los Angeles Superior Court on May 28. Mickey didn't show up to contest the charges a tearful Betty Jane made from the stand. The judge granted an interlocutory divorce decree (final in a year) and approved a property settlement giving Betty Jane $12,500 a year for ten years, $5,000 a year child support, $25,000 for the purchase of a home, and $750 a month rent money on her present house until she was able to buy one. In addition, Mickey was to pay her attorney fees.

She was also given custody of Mickey Junior, who was two and one-half, and Timothy, who was seventeen months.

NOW THAT MICKEY was single again, he was also homeless. Of course he was welcome to continue living with Nell and Fred Pankey in the house he had bought for his mother. But somehow living with one's parents didn't seem the proper life-style for a major movie star who was twenty-eight years old. On the other hand he didn't like living alone, so he decided to find a roommate. A male roommate. If you split up with a male, you weren't expected to pay him alimony or child support.

A few days later, Jimmy Cook got a call from his old war buddy Mickey Rooney, who told him, "I just broke up with Betty Jane for good. How would you like to take an apartment with me?"

Much as he enjoyed Mickey's company, Cook wasn't sure. He'd disturbed his tranquility by making room for Mickey on a couple of occasions when he'd broken up with Betty Jane. Now he was in a smaller place, and he'd have to move to a larger one to accommodate Mickey. "I don't know," Cook said, hesitantly. "I'd like to, Mick. But you know. You'll meet another girl, and in two months you'll be married again."

After Mickey swore to Cook that he not only wouldn't be married in two months but it was quite likely he would never marry again, the two moved into the Argyle Apartments on Fountain Avenue in West Hollywood.

The place they chose was roomy, with two bedrooms, ideal for bringing girls in. According to Cook, Mickey was a good roommate and a "pretty good cook." Unlike Betty Jane and Mickey, he and Mickey had much in common. Neither was excessively neat nor excessively sloppy. They liked girls, booze, and carousing in moderation. Though Mickey had hit the bottle pretty heavily when he was breaking up with Ava, "he only drank a little when he was with me," Cook recalls. "A couple of drinks a night would take care of the two of us. But he was still carrying the torch for Ava. He'd do things like stopping by her place at eight o'clock in the morning and wake her up. She'd be friendly to him, but that was about it."

After ten months of marriage, Ava had divorced Artie Shaw. But by Mickey's "odd couple" period she was in the throes of an affair with Howard Duff. So even though Howard Hughes and Artie Shaw were out of the picture, there was still no chance for Mickey.

"He never got over her, I don't think," Cook says of that period. "I think that's why he got married so many times. He was always looking for another one just like Ava."

154

14

NEITHER WAS 1948 a banner year for Mickey professionally. In the two films in which movie fans saw him, *Summer Holiday*, which had been on the shelf for a year and a half, and *Words and Music*, in which Mickey played Larry Hart, he less than bowled over the critics. Of Mickey's performance in *Summer Holiday*, Bosley Crowther wrote: "He makes puppy love with burlesque shyness, he wears his clothes in exaggerated style, and he acts the big cheese in his household exactly as Andy Hardy does." But when it came to *Words and Music*, Crowther was downright vitriolic: "As played by Mr. Rooney, the deterioration of Mr. Hart deserves some sort of recognition as the year's prize grotesquerie . . . His florid flings at gay abandon, his puff-eyed pleas for sympathy, and his final, groping trek from the hospital to the theater (in the rain, of course) are among the most horribly inadequate and embarrassing things this reviewer has ever watched."

Although *Words and Music* did nothing to enhance Mickey Rooney's reputation as a performer, it wound up making a lot of money for MGM, which was about all Louis Mayer and Benny Thau could ask of any picture.

Way back in the spring of 1948, even before Mickey took a lambasting from the critics in *Words and Music*, it was becoming evident to his bosses, and in fact, most of the industry, that Mickey Rooney, at the ripe old age of twenty-eight, had finally arrived at the "awkward age." Because of Mickey's enormous talent, verve, and box-office appeal, it had taken him longer than most juvenile actors to reach that unhappy plateau where he was too battle-scarred from life to be accepted in the role of an innocent teenager

155

and not tall enough to compete with the likes of Gable, Tracy, and Stewart for romantic leads. Maturity had overtaken Mickey's face; he was more gross than cute, making it difficult for the studio to find roles to commensurate with the enormous salary he was getting.

As a result, Metro took advantage of the forty-week clause in his contract, and kept Mickey on layoff without salary for more weeks in 1948 than his alimony payments could stand. *Words and Music* was his only picture that year, a vast difference from the nine features in which he had starred in 1939.

Aside from the lost income, Mickey simply didn't like not working. Which was why, one day in the spring of 1948, while he and Mickey were sitting in their office on Sunset Boulevard, Stiefel suggested they take advantage of the clause in Mickey's contract that permitted him to do radio thirty-nine weeks a year.

Mickey had always wanted a radio show of his own, but so far there'd been no takers. There'd been interest, but somehow something always seemed to happen to prevent the actual consummation of a radio deal.

"We just have to get you into radio," Stiefel said. "You *sound* as young as ever."

That made sense to Mickey, but first they had to have an idea, and then they had to sell it to a radio network. Stiefel didn't believe that would be any problem, because he had already come up with a very salable idea—Mickey would play Andy Hardy in a half-hour weekly radio situation comedy.

"You've got a built-in audience out there just waiting to hear their old friend Andy Hardy on radio," Stiefel said enthusiastically. Mickey agreed it was a terrific idea. There was just a slight problem. They'd have to get the rights from Louis B. Mayer—who hated radio because it competed with pictures.

Being a man whose middle name was chutzpah, Stiefel was sure he could handle "Uncle Louie." The following day, after an appointment with Mayer had been arranged, Stiefel, Briskin, and Mickey filed into the studio head's cavernous office on the third floor of the Thalberg Building on the Culver City lot, ready to start wheeling and dealing.

Mayer was sitting behind a huge white desk that matched the rest of the decor. As the late comedian George Jessel once remarked about a similar decorating job, "There was so much white in the room you could go snow blind." Mayer greeted them wearing a defensive smile, and with a wary voice. He knew from past experience that Stiefel wasn't there with his lawyer and client to do him a service.

156

Following the usual opening amenities, Stiefel got down to business. "I'll tell you why we came, L.B. We want to put the Hardy series on radio, with Mickey starring."

Mayer scowled but said nothing. Stiefel continued uneasily: "Of course we'll give the studio full credit, and a royalty."

Shooting Stiefel a hostile glance, Mayer turned to Mickey and, in a voice dripping with false kindliness that belied the anger in his eyes, said, "You know, Mickey, you've always been one of my favorite people. I look upon you as I would my own son. And you're a great actor, and I'd like to help you out. But you have to understand, an Andy Hardy radio show would detract from the value of the pictures."

"But you already announced to the trades you're not going to make any more Hardy flicks," Stiefel reminded him.

"Suppose I change my mind?" Mayer tossed back.

"In that case," Mickey said, "you can get Butch Jenkins to play Andy Hardy."

Mayer was livid. He wasn't used to having an actor talk "fresh" to him—especially one who was barely over five feet tall—and he threatened to throw Mickey right out of the office.

Mayer was built like an ox, and though he was nearing seventy, he was still quite strong. But Mickey wasn't intimidated. Leaping out of his chair, he dared Mayer to make good his threat. Mayer remained in his chair, scowling and fuming at the upstart.

Finally he replied in an unctuous tone, "You know what I've done for you, my son."

"No, but I know what I've done for you," Mickey retorted. "I've made you millions."

And with that he stormed out of the office, slamming the door.

Mayer was in such a rage that he refused to say anything further to Briskin and Stiefel except that he was putting Mickey on suspension. In short, the conference was over and, quite possibly, Mickey's movie career—at least at Metro. If Mickey had still been number one at the box office, he might have gotten away with telling off the most powerful man in the industry. As it was, if he didn't want to remain on suspension indefinitely, he'd have to go back to Mayer and beg.

Much as it was against Mickey's proud nature to apologize to Mayer for something that he didn't believe was his fault, logic—not to mention his bank account—told him he'd better.

But Stiefel was against it. He saw this as a way of getting Mickey out of his MGM contract and going completely independent. "We'll make a settlement with Metro, and make pictures on our own. That

157

way you'll be getting some real money. A hundred ... a hundred and fifty thousand a picture."

It sounded good to Mickey, who was always a better actor than he was a businessman and very emotional after the Mayer confrontation. In his eagerness to get back at Mayer for threatening to throw him out of the office, he didn't stop to think what he would be giving up if he left MGM: $5,000 a week for forty weeks a year; a pension plan that would have given him $49,000 a year at retirement—if he just stuck it out at MGM for four more years; and smart people looking out for his interests, including a powerful publicity department headed by Howard Strickling, the best man in the business.

Friends like Nick Sevano, who was managing Frank Sinatra at the time, and Mickey's stepfather, Fred Pankey, who was handling the books for Mickey Rooney, Inc., all advised Mickey to make peace with Louis B. Mayer. "When Mickey came to me one day," Sevano recalls, "and told me about Stiefel, I called Sam, and as much as I liked him, I chewed his ass out. I said, 'Sam, you know what you're making this kid do?' And I reminded him that Mickey would be giving up the five grand a week and the pension. But Stiefel already had two outside pictures lined up for Mickey to do for United Artists—*Quicksand* and *The Big Wheel*. Stiefel promised Mickey he was going to get him a hundred and fifty thousand a picture. And Stiefel had a couple of other pictures he wanted Mickey to do independently, too. Which meant Mickey was looking down the road at what he thought was four or five hundred thousand dollars. So when I told Mickey not to leave Metro, to think of what he was giving up, he said to me, 'Listen, Nick, I wouldn't make that at MGM in ten years.' So he went ahead and told Stiefel to do what he could about getting out of the Metro contract."

Mayer, however, wasn't about to relinquish a talent like Mickey who'd made so much money for him in the past—at least not without a fight. Whether Mickey liked it or not, he was contractually tied to MGM for the next five years. If Mickey insisted on leaving MGM, he'd have to buy his way out.

When Sevano heard that Metro wasn't going to roll over and play dead for Stiefel, he persuaded Mickey to retain Greg Bautzer, one of the highest-priced and most-respected attorneys in the movie business, to renegotiate the deal for Rooney, Inc. A good thought, but Bautzer had a weak hand to play.

The negotiations dragged on throughout the spring and most of the summer of 1948.

Louis B. Mayer was playing dog-in-the-manger with a doggedness that would have bored the average dog to death. Finally, on August 2, it was over.

What may have, at first glance, looked like a victory for Rooney, Inc., was actually a rout for the other side. Judging from the terms of his new contract, Mickey might have been better off just to give Mayer a pound of flesh.

In order to get out of his old MGM contract, Mickey had to agree to terms outlined in a memo from Floyd Hendrickson to Benny Thau on July 30, 1948. Minus the legal mumbo jumbo, the most salient points of this were:

(1) Mickey had to forgo his $5,000-a-week salary for forty weeks and accept $2,500 for twenty weeks instead;

(2) Mickey had to give Metro a note for $500,000, "which indebtedness would be reduced by $100,000 for each picture he completed under the new picture agreement," which would call for six-month options instead of yearly options;

(3) Mickey would receive $125,000 for each picture he made under the new agreement, but $100,000 of that would go to pay off the $500,000 bond he had posted. In actual cash he would receive only $25,000 per picture;

(4) In the event Mickey defaulted under the picture contract, Metro would have the right to hold him to the old picture contract and enjoin him from rendering services of any kind to anyone else during his failure or refusal to perform services;

(5) Moreover, if Metro exercised its right to terminate the five-picture agreement by reason of Mickey's failure or refusal to work, the unpaid balance of the $500,000 was to be paid in cash to the studio upon "demand."

By the average journeyman actor's standards, $25,000 a picture wasn't exactly slave wages in 1948. However, under the terms of Mickey's partnership agreement with Stiefel, he had to give him half. Then William Morris took another ten percent off the top, leaving Mickey with just $10,000 to pay his living expenses, alimony, child support, income taxes, and racetrack losses.

If he made five pictures in one year for Metro, he'd personally wind up with fifty thousand, before taxes. And that wasn't about to happen. With Mayer still angry with Mickey, he wasn't making any great effort to find a vehicle for him to star in at MGM. As a matter of fact, Mayer wasn't thinking very much about Mickey at all. Mayer was beginning to have his own problems.

Because of its huge overhead and a general depression in the movie business, MGM was beginning to lose money steadily for the first time since Louie B. Mayer had been in charge. Moreover, Leo hadn't been collecting it's usual lion's share of the Oscars at Academy Award time. In 1948 Nicholas Schenck, president of Loew's, Incorporated, brought Dore Schary, who had written *Boys Town*, back to Metro to oversee all production in collaboration with Mayer. An ambitious man, Schary wasn't satisfied with corunning the studio; he had his sights on Mayer's job.

While the boys in the upper echelon were busy playing musical executive chairs, nobody was paying any attention to little Mickey Rooney, except possibly Herman C. Biegel, whose job it was to administer the pension plan. Just one week after the story of Mickey's new deal appeared in *Variety*, Biegel sent off a memo to Eugene Leake, the plan's keeper of the funds, which said, "After going over Rooney's new contract, it is my opinion that he is no longer a full-time employee of Loew's. Therefore his membership in the plan has been terminated as of June 25, 1948."

At the time Mickey couldn't have cared less about losing the pension plan, if indeed anyone at Metro bothered to notify him. He was only twenty-eight, and eager to start making movies for himself under the banner of Mickey Rooney Enterprises, which Stiefel had let everyone believe he was going to finance with his own millions.

But according to Mort Briskin, the other partner in the venture, "Stiefel didn't want to take any risks with his own money. So I had to go out and get independent financing for our projects. For example, I was the one who found Harry Popkin. He put up most of the money for *The Big Wheel*. Once we had the money, United Artists agreed to release it. So in reality Stiefel was in on a free ride. He got other people to put up the money, and he took forty percent of the profits."

Raising the money for *Quicksand* and *The Big Wheel*, and getting a major distributor for them took time, however,—time when Mickey wasn't making the big money he was used to. This was something he could ill afford with all his expenses.

In December of 1948, tired of waiting for Stiefel to set a picture deal, Mickey accepted engagements to play the Hippodrome Theater in Baltimore for $10,000 a week for two weeks, and the State Theater in Hartford, Connecticut, at $12,000 a week for two weeks. That was big money for personal appearances in those days and proved that Mickey was still something of a box-office attraction.

But it did nothing to ease Mickey's rapidly growing fears, nurtured while lying awake nights in various hotel rooms, that he had perhaps made a mistake of gigantic proportions by joining forces with Samuel H. Stiefel. What did he have to show for that alliance except a company that couldn't get a picture off the ground, a partner who was pocketing half his earnings, a contract with Metro that was virtually worthless, and a load of debts?

By the time Mickey returned to the Coast in mid-January, he was convinced that he could no longer afford to have Stiefel for a partner. Mickey's stepfather, Fred Pankey, who'd been the book-keeper for Rooney, Inc., also was of the opinion that Mickey ought to dump Stiefel. According to Pankey, Stiefel was no longer letting him examine the books, so it was impossible to determine just where Mickey's money had gone.

However, when Mickey notified Stiefel of his decision to dissolve the partnership, Stiefel informed him that there were commitments to honor first. While Mickey had been away, Stiefel had completed the deal with United Artists for him and Mort Briskin to coproduce *Quicksand* and *The Big Wheel*. When Mickey asked what would happen if he refused to play in those pictures, Stiefel said to him, "You could get sued for breach of contract."

WHILE MICKEY WAS contemplating breaking away from one partner-ship, he was on the verge of becoming entangled in another one—this one of a more personal nature.

For eight months, Mickey had remained true to his word to Jimmy Cook: he'd stayed clear of any serious commitment to members of the opposite sex. This exercise in willpower had sur-prised not only his saxophonist roommate, but Mickey as well. Since his divorce from Betty Jane, Mickey had chased, but had never come close to getting caught—until Nick Sevano introduced him to a rising young actress named Martha Vickers at a party at Ciro's one night in January of 1949.

It was a typical Hollywood party. Plenty of booze, women, and song, but Mickey was not in a very festive mood as he sat in a corner brooding about his career troubles and trying to wash them away with one martini after another. The booze left him vulnerable to anyone who would listen, but especially to an attractive girl who would hear out his sad tale. As a result, his guard was completely down when Nick Sevano led Martha Vickers over by the hand and introduced her to Mickey.

Martha was twenty-four years old, beautiful, auburn-haired, and only five-foot-three-and-a-half-inches tall. For a change, this ap-pealed to Mickey. It wasn't easy to find a girl who didn't make him look like a midget. In addition, Martha wouldn't have been after his money (if he had any, that is) because she had her own career going. Although she'd appeared in other films, her most memorable screen appearance to date was as the sultry second lead in *The Big Sleep* for Warner Brothers, which had starred Humphrey Bogart and Lauren Bacall.

The chemistry between them seemed to work from the start. After she accepted his invitation to sit down with him, Mickey realized that they had a lot more in common than the same first initials. Martha wasn't a "hick," and she was familiar with the divorce scene. Her first husband, whom she was in the process of divorcing, was a film publicist named A. C. Lyles, Jr.

"Mickey went crazy when I first introduced him to Martha," Nick Sevano recalls. "He wanted to marry her right away."

But unless he wanted to elope with her to Vegas or Juarez, he couldn't marry her before June when his second divorce would become final. As a matter of fact, hers would not become final until several months after his marriage was officially over.

But from the moment Mickey first gazed into her hazel eyes, it was apparent to Mickey that Martha was meant for him. She was easy to talk to. She was a good listener. She admired his talent. She cared enough about him personally to tell him that he shouldn't drink so much, even as she had a few herself.

Moreover, she built up his ego as he spewed out his troubles to her, wondering aloud if he'd ever again appear in another hit picture. She consoled him by saying that soon he'd be king of the movie hill again.

"I respected and admired Mickey at our very first meeting," Martha told a friend, Frances Lane, with whom she had double-dated a few weeks earlier. "I had always been a faithful fan of the Andy Hardy series, and was impressed that Mickey was actually modest and not noisy and all over the place as some people have said. He is very intelligent and quiet—unless his mood is for fun or there are some hot drums he can play."

Two days later, Mickey phoned Martha at her home in the Valley, where she still lived with her mother and father James and Frances MacVicker, a handsome couple in their forties, and her younger brother, Jimmy, and asked her for a date. "That first date, however, was a little strange," Martha related to her friend. "We were to meet another couple at Chasen's. The other boy, Dick Morley, was alone, because his date was sick, so we became a threesome. Mickey had hurt his leg since I'd last been with him, and when we went on to the

Beverly Wilshire to see Kay Thompson's act, I danced with the other boy. Mickey seemed very quiet and very thoughtful."

Judging by Mickey's subdued behavior, Martha felt she was making no impression on him whatsoever. And by the end of the evening, when he dropped her off, she was sure she had struck out with him. He told her he was flying to Texas in the morning and that he would phone her when he got back. But he didn't give her a clue as to when he would be coming back—what day or even what month.

But to Martha's surprise, Mickey phoned the next morning. "I'm not going to Texas," he told her. "I couldn't get you off my mind. Martha, I think you're the nicest girl I ever met. Would you please have dinner with me again tonight?"

As a change of pace, Martha invited Mickey to have dinner with her and her family at her house in the Valley. That sounded good to Mickey, and she gave him the time to be there and her address.

The MacVickers had a comfortable, ranch-style home, and Mickey was impressed with Martha's parents. James MacVicker, a modestly successful sales representative for a Japanese steel firm, was very interested in the things Mickey loved to do outdoors— deep-sea fishing and duck hunting. His wife, Frances, was a lovely hostess and a good cook.

"Mother had cooked a ham, and I fixed the candied sweet potatoes with marshmallows, and a salad," Martha said to her friend. "My brother Jimmy brought his girl over, and we served dinner buffet style. Mickey was surprised that I had cooked most of the dinner, and complimented me on being such a good cook. But he didn't eat very much. In fact, Mother was a little upset that he had eaten so little."

There was nothing wrong with Mickey, however. He was just more interested in discussing hunting and fishing with Martha's father who, after they got up from the table, dragged out all his hunting and fishing equipment and showed it to Mickey.

"Do you like to hunt and fish, too?" Mickey asked Martha.

Martha really didn't—her sport was horseback riding. But she wasn't going to admit that to Mickey and take the chance of turning him off. And neither was her father, who, after exchanging a conspiratorial wink with his daughter, started telling Mickey some tall tales about all the big fish Martha had landed.

Mickey was impressed that he had finally found a girl who seemed to enjoy the same outdoor activities he did. At the end of the evening he invited the whole MacVicker family over to his place—a little bachelor's house he was renting on Laurel Canyon—for a duck dinner on the following night. "I'll cook," he told them. This was no idle boast. One of Mickey's hobbies was cooking, and he knew a special way to prepare wild duck.

That evening was such a success that, the very next day, Mickey introduced Martha to his mother and stepfather, Nell and Fred Pankey. Then the four of them went to the races together.

Soon Mickey and Martha were seen everywhere together and became an "item" in the Hollywood gossip columns. Friends were predicting that wedding bells would soon be ringing in their future.

Mickey must have thought so too. He gave up the bachelor house and moved back in with his parents. No use paying rent on a bachelor pad, when he'd soon be having to buy a house.

SHORTLY AFTER HE and Martha started going steady, Mickey became determined to leave Stiefel. He called on Johnny Hyde, his former agent at William Morris, and told him that he was thinking of leaving Stiefel, and why. Hyde, who'd always been fond of Mickey, was anxious to get his old client back. He agreed that Mickey's career was going nowhere with Stiefel and advised him to return to William Morris for representation. It even seemed possible that he could get Mickey out of the *Quicksand* deal.

Mickey was elated that William Morris still wanted him, and signed with the agency immediately.

On February 1, 1949, the following appeared in a piece on page one of *Daily Variety*:

ROONEY CUTS AWAY
FROM SAM STIEFEL

Rooney was dissatisfied with the financial returns he had been getting out of Rooney-Stiefel Corp. . . .

Actor was set in a deal Stiefel made with United Artists for release of *Quicksand*. However, he is now negotiating with King Bros. to make a picture, with Lou Rantz repping the Kings, to put together a package and also negotiating with RKO for a releasing deal for the Kings and Rooney . . .

Since William Morris now is repping him, naturally Rooney will try to by-pass the Stiefel *Quicksand* deal.

UNFORTUNATELY, ALL THE King Brothers' horses and all of William Morris's men couldn't do anything about extricating Mickey from

Quicksand and *The Big Wheel* (the other picture Stiefel had negotiated with United Artists). However, the agency did start negotiations to get Mickey out of his partnership with Sam Stiefel. The result of several weeks of dickering was that in return for dissolving the partnership Mickey agreed to appear in three pictures for Sam Stiefel.

"These pictures—*Quicksand* and *The Big Wheel* plus another one—became the basis of his settlement with us," reports Mort Briskin from his home in Beverly Hills today. "Mickey agreed to make both of them, and another one, for a very limited amount of money. I believe it was around $25,000 a picture. The third picture—*Frances the Mule*—never did get made. Even though I had optioned the story, Stiefel didn't have any faith in it and refused to put up his own money. So I dropped the option, and Universal bought it immediately."

That's the way Mickey's luck was running in those days. The one picture of the three he wasn't forced to make turned into a blockbuster for Universal and made a star out of Donald O'Connor. Mickey, meanwhile, was stuck in two cheapies that did nothing for his career except confirm what most insiders in the business were already thinking—that Mickey Rooney was washed up. And to many of these people it served him right for turning like an ungrateful child on the studio that was responsible for making him kingpin of the box office before he was even old enough to vote.

There was nothing notable about *Quicksand*, and the most noteworthy thing about *The Big Wheel* was that Mickey did something he ordinarily hated to do: he gave somebody's girlfriend a walk-on part in the picture.

"The somebody was Mickey's agent, Johnny Hyde," Nick Sevano says. "Johnny Hyde came to me and said he had this girl, Norma Jean, he wanted to get some film on so he could use it for a screen test. But he hated to ask Mickey, because Mickey would promise him and then not go through with it. So he asked me to ask Mickey. And I finally got Mickey to say okay."

As a result, Johnny Hyde's girlfriend made her debut in *The Big Wheel*, in a crowd scene at the Indianapolis racetrack. "If you blinked, you would have missed her," Sevano continues. "And, oh, yeah, Norma Jean eventually changed her name to Marilyn Monroe."

If the reason for Mickey's sudden ebullient spirits wasn't apparent to his casual acquaintances, it was no mystery to his intimates. Mickey was always happiest when he was in the courting stage of a

165

romance. After his initial impulse couldn't be satisfied, Mickey decided not to rush into marriage, or even into Martha's bedroom—trying to assess his true feelings about her. Was it simply physical attraction or was it the kind of love that would last? So he curbed his desire and for a while just enjoyed her companionship. Mickey took her to athletic events and to his favorite restaurants and drinking spots where they engaged in lively philosophical discussions about life, love, and why their past marriages had ended in failure.

Martha had always preferred wearing comfortable clothes: skirts, sweaters—and flats. Since Mickey also wore sports clothes most of the time, Martha assumed he approved of her attire. But one night, Mickey said to Martha, "Sweetheart, you know you and I are exactly the same height. But I like girls in high heels. Don't wear flats for me any more."

The following day Martha threw away her flats and went out and bought a whole new wardrobe and a closetful of pretty high-heeled shoes. Mickey should have read the signs. "I just knew in my heart there would never be another boy like him," Martha confessed to Wally and Marcy Cassell, close friends of Mickey's.

One night in April, Mickey said, "We must be in love."

"I guess we are," Martha replied.

"I suppose we should get an engagement ring," Mickey said.

"If you say so," Martha said, trying not to sound too eager.

The next morning, Mickey phoned Martha from a jewelry store in Hollywood, "I'm looking at our ring," he said. "I've got one all ordered."

Once Mickey had slipped the large, emerald-cut diamond, engagement ring on Martha's finger, he couldn't wait for her divorce to become final at the end of the year to marry her.

"So I arranged for Martha to get a Vegas divorce" Cassell remembers today. "She could get one there after just six weeks of residency. Marcy and I drove them to Vegas, and I put her on an exclusive guest ranch owned by some friends of mine there. They had about 450 acres, but no slots, no gambling. Just horses. And quite secluded. Martha waited the six-week period there, while Mickey commuted back and forth to Los Angeles, where he was shooting a picture."

Las Vegas may have been the place to get a "quickie" divorce, but it was not the ideal surroundings for a fellow like Mickey to be spending his leisure time. "The first weekend I took him and Martha there," Cassell recalls, "Mickey went into one of the casinos and dropped $3600, which he couldn't afford, and was writing markers for it. He was so busted at that point that I knew he didn't have a quarter in his checking account to cover the markers. So I had to go out and get the markers back for him—the pit bosses cooperated with me because he was a celebrity and they liked the little guy. After all, they weren't going to go out and put Andy Hardy in a cement block."

The fact that he had no money to gamble with never stopped Mickey. "A couple of weekends later we were having dinner and watching a show at the El Rancho," says Marcy Cassell. "We were going to split the check, so we gave Mickey our half, which was about fifty dollars, and he left, while Wally and I stayed on a little longer and danced. But later when we were going out the door the maitre d' grabbed Wally's arm roughly and said, 'Hey, buddy. You're not going without paying the check, are you?' Surprised, Wally told him that Mickey had already paid it, but the maitre d' said, no, he hadn't. So we paid it, and then went out to look for Mickey. We found him at the crap tables, using our half of the dinner check to finance his gambling."

IT WAS A good thing it only took six weeks to get a Vegas divorce.

Martha's divorce came through at the end of May, just five days before Mickey's California divorce from Betty Jane became final. By then, Mickey was in favor of a simple wedding in Vegas. He couldn't afford anything fancier. But Martha had her heart set on a church wedding in Southern California because she wanted her folks to witness it. So, compliant as Mickey was—at least at that stage of the wedding game—he acquiesced.

There was one final hitch: it wasn't easy to find a minister willing to splice a one-time and two-time loser. After being turned down flat by several churches, Mickey finally met with success at the Christ Memorial Unity Church of North Hollywood, the home grounds of the Reverend Herbert J. Schneider. The nuptials took place on June 3, at five in the afternoon, just six hours to the minute after Mickey had picked up his final divorce papers from Betty Jane (who, incidentally, married band leader Buddy Baker just five days later).

It was a double-ring ceremony, and despite the fact that Mickey, at age twenty-nine, was an old hand at getting married, his hand trembled as he placed the ring on Martha's finger. Martha was almost as shaky as she slipped a twin band on Mickey's wedding finger. The rings were engraved, *Today...tomorrow...always... I love you. M.R. to M.R.*

After the Reverend Schneider pronounced them man and wife, the new Mrs. Rooney, who towered over Mickey in her spiked heels, stooped down, took his puckish face in her lace-gloved hands, and gave him a loud kiss on his lips. Following a second kiss, the happy couple grabbed hands and hurried up the aisle and out onto the sidewalk. There they waved to the crowd, hopped into a shiny green convertible, and roared away for what Mickey said to the press was to be a little "complete privacy."

Later, they returned to a champagne reception at the church, where Mickey made the first cut into a three-tiered wedding cake and announced to the amused guests, "I've got me a wonderful girl this time. If I don't make this one last, there's something wrong with me."

Then he and Martha guzzled champagne with their friends, relatives, and Sam Stiefel until the wee hours.

If it seems odd, after some of the allegations Mickey had made about him in the press impugning his honesty, that Sam Stiefel was among the select few invited to the wedding, you don't know Mickey. It wasn't in his nature to hold a grudge for very long.

"Besides, Sam and I paid for the wedding," Mort Briskin says, with an amused grin.

Mickey at age three.

Mickey and Coleen Moore in *Orchids and Ermine*, a 1932 film. Mickey is playing a hogman from Walla Walla.

(above) Mickey (in checked shirt and derby) doing a little slave driving in one of the early Mickey McGuire comedies. *(Marvin Paige Motion Picture & TV Research Center)*

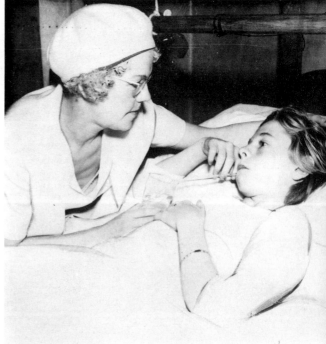

(right) Mickey's doting mother, Nell, playing nurse to her hospitalized son after Mickey broke his leg in a toboggan accident at Big Bear Lake in the mid-thirties. *(Marvin Paige Motion Picture & TV Research Center)*

Mickey and Judy Garland boning up on their lines for *Love Finds Andy Hardy,* their first film together.

Mickey and Esther Williams cheek to cheek on the set of *Andy Hardy's Double Life.* It was Miss Williams's first picture.

(left) Mickey and Judy Garland watching Bill Tilden at the tennis matches at the Ambassador Hotel in 1940.

(facing page) Mickey and top banana father Joe Yule singing a little harmony on the Andy Hardy set. *(Marvin Page Motion Picture & TV Research Center)*

Left to right: Bob Hope, Mickey, Judy Garland, and Jackie Cooper at Coconut Grove c. 1938.

(above) The wedding party at Ballard, California. From left to right, front: Ava's sister Bappie, Les Peterson, Mickey, Ava, Nell Pankey, and Joe Yule. Behind the bride and groom are the Reverend Lutz and his wife, and hidden behind Nell is her second husband, Fred Pankey. *(Courtesy Les Peterson)*

(right) Mickey and his new bride, Ava Gardner, enjoying a picnic on the putting green at Lakeside, between rounds. *(Photo by Bill Chapman)*

Mickey and movie father Lewis Stone. *(Marvin Paige Motion Picture & TV Research Center)*

Mickey entertaining the troops at St. Gertrude, Belgium, while touring the front with his three-man "jeep show" during World War II. *(U.S. Army photo)*

(facing page) MGM's famous "stock company" wishing Lionel Barrymore a happy 60th birthday. Left to right, front: Norma Shearer, the birthday boy himself, and Rosalind Russell. Left to right, rear: Mickey Rooney, Robert Montgomery, Clark Gable, Louis B. Mayer, William Powell, and Robert Taylor. *(A MGM photo)*

(above) Mickey and his second
wife, Betty Jane Rase, former
Alabama beauty queen winner,
enjoying a day at the races in
spring 1946. *(Photo by Walt
Davis)*

(right) Mickey and his radiant
third bride, actress Martha
Vickers, after tying the knot at
Christ Memorial Church in June
1949. *(Marvin Paige Motion
Picture & TV Research Center)*

Mickey and fourth bride, actress Elaine Mahnken, debarking from their chartered plane after their 1952 elopement to Las Vegas. *(Photo by permission of Los Angeles Herald Examiner)*

(below) Barbara and infant son Michael Joseph Kyle Rooney in St. John's Hospital on the day after he was born, April 2, 1962. *(Marvin Paige Motion Picture & TV Research Center)*

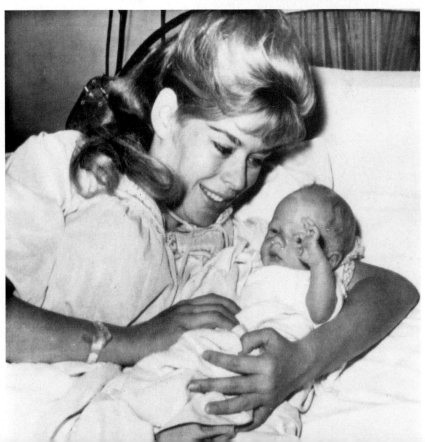

(top left) Mickey talking with the funeral director at Forest Lawn, following his wife Barbara's funeral. At Mickey's left is Red Doff, his business manager, and behind him to the right is Mickey Rooney, Jr. *(Marvin Paige Motion Picture & TV Research Service)*

(top right) Mickey going through a car wash for a comedy bit in the TV series "Mickey," 1964, on ABC. *(Photo by Arthur Marx)*

(below) Mickey cutting his sixth wedding cake with his new wife Margie Lane, September 1966. *(AP/Wide World Photos)*

(left) Mickey and seventh wife Caroline Hacket in May 1969. *(AP/Wide World Photos)*

(below) Left to right: "This Is Your Life" host Joe Campanella, Mickey's agent Ruth Webb, Mickey, Sig Frolich, Mickey's eighth wife Jan Sterling, longtime friend Sidney Miller, and director Les Martinson having a little get-together after the show. *(Courtesy of Ralph Edwards Productions)*

(facing page) Mickey opening *Sugar Babies. (Courtesy Sugar Babies Company)*

(left) Mickey and Ann Miller doing their schoolroom sketch. *(Courtesy of Sugar Babies Company)*

(below) Mickey cutting a rug with Ann Miller in the finale number of *Sugar Babies. (Courtesy Sugar Babies Company)*

A mature Mickey Rooney grinning over his new success. (Courtesy of Sugar Babies Company)

15

THERE WAS NO out-of-town honeymoon for Martha and Mickey, because of *The Big Wheel*. Instead, Mickey and "Mart," as he affectionately called his new bride, moved into a small bungalow, formerly the home of Spencer Tracy, at 4723 White Oak Avenue in Encino. If it was a modest place by movie-star standards, the bungalow was cheerful and comfortable and spacious enough for newlyweds. It even had the obligatory swimming pool, though a tiny one, in the front yard.

But the important thing was that his home was in Encino. For some reason, Mickey always felt impelled to live close to his roots. Besides, this way he could go home to Mama in case Martha became fed up with his eccentric life-style and banished him from their house.

He must have had a premonition that that would be the case. Or else was getting to know himself a little. At any rate, despite Mickey's frequent avowals to friends, relatives, and the press that this "one is going to stick," his marriage to Martha Vickers turned out to be a rerun of his first two. As usual, Mickey entered the union with the best of intentions. Unfortunately, he brought to this marriage the same problems that had derailed the other two—a wandering eye, a restless nature, a bad temper, and an almost suicidal impulse to throw money away at the racetrack.

Notwithstanding all those negatives, he loved Martha—in his own way. But according to friends who've known him throughout his many marriages, he believed his obligations to a wife stopped short of having to be with her when he had more exciting things to do.

169

"Mickey considered himself a free soul," Cassell asserts today. "He was a sweet little guy, and fun to be with. But with his wives he felt he could do anything he pleased: leave them alone, or go anywhere he wanted with anyone he wanted any time he wanted as long as it made *him* feel good." Mickey's was an attitude that a lot of husbands understand and perhaps secretly wish they could get away with in their marriages. But few besides Mickey dare to live that way. It was his downfall with women, though interestingly enough most of his wives had to be aware of these faults before they married him.

"How could they not be with his track record?" asks Dick Quine. "The problem was always the same. His frenetic existence. It was impossible for a wife to keep up with him. But as I say, how could they not have known before they married him? I feel he's taken a bum rap about being a lousy husband. I think a lot of the women used him to get somewhere ... After all, he was a tremendous star ... And still is. He had clout in the business or at least they thought he did."

From the distaff side comes another perspective.

"I can't think of two more revealing anecdotes to illustrate Mickey's attitude towards marriage and women than the ones I'm about to tell you," declares Marcy Cassell who, together with her husband Wally, was Mickey's constant companion during the Martha Vickers marriage.

"One night," Marcy continued, "Wally and I were sitting around our living room after dinner with Mickey and Martha, when the men started talking about going to New York to raise money for a picture Mickey wanted to produce. Suddenly Mickey jumped to the phone, called an airline, and started making plane reservations for him and Wally. 'Hey, buddy, just a minute,' I yelled at Mickey, 'my husband and I never go anywhere without each other. So if he goes to New York, we're going to go together.' And then I added, 'And you're not going to leave Martha home alone, either.' 'I'm not?' He looked at me kind of shocked, 'No, you're not.' I was never afraid to jump on him like that. But Martha, during this whole scene, just sat there very quietly, afraid to make any waves at all. That's the kind of girl Martha was. Very quiet and reserved, almost afraid of her shadow, afraid to stick up for herself if Mickey treated her inconsiderately, which he frequently did."

On another occasion, according to Marcy Cassell, she, Wally, and Mickey were sitting in their living room one Saturday night, watching the "Perry Como Show." As Como finished crooning a very schmaltzy ballad, Mickey shook his head in amazement and exclaimed, "How can a guy sing like that when he's been married to the same broad so many years!?" Mickey and Martha had a child right away, but pregnancy only compounded the problems.

While Mickey loved children, he most definitely did not love the gestation period. As it had happened twice before, as soon as his wife turned in her swimsuit and party dresses for maternity clothes, Mickey started looking for reasons to duck out of the house in the evenings.

Like his other wives, Martha found his behavior hard to cope with. Her way was either to anesthetize herself with liquor or else give him the "silent treatment" and become unresponsive to his demands in bed. "She was frigid," Mickey told author Roger Kahn, who ghosted his autobiography in 1965. The natural result of all this was that Mickey would look for sex elsewhere. And usually get it.

ON TOP OF Mickey's chauvinist behavior toward women, his new marriage had to cope with not one but two careers that were turning sour. Martha's career, which had started out in such a blaze of glory, had sputtered badly since *The Big Sleep*. She had acted in only three films since 1946: *Love and Learn, Ruthless,* and *Bad Boy,* three grade-B turkeys. And pregnancy didn't make it any easier to obtain leading-lady roles.

Mickey's career had lost most of its impetus and luster by then, too. Both *The Big Wheel* and *Quicksand* were the kinds of film that could keep an actor connected with them on layoff permanently, and no one was more aware of this than Mickey himself who, at the ripe old age of thirty, was a battle-scarred veteran of show business. He finally managed to break the Stiefel connection in March 1950. According to Mort Briskin, "There was no animosity between Mickey and Stiefel over the breakup." And Mickey told Hedda Hopper: "I went down the sewer with Stiefel. Sam Stiefel and I made some lousy pictures. He's back in Philadelphia now, but there are no hard feelings between us. When trouble arises between two people, I've learned its best to shake hands and go to a neutral corner."

But privately Mickey had grown extremely bitter about Stiefel. He felt that Stiefel had more than gotten even with him for the money he had loaned the Rooney family during the war. He believed that Stiefel had given him extremely bad advice in telling him to leave Metro. He further believed that Stiefel had milked him for $346,513.12.

171

Mickey had a career to salvage, and the ideal way to accomplish that would have been to return to Metro-Goldwyn-Mayer and admit to Louis B. Mayer that he'd made a mistake—on his knees, if necessary. However, Mayer, who'd been Mickey's champion for almost his entire career, had been supplanted by Dore Schary, who had his own way of running the studio. For example, he didn't believe that the "star system" worked any longer. According to him, moviegoers wanted to see "meaningful" stories and didn't give a damn about who was in them. Mickey didn't like message pictures. He also didn't like Dore Schary.

Notwithstanding, he decided to return to the Culver City lot, admit to the new man in charge of production that he'd made a giant boo-boo in breaking his contract, and ask to be taken back.

Schary, a man with the kindly demeanor of Uncle Dan Beard, founder of the Boy Scouts of America, was cordial enough in greeting the former box-office kingpin.* But after Mickey had told his story with all the humility he could muster, Schary said, "We'll see if we can find something for you, kid." And with that, he showed Mickey to the door.

Contractually, Mickey was loosely tied to MGM under the terms of the 1948 settlement worked out by Greg Bautzer. But the catch in that agreement was that if they didn't have anything for him, they didn't have to use him. In other words, it wasn't a play-or-pay deal. If Metro didn't feel like playing, it didn't have to pay. Mickey left Schary's office as deflated as a flat tire.

"Things were very bad for Mickey in 1949 and most of '50," Wally Cassell recalls. "He was in bad shape and quite broke. He'd be over to our place to dinner many and many a night before he was married to Martha. And then while he was married to Martha it got worse. He used to tell me he couldn't get arrested."

After listening to his complaints about the business, Cassell finally said to Mickey, "My God, a man with your talent. Why don't you call the Bank of America and get hold of Gianinini [founder of the Bank of America]? With your name, I'm sure you could get backing for a film in five minutes."

"Really?" Mickey exclaimed.

"Sure," Cassell said. "Just get a script."

"I've got a script. I wrote it myself."

Unfortunately, it wasn't as easy as that. The Bank of America was

---

*Without Mickey Rooney in the film, it's doubtful if Schary would have won an Oscar for writing *Boys Town*.

interested—if Mickey could come up with the front money, or about $350,000.

"Hell," Mickey lamented to Cassell. "Where am I going to get that kind of money?"

Luckily, Cassell had a friend in New York named Andy Paolillo who'd become wealthy during World War II making nylon parachutes for the government. With the leftover nylon, he manufactured the first nylon brassieres after World War II and made millions.

"Well, my friend Andy had more money than Carter has pills," Cassell relates today. "After I got hold of him a few days later he said he'd put up the money for a picture. He'd barely heard of Mickey Rooney and didn't give a damn about him, but he wanted me to become a big star. I told him, no, I didn't want that. I never wanted my name above the title. I just wanted to keep on working, and to get my friend Mickey back in pictures again.

"Anyway, Andy agreed in principle, and Mickey and I were supposed to go to New York and spend a few days on his yacht talking with him. But the morning we were supposed to leave, we first had a meeting at William Morris with Martin Gang, Mickey's lawyer, to discuss the business aspects of the deal. The meeting was called for nine o'clock. But when I got there around nine-fifteen, there was no Rooney and no Martin Gang. I waited about fifteen minutes, and then I called home and spoke to Marcy to see if she'd heard anything from Mickey. She hadn't, so I told her I'd wait another ten minutes and then to hell with him."

At nine-thirty, Cassell received a call from Marcy. "Fred Pankey just called," she told him, "and said the deal is all set, and to meet Mickey at Lakeside Country Club."

"What's all set?" Cassell asked.

Marcy didn't know anything more about it, so Cassell dialed Fred Pankey's number.

"Well, the deal's all set," Pankey said over the phone.

"What do you mean it's all set?"

"Well, Mickey's already talked to Martin Gang. The figures are all set. Mickey's going to get $125,000 as base pay plus a percentage. He's already hired Mort Briskin to do the producing. He's already got a director . . . I think it's Richard Quine. He's already got a cast . . ."

"Wait a minute," said Cassell somewhat angrily. "What happened to Wally Cassell in that deal?"

"Nothing was mentioned about you," Pankey replied.

173

"Well, you call Mickey at Lakeside and tell him he's a stupid fucking idiot and the deal is off," replied the usually mild-mannered Cassell.

"I then phoned my friend in New York and told him this thing is all one-sided, it won't work," Cassell says. "I told him, to quote Sam Goldwyn, 'They've included me out.' And they haven't included you either for putting up the money. So let's forget the whole thing. And if they should call you, tell them the deal is off unless they talk to me.' Which they never did. And that was the end of that."

Though they continued to see each other socially, Mickey's and Wally's friendship was never as close from that moment on. "The years have passed, and we've both done all right since then, but I've never forgotten that incident," Cassell says today.

Even before the year 1949 drew to a close, Martha's and Mickey's marriage seemed on the verge of total collapse, too. Drinking had become a serious problem with Martha. "Beulah, her maid, used to call me all the time, unbeknownst to Martha, and tell me that she was terribly concerned about Martha's drinking," Marcy Cassell recalls. "She'd also tell me about the terrible depressions Martha was going through because of the way Mickey neglected her."

When Martha had too much to drink in the evenings, she'd often start riding Mickey about how paranoid he was becoming about his waning career. She said he was blaming everyone but the person who should be blamed—himself. Mickey would counter by losing his temper and threatening to quit the business.

If he expected sympathy, what he received instead were sharp little taunts of agreement. "Maybe that would be a good idea, Mickey. Why don't you go ahead and quit? You could be a milkman, or something like that."

Her attitude only exacerbated the ill feelings he was beginning to harbor toward her. Six months into the marriage he knew she wasn't right for him, and vice versa. Moreover, he felt a horror and disgust with himself for letting another marriage fail. If he'd been working steadily, he might not have had time to notice. But the way things were, he had plenty of time to sit around and feel sorry for himself.

EARLY IN 1950, the work drought appeared to be over when Mickey was hired to play the lead in two low-budget pictures: *He's a Cockeyed Wonder* for Columbia, and *Fireball* for Twentieth Century-Fox. Neither film was destined to make motion-picture history, but at least they gave Mickey a legitimate excuse to get out

174

of the house and away from Martha. By then, however, they were together largely because she was going to have a baby sometime in the spring.

According to Martha's doctor, the baby was due in the middle of March. But the baby was three weeks late, and during that time "I don't think I saw Mickey at all," Martha recalled sometime later.

On the thirtieth of March, Joe Yule died of a heart attack in Santa Monica Hospital. Although Mickey hadn't seen much of his father in recent years, he was quite broken up, according to Dick Quine, who attended the services with him.

Mickey telephoned Martha the day before the baby was born, "and I told him the doctor had said it would be soon, and he said he was very busy and had to go to a party." Mickey still hadn't returned home when Beulah drove Martha, who had finally gone into labor, to the Valley Hospital at four A.M. on April 13, 1950. Finally a friend located Mickey for her, and he arrived at the hospital at five that afternoon.

The baby, a boy, was born at seven o'clock. He weighed seven pounds three ounces, and Mickey and Martha named him Teddy Michael. Then they made up and decided to give their marriage another try. "I didn't want Teddy to be the victim of a broken home so early in his life," was the reason Martha gave to her best friend.

EVEN WITH THE bad scripts he had to contend with in *He's a Cockeyed Wonder* and *Fireball,* Mickey never let his enthusiasm pale. Perhaps he tried a little too hard to overcome bad writing with his overacting—that seemed to be the general consensus of the critics.

Written by Jack Henley, whose major credits had been on the *Blondie* series, *He's a Cockeyed Wonder* opened, late in 1950, to unanimously bad reviews. "In *He's a Cockeyed Wonder,* Mickey Rooney misses on all counts," *Variety* wrote. "A witless farce dealing with an ineffectual sputterer who wins his lady love [Terry Moore]."

Fireball, which was made under the Twentieth Century-Fox banner, didn't please the critics, either. "Never let it be said," wrote *The New York Times,* "that Mickey Rooney doesn't try . . . Mr. Rooney is the whole show, seems completely aware of it, and does everything but swallow the camera to prove it."

These films fared at the box office about as well as they did at the hands of the critics. As a result, Mickey wasn't the hottest thing in show business in the year 1950.

Except for Teddy's arrival, 1950 was a bad year for the Rooney's all around. Between the poor reviews his latest pictures were getting, the death of his father, and a marriage that, despite the efforts of both participants to hold it together, was crumbling faster than a sand castle at high tide, Mickey was beginning to wonder what he had done to make the gods so angry. Mickey may not have been a saint, but he wasn't the worst person in the world, either. At least to his way of thinking. What if he did stray from home occasionally? What if he did become moody and ill-tempered because his career wasn't what it used to be, or his income, either? At least he was trying. God knew, he was trying.

But things only went from bad to terrible. With the failure of his own company went all the money he had (except for his trust funds, which couldn't be touched until he was sixty). Lawsuits were instituted against him for tax liabilities the company had incurred. Worse, he suddenly began to discover that he had been forgotten by the industry he had helped survive the Great Depression.

He suffered a series of unpleasant surprises: stars and executives who once had fawned on him now gave him a quick brush-off; and news photographers who formerly had mobbed him at big premières now didn't notice him in the crowd—provided he got invited to the premières in the first place. "My pride was hurt," says Mickey. "I wanted to be wanted and needed, but I didn't know how."

Mickey's most stinging personal humiliation during that period was connected with the Academy Awards. Mickey had been invited to be a presenter. Touched that he should still be considered a personality despite his sagging fortunes, on the evening of the gala show he dressed in his seldom-used tuxedo.

"The tuxedo didn't fit so good any more, but there was nothing I could do about that," Mickey told a writer who was interviewing him years later for *McCalls* magazine. "I was finishing dinner with Martha, who was my wife at the time, when I got a call from Johnny Green, the Academy musical conductor. It was twenty minutes before I was due to leave for the theater. Green said he didn't know how to say this, but that the Academy had changed their minds about having me take part in their show, and had elected him to break it to me. It seems, I'd been married so often that I was a bad representative of the picture industry. When I realized what he was trying to tell me, I blew. Boy, how I blew! I told him where the whole Academy could go, and I resigned then and there at the top of my lungs. Then, after I'd hung up, I cried."

Who could blame him? Having been snubbed by the Academy and ignored by the major film studios, he was, at the age of thirty, stuck with only the remnants of what was once a spectacular career.

Such rejection didn't improve his disposition when he was in the company of Martha—or anyone else. All his life he had been given to brief but violent outbursts of temper. Now it was happening more frequently and not only in the privacy of his home. For example, he once flew into a blind rage after missing an important putt on the fifteenth hole of Lakeside, in Toluca Lake, where he was a member, and kicked apart a drinking fountain that was on the sixteenth tee. For his unsportsmanlike conduct, the club fined him six hundred dollars, and asked him to apologize to the membership or get out. Unwilling to pay and refusing to apologize, Mickey furiously resigned. His resignation was promptly accepted, and he has never been allowed to rejoin. (When a new water dispenser was built on the sixteenth tee, it was unofficially dubbed, The Mickey Rooney Memorial Drinking Fountain.)

Snubs and tantrums notwithstanding, Mickey, much to his credit, has never really been out of work for any extended period in his career. Since his first appearance in a feature for Universal in 1932, there wasn't a year until 1970, including the war years, when his face hasn't been seen on the silver screen by the public in at least one film, and frequently in two or three. No, his problem hasn't been that he couldn't get some kind of employment. His problem was that he always spent money faster than he could earn it. Sometimes, he was reduced to taking any job offered to him, no matter how lowly. What was offered to him, that summer of 1950, was a job emceeing the "Hadacol Caravan," an updated medicine show sponsored and backed by Dudley LeBlanc, a Louisiana state senator who manufactured Hadacol Tonic, an elixir that was supposed to cure all ailments. If one had no ailments, it could be used as a general pick-me-up. Eventually, the federal government forced Hadacol off the market because of its high (about twenty-six percent) alcoholic content. But before that, it enjoyed a certain vogue among health fanatics.

Senator LeBlanc threw a lot of muscle behind promoting Hadacol to the down-home folks. The "Hadacol Caravan" had a huge, expensive cast, headed by the popular singer Connie Boswell and Mickey Rooney, who, in turn were supported by Roy Acuff and the Smokey Mountain Boys, Minnie Pearl of the Grand Ole Opry, Dorothy Dorben's Chez Paree Girls, Buglin' Sam DeKemel, Sharkey and his Kings of Dixieland, and Gene Meyer's Caravan Orchestra. The talent-studded show, which eventually played fifteen cities in seven Southern states, opened in City Park Stadium, New Orleans, before a packed house of seventeen thousand country-music fans. The price of admission was a box top from a bottle of

177

Hadacol. The performers, however, were paid in cash. Mickey knocked down about $7,500 a week and, according to the *Variety* review on August 30, 1950, was worth every penny of it.

By the time Mickey returned to the Coast fifteen weeks later, Martha was fed up and announced to Mickey that she wanted a divorce. Mickey said fine and moved out of the house on White Oak and into his mother's and Fred Pankey's new house on Dickens Street in Sherman Oaks. Nell had sold the house on Densmore because it was "too much house" for the two of them. Besides, Mickey needed part of the cash she realized from the sale.

On December 16, however, just nine days before Christmas, Mickey and Martha called a truce, and he moved back into the White Oak house. Since the separation had been reported in the newspapers, Martha thought it best to keep the press advised of their reconciliation. "We thought it a shame to spoil the baby's first Christmas," she told Hedda Hopper. "We're going to see if we can't be a little more sensible and hang onto our tempers."

But shortly after the first of the year, they split up again, with Martha declaring to the press that she was going to seek a divorce because "Mickey doesn't like the restrictions of marriage." No divorce papers had actually been filed, however, and on March 8, 1951, readers of the *Los Angeles Times* were treated to a further installment of the Martha and Mickey "soap."

> Mickey Rooney and his estranged wife, Martha Vickers, will leave on a second honeymoon in a few weeks, MGM has announced. A studio spokesman said the Rooneys kissed and made up, and decided to put their San Fernando home up for sale, so they can start fresh in new surroundings.

Lack of cash flow was the principal reason, but luckily the gods, or at any rate, Dore Schary, intervened in time for them not to have to put their house on the block.

Mickey was called back to MGM to star in *The Strip*, under the terms of the settlement that Bautzer and Stiefel had worked so diligently to "win" for their client. *The Strip* was the first picture Mickey had made for his alma mater since 1948. It was a low-budget musical, with Mickey playing a band drummer falsely accused of the murder of a racketeer. There were enough good music and cabaret spots for Vic Damone, Louis Armstrong, Jack Teagarden, and Earl "Fatha" Hines to make the film enjoyable entertainment and a pretty good money-maker, despite its melodramatic, old-fashioned plot.

Although the reviews and public reaction were quite good, Mickey was again put on the back burner at Metro.

Though he was without a pay check, Mickey was technically still an employee of Loew's, Incorporated. This made him a relatively easy target for the process server that Betty Jane Rooney put on his tail in the middle of April with a Writ of Execution by the County Clerk of the Superior Court of California, demanding "$3,541.14 in back alimony and child support payments."

When Mickey was unable to come up with the cash requested in a month and a half, Betty Jane proved that, unsophisticated country girl or not, she knew how to deal with an ex-husband who welshed on his financial obligations.

On May 29, a letter arrived at MGM from the office of Sheriff Eugene W. Biscailuz, attaching anything owed Mickey by MGM. It was a lucky thing for Mickey that he'd already received his salary for his acting chores in *The Strip*.

Mickey was able to get Betty Jane off his back temporarily with a couple of token payments, and a solemn promise from his attorney that he would pay back the rest of his arrears as soon as he started working again.

Fortunately, this was almost immediately.

"In the spring of '51 we made a three-picture deal for Mickey with Columbia," Nick Sevano remembers. "Harry Cohn still had great faith in Mickey as a talent, and thought he could bring his career back to where it was, and was willing to pay him $75,000 a picture over the next three years to prove it."

The first Rooney flick was supposed to go into production only eight weeks later. In those days every major studio had to make a quota of films in order to meet the demands of the distribution office in New York City. They had to make a picture even if they didn't have an idea for one.

"Harry Cohn didn't have a vehicle for Mickey," recalls Jonie Taps, who produced the three films Mickey made for Columbia under his new contract. "So Harry went to Eddie Small and said, 'Eddie can you make these pictures for me?' Eddie wasn't interested but said, 'You've got a man here who can—Jonie Taps.' So Harry sent for me, and said, 'Jonie, we've got this three-picture deal and we're supposed to start one of them in eight weeks and we don't have a script yet. Not even an idea. Do you have any?' So I told him, 'Sure, why don't we put Rooney in an army picture. Abbott and

Costello are making a fortune making Service pictures over at Universal.' So Harry said, 'Fine, what'll we call it?' And I said, 'Let's call it *Sound Off*—because I owned a song with that title when I was in the music publishing business.

"I was assigned two young kids Mickey had requested—Blake Edwards and Richard Quine—to write the script, and Quine to direct. Blake and Dick were friends of Mickey's from MGM, and Mickey had faith in their ability. They came up with a helluva script, too."

While they were writing, however, Mickey didn't dare sit around letting the grass grow under his golf shoes—not with the sheriff pressing him for back alimony. So while he was waiting, he took an acting job in a low-budget Western called *My Outlaw Brother*, for Eagle-Lion.

My Outlaw Brother did nothing for Mickey's reputation as an actor. "As the New York tenderfoot, Mr. Rooney is about as convincing as the Mexican sombrero he wears," *The New York Times* wrote.

Because it had no pretensions of being anything but a low-budget musical, *Sound Off* was treated with more tenderness by the critics. Said *Variety*: "... a bright film musical ... Rooney socks over every line, scene and song."

It's a tribute to Mickey's ability as a performer that he didn't allow what was taking place in his private life to interfere with the enthusiasm he exuded on the screen. Martha had filed for divorce on June 11, 1951, charging Mickey with "extreme mental cruelty" and asking for custody of their son, Ted Michael, who was then fourteen months old.

While Mickey's attorney, James Needleman, was working out the details of the property settlement, which took the rest of the summer, Mickey moved back in with his mother and Fred Pankey. There he remained until he finished shooting *Sound Off* at Columbia at the end of August.

According to Dick Quine, Mickey was in a state of depression all during the filming of *Sound Off*, because he felt that there had to be something wrong with him that he couldn't make a marriage work. "One day, when I was on the set waiting to make our first shot, Mickey called in sick and said, 'I can't make it, Dick, I can't make it,'" Quine recalls. "'I'm sick.' [he said.] I said, 'Come on, Mick. You can handle it. You were all right last night.' But he told me he wasn't kidding, he really was sick and couldn't make it. So I told him I'd come out and see him. So I left the stage, left the crew and everybody, and got in my car and started racing out Ventura Boulevard in the direction of Dickens Street. I got about halfway there when I saw Mickey coming at me from the other direction . . . around seventy miles an hour. He'd changed his mind about being sick, and was on his way into the studio."

Quine doesn't believe Mickey was drinking heavily on those days. "His problem was that he was having trouble sleeping. When Blake and I would go out to dinner with him after a day's shooting," Quine says, with an amused twinkle in his eyes, "we'd slip a couple of phenobarbitals into his drink. That way he'd be sleepy after dinner and go home to bed instead of roaming around the city half the night getting into trouble."

Dick Quine called it a "wrap" on the set of *Sound Off* on August 28, 1951. Less than a month later, on September 25, Superior Court Judge Clarence Kinkaid called it a "wrap" on the Martha Vickers-Mickey Rooney marriage. Mickey let Martha's accusations on the witness stand go uncontested. "Was your marriage at all harmonious and peaceful?" Martha's attorney, Stanley Fox asked.

"No, I'm afraid it never was," Martha testified in a quiet voice.

"What exactly do you mean by that?" Fox asked.

"Well, Mickey had a very bad temper. He seemed to look for reasons all the time just to pick a fight—simply for an excuse to leave the house. He spent most of our married life away from home. And it was the worst when I was expecting our child. Many times he would get in an argument and say he wanted a divorce or wanted me to leave him, and would storm out of the house—and I'd not see him for three or four or five days. Then he'd just wander into the house like nothing had happened at all and ask for his dinner or something."

"Can you tell the court anything else about Mr. Rooney?"

"Yes," Martha replied. "He was extremely abusive, and sometimes was drinking."

As compensation for the abuse Martha claimed to have taken from Mickey, the court awarded her $2,000 a month alimony for the rest of the year; $1,875 a month for the following year; $1,750 a month until July of 1955; at that point, payment would drop to $950 a month for six months. In 1956, she would be entitled to $750 a month; in 1957, $600 a month; in 1958, $450 a month, and in 1959, and from then on, $300 a month unless she died or remarried. In addition Martha was given custody of Teddy, and $150 a month for child support. Mickey was allowed to keep his house on White Oak in Encino, although its furniture, except for his piano, went to Martha.

Just how long Mickey would be able to afford even the tiny house on White Oak was a moot question after the division chief of the Internal Revenue Service notified Metro-Goldwyn-Mayer Studios, on October 31, that Mickey and Martha Rooney owed the government a total of thirty-five thousand in back income taxes. "You are further notified that all property, rights to property, moneys, credits and/or blank deposits now in your possession and belonging to the aforesaid taxpayer, and all sums of money owing from you to the said taxpayer, are hereby seized and levied upon for the payment of the aforesaid tax deficiencies, together with penalties and interest. /s/ R. A. Riddle, Collector of Internal Revenue."

Mickey went to the one person in the world he could always depend on for support when things were going badly, Sig Frolich. "I have to get out of town," he told Sig, "and you're coming with me."

Together they flew to Houston, Texas, where Mickey checked them into a suite in the Shamrock Hotel, Houston's splashiest inn for the weary traveler. There was no particular reason for choosing Houston other than it was halfway between the west and east coasts, and a perfect place to hide from the media, ambitious starlets, or any other kinds of temptation.

After checking in, Mickey took a number of sleeping pills and spent the next two weeks in hibernation, according to his recollection of that period in his autobiography. He didn't swallow enough pills to kill himself, just enough to put himself into an unconscious state for twelve- and fourteen-hour stretches. Then he'd gulp down another handful of pills and drop off into the arms of Morpheus again.

Concerned that Mickey might knock himself off, either intentionally or unintentionally, Sig Frolich managed to get some food into his diminutive sidekick's stomach—which seemed to have saved his life. God must have wanted to see *Sugar Babies,* too.

Finally, after two weeks, Mickey woke up one morning with a smile on his face, and announced that he was through feeling sorry for himself. He told Sig to pack, they were catching the next plane for Hollywood.

ANNOUNCING THAT HE was through with marriage for good, Mickey thanked Sig at the other end of the flight for his loyal support and ministrations, slipped him a few bucks, and then contacted another close friend, Don "Red" Barry, the Western character actor, and asked him if he would like a roommate.

"Sounds good to me, pardner," Barry replied. And the two of them set up bachelor quarters in a small apartment in Hollywood.

Using his Hollywood apartment as his home base, Mickey worked at the studios, squired sexy women around town, became involved with a notorious New York call girl, played golf at a public course in the Valley, went to the races, and in general "put on a happy face" for the Hollywood home crowd.

By this time, however, friends were beginning to wonder if Mickey had the capacity to be happy, especially sharing his life with a woman. He seemed to have all the wrong values.

"When Mickey's marriage to Martha Vickers was going so badly," states Wally Cassell, "Mickey used to say to me with envy in his voice, 'Hey, Wally, I've got to get me a redhead just like you have. You've got a wonderful marriage.' And I'd say, "Look, Mick, the color of Marcy's hair has nothing to do with it.' And he'd look at me as if I was nuts and say, 'Bullshit, it's got everything to do with it!'"

16

ON JANUARY 8, 1952, Mickey finally cut the umbilical cord to MGM by signing an agreement with the studio that officially ended their long association. According to the agreement, neither side had any claim on the other, with the exception that Mickey agreed to appear in one last film for Metro-Goldwyn-Mayer, to be decided on at some later date mutually agreeable to both parties. The previous contract, which had called for five pictures, only one of which Mickey had made, was abrogated by mutual consent. In a way it was a victory for Mickey not to have to make three pictures at the low rate of $25,000 per picture; on the other side of the coin, it couldn't have boosted his self-image when he realized that the most important studio in Hollywood no longer had much interest in him.

Mickey still had two more films to go under his nonexclusive contract with Columbia. The second of these was *All Ashore,* a picture with a Navy background, starring Mickey and singer Dick Haymes. *All Ashore,* a navy farce, was made by the same team responsible for *Sound Off.* Most of the ship stuff was shot on location at Catalina Island. Catalina, with its yacht harbor at Avalon and its waterfront dives, was a drinker's paradise. This had studio boss Harry Cohn a little worried; Mickey's reputation had not gone unnoticed by him.

"So Harry said to me," producer Jonie Taps remembers, "you'd better go over with them, Jonie, and see that they don't get in trouble. So I went to Catalina with them, and the first guy to get drunk was, of all people, Jonie Taps. Mickey Rooney had to put *me* to bed. And when he did, he said, 'This is the last time on this trip you're going to get drunk ahead of me, Jonie.'"

185

Somehow the picture got made, and for what it was supposed to be, it wasn't bad. However, it's not even mentioned in most film guides.

The year for Mickey to spend his acting days in the uniform of his country seemed to be 1952. In addition to starring in *All Ashore*, he appeared with Bob Hope in *Off Limits* for Paramount. A comedy about Navy shore patrolmen, *Off Limits* was written off by film critics.

Toward the end of summer, Mickey started dating stripper Tempest Storm. Mickey was thoroughly familiar with what it took to woo a stripper. One of the things was a floor-length mink coat that "set him back ten thousand dollars," according to one of his managers. Of course he made only a small down payment, but it was a serious enough investment to convince friends that Mickey would soon be escorting the young lady to the altar.

But as fate would have it, Tempest Storm was not destined to be Mrs. Mickey Rooney, number four. It's doubtful if Mickey even continued making the payments on the coat after a tall, statuesque, redhead named Elaine Mahnken caught his eye at a Woodland Hills driving range one afternoon in early fall.

Twenty-three years old and a one-time Compton Community College beauty queen, Elaine had recently been divorced in Butte, Montana, from Dan Ducich, a former Compton and Utah State basketball star, who'd been convicted of armed robbery in Los Angeles in 1949 and placed on five years probation.

Mickey, who was living in a small house in Woodland Hills by now, had gone to the driving range to improve his golf swing, not to look for a wife to deplete his bank account further. However, when Mickey looked away from a golf ball he had just driven two hundred yards down the range and saw Elaine's sexy figure clad in slacks and a blouse and topped by flaming red hair, his heart started to go pitter-pat again.

"His divorce from Martha had just become final, I believe," Elaine says, recollecting her first meeting with Mickey, "and I was living in Woodland Hills with my mother and taking golf lessons a couple of times a week at the Woodland Hills driving range. Anyway, I was practicing by myself that day, and Mickey came over—I had a little dog with me, Pepy, a Maltese terrier, that I had brought from Montana, and Mickey flipped over him. He loves animals, you know, he has a great way with them. He gives them a lot of baby talk and animals love that . . . and him. So you know there's a lot of good

186

in Mickey because of that. As far as his being partial to redheads, I don't know. He just likes any pretty girl, period. Anyway, Mickey made a fuss over Pepy, and then offered to show me how to hit the ball. So I bought another bucket and he stood there and drove them all out for me. After that, he invited me to dinner."

That was the beginning of a romance that would lead to one of Mickey's longest marriages. "We were together every night for about a month," remembers Elaine, who today, more than thirty years later, is still enormously attractive. "And every night he proposed to me. And every time he proposed I would say, 'No, Mickey, I'm not in love with you.'"

But little by little she was won over by his persistence, charm, and the fact that the name Mickey Rooney still had a certain amount of glitz to it. "Mickey has quite a way about him," declared Elaine when I interviewed her in the kitchen of her comfortable, ranch house in San Fernando Valley. "When he was doing the *Andy Hardy* series—I was just a kid then—my whole family just adored Mickey. I think one of the reasons they did, aside from his talent and charm on film, was because he looked just like my kid brother at his age. So I felt I already knew Mickey when I first met him. And my whole family felt they knew him, but they of course really didn't know him, and neither did I. But I thought I did, and I felt comfortable with him. Also, I was quite in awe of his musical talent. While we were dating he used to sit down and play the piano at his house, and he'd make up lyrics, and they were beautiful. And I thought, 'This man must have a beautiful soul.' I fell in love with that talent. It made me feel good. I believed that together we could be good, though I was not in love with him. But that didn't seem to bother him, and he kept saying 'You can learn to love me.' And I did. I was never madly in love with him, but I loved him in a particular way."

By the time the couple had been going together for about a month, Mickey, according to Elaine, knew everything there was to know about her past and present: the fact that when she was seventeen she had done some nude modeling for one of the most respected photographers in Hollywood, Theda Emerson Hall, and that her form had shown up on a calendar; that she had been selected by Warner Bros. to take acting lessons from Sylvia Rosenstein, a well-known drama coach; that she had married her high-school sweetheart, a Montana boy, who later got into trouble over a gambling debt; that finally she divorced him and returned to Hollywood to resume her acting career; and at the time they met she was working as a carhop at Dolores Drive-In restaurant at night so she could support herself while she went out on interviews during the day.

But Mickey denied that he was aware of Elaine's past before he proposed to her. In his 1965 autobiography, he claims to be "surprised by it, and blames part of the problems in our marriage on my past," Elaine maintains today, unable to conceal the irritation in her voice, though she still insists she's fond of Mickey. "Well, it is true that I did pose nude that one time, with my parents' permission, because I was only seventeen. They were very tasteful shots, and I'm not ashamed of them. They weren't pornographic, and I see nothing wrong with showing off a good body, if you happen to have one. Also, his description of me as a 'carhop' seems a bit of a put-down. Yes, I did work at that at times, but it was more accurate to consider me an actress who was working as a carhop until I could get started in Hollywood again.

"Anyway, Mickey knew more about me than I knew about him when he proposed to me. I certainly didn't know he was in any kind of financial trouble. While we were dating, he used to drive me down Tarzana Boulevard and say to me as he pointed out the car window, 'I own this side of the street and I own that side of the street,' and went on like that. It sounded as if he owned all of San Fernando Valley. Not that that had anything to do with my feelings about him, but he did act the big shot for my benefit."

One evening while they were dining at Don the Beachcomber's about a month after they first met, Elaine surprised Mickey by answering "yes" to one of his continuing marriage proposals. Mickey was so delighted that he chartered a private plane, and within an hour he, Elaine, and Gene and Sylvia Kahan, close friends of his, were on their way to Las Vegas. There, at one in the morning, he and Elaine were married at the Wee Kirk of the Heather, with Gene Kahan acting as best man. Afterwards they checked into the El Rancho Vegas, where they registered as Mr. and Mrs. Joseph Yule. (Mickey still hadn't changed his name legally to "Rooney.")

The events of the day were so sudden that Mickey didn't even have time to buy Elaine a wedding ring before taking off for Las Vegas. "We used friends' rings for the actual ceremony," she recalls. "But after we were married and back in town, living in Mickey's house in Woodland Hills, Mickey wanted me to have a diamond ring that I could splash around for his friends' benefit—personally I would have been happy with a plain gold band. So he went out and bought diamond wedding and engagement rings. Not long after that they came around one night to take the rings right off my hand. The people Mickey had bought the rings from, that is. He hadn't paid for them yet—not even a down payment. I knew then that he was not the 'big shot' he had professed to be when we were dating. As it happened, they didn't take the rings off my fingers. We made an agreement that night as to how we would pay for them. And I stuck with the agreement and saw that they were paid for— eventually."

For the first two years of their marriage, Mickey and his new bride were content to live in his house in Woodland Hills. "It was a small house—not the kind of a place you'd expect to find Mickey living in—but a nice house, in a typical 'Valley' neighborhood," Elaine remembers. "Nice living room, nice master bedroom, a servant's room, a nice yard with swimming pool, all fenced in, which was just perfect for the dogs. Besides Pepy, I had two collies.

"When I married him, Mickey had a house man, a nice elderly gentleman named Arthur Baker . . . Mickey didn't want me to do a darn thing around the house. Cook or clean or any menial work. And if I started to do something, just to keep myself busy, he'd stop me and say, 'I pay someone to do that.' . . . he had a certain life-style and I had to fit into it, and having a house man was part of it, even if he couldn't afford one."

No matter how tough times were, or how many creditors were knocking at the door, Mickey always had to have a valet to take care of his extensive wardrobe and to look after the house. "Mickey couldn't have cared less about creditors," Elaine says. "While they were dunning him for bills, he'd be out buying two new Jaguars . . . When we were first married, I remember going down to the service station on the corner to get a tank of gas, and when the attendant found out my name, and that I was married to Mickey, he said, kind of reluctantly, 'Your husband hasn't paid his bills here in six months. Could you do anything about it?' And I assured him I could, and I went home and saw that he was paid. I stopped that kind of thing and saw that people were paid."

AFTER A FEW months, Elaine's father, Fred, came to stay with the newlyweds. When Mickey invited him to live with them permanently, "because they got on real well," Elaine says, "Mickey gave my daddy the second bedroom and had another room built over the garage for Arthur Baker."

Mickey "adored" Elaine's father, according to her, and let him live there as part of the family, although he did pay him an insignificant amount of money to work around the place as a handyman and gardener. But basically he was Mickey's surrogate father, and they were "inseparable buddies," Elaine says. "But Mickey didn't accept the rest of my family. He wanted to keep himself separate from them, because he said he had so many wives and so many mothers-in-law that he couldn't handle any more. For that matter, he never saw a great deal of his own mother, either, even though she moved quite near to here, in a small house over on Dickens Street. Whenever we'd go to visit Nell, Mickey would stay about ten minutes and then say, 'Let's go.' And I'd say. 'Don't you want to stay and visit with your mom?' And he'd shake his head 'No,' and we'd go. So I never really got to know Nell. I was anxious to know her and like her. But she was very leery of me. Which is normal after her son was married that many times.

"But to get back to my daddy, Mickey loved him and vice versa, and they went everywhere together. If I didn't want to go to the track with Mickey, which was usually the case, although Mickey always invited me, the two would go by themselves. So my heart was sick after I read in his book what he wrote about my daddy—'You shouldn't hire relatives.'"

In his autobiography, Mickey implied that he didn't get his "money's worth" out of Fred, and wrote, "It's not always a smart idea to hire in-laws."

To this day, Elaine resents that crack about her father, who is still alive. In calling Mickey's assertion a lie, she says, "About the time my daddy would start to do something around the house or in the yard, Mickey would say, 'Aw, forget that, Fred. Let's go to the races.' And off they'd go."

Mickey had plenty of time for the races in the months immediately following his marriage to Elaine, because except for a trip with the USO to Korea in December of 1952 to entertain the troops, for which he got nothing except his traveling expenses, he was out of work.

But the bills continued to pour in. "I really felt sorry for Mickey after I found out he was in financial trouble, and I heard all his tales of woe about how everyone was taking advantage of him," Elaine says. "I made up my mind that I was going to get him out of debt. So I spent over two years working at my desk, paying the bills. I always paid the alimony first and got that out of the way before we even put food on our own table. The government was constantly after him and taking big chunks of money from his salary whenever Mickey made any. And he made considerable. Never less than $150,000 a year the whole time I was married to him. And we managed to meet the government's demands, God only knows how."

Mickey's marriage to Elaine was beset with other difficulties, both real and imagined, almost from the start. A few weeks after the wedding, Mickey started hearing gossip from his friends that Elaine had been seen with someone who looked suspiciously like her first husband, Dan Ducich. Mickey tried to ignore the gossip, but finally it started eating away at him, and he confronted Elaine with it.

Elaine admitted she had seen her former husband a couple of times. "Dan felt I would end up being hurt by being married to Mickey, and he wanted me to come back to him," Elaine says in a very straightforward manner. "There was nothing romantic about our meetings. We simply talked, and I conducted myself as a lady. We never did anything that I would be ashamed of. I was married to Mickey, and I took my vows seriously. But Dan wanted something else of me, too. He'd gotten into real trouble in Las Vegas . . . he owed them a lot of money up there, and they were threatening him. So he came to me and asked me if there was anything I could do personally to help him. He knew that I had access to a certain amount of money, being married to a movie star. So I went to Mickey, and I told him Dan's problem about his needing money. And did he think he could help? As one human being to another, I saw nothing wrong with that. But Mickey didn't think it was his problem to help out my first husband, and would do absolutely nothing about it. It ended up with Dan getting killed by the mob a few months later—shot in the head. It was a terrible tragedy because he was basically a nice boy, who'd gotten into trouble and couldn't get out of it by himself."

Mickey didn't see it that way, and claims that his marriage to Elaine was never the same after that.

Elaine, however, contends that "If Mickey was unhappy with me that early in the marriage, he'd had to have been a fool to stay with me for the next seven years." Mickey's answer to this is that he was terribly afraid of another divorce, just two weeks after the marriage, and how it would look in the headlines. Consequently he stuck it out. He also charges that the reason Elaine didn't leave him when she knew the marriage was on the rocks was because she was insecure and terrified of poverty, having come from a poor family. Moreover, she thought she could get into films through him.

Elaine disputes that, pointing out that her mother, with whom she lived before marrying Mickey, had been a successful animator at Walt Disney's for fifteen years and was well able to take care of the family. In addition, says Elaine, "I'd always been able to support myself, either through modeling or acting. I'd never been afraid of working, and I'd never been afraid of poverty, either. Moreover, if it was just support I was looking for, I could have married any number of men in Hollywood who would have given me a more comfortable, worry-free life than I had with Mickey. Any good-looking girl can. But I really was fond of Mickey. I had real compassion for him and his problems, and I still do. Personally, I think Mickey should have considered himself lucky to have somebody like me who was interested in making a nice home for him, who cared about him, who cared about his animals, who cared about the family, and tried to pay the bills."

It became less of a problem to pay the bills as 1952 drew to a close. Two days before Christmas, Mickey was notified by MGM that he was supposed to report to the studio shortly after the first of the year to begin filming *A Slight Case of Larceny*, in which he would costar with Eddie Bracken. He was to be paid under the terms of his settlement contract, $25,000. But at least, and at last, his appearance in it would wipe the slate clean of any further obligations to MGM.

A Slight Case of Larceny turned out to be only partially successful when it was released later in the year. "A mildly innocuous programmer for the family trade that might have some marquee value in the names of Mickey Rooney and Eddie Bracken," *Variety* wrote.

Following *A Slight Case of Larceny*, Mickey's film career took an upward turn—possibly due to the entrance into his life of Maurice Duke. Duke walked into Mickey's living room in Woodland Hills one afternoon and announced that he wanted to manage Mickey. "I'll get you started again," he promised confidently.

A former professional harmonica player who had turned to managing show business personalities when he discovered there was no great demand in the theater for a harmonica soloist, Duke had been a friend of Mickey's for several years, and had watched his career go slowly downhill. But he had enormous faith in Mickey's talent. ("Let's face it," Duke says, "Mickey's one of the five greatest actors living today.") And he believed he could help him.

The timing was perfect. Mickey had just fired Nick Sevano "because I wouldn't agree with him about what he wanted to do with his career," Sevano says today. "For example, he wanted to direct and I thought he was a lousy director because he had no discipline. Anyway, we parted."

For a time, Maurice Duke brought Mickey some luck. If not luck,

192

at least employment. That spring he starred in *The Twinkle in God's Eye* for Republic, and while he was on the lot Mickey came up with an idea for a picture for Sabu, the Elephant Boy, which they let him produce. It was called *Jaguar*. Mickey didn't appear in it, but Duke got him a percentage of the profits as well as a small producing fee. Mickey had a profit-sharing deal on *The Twinkle in God's Eye* also. But there weren't any profits, and Mickey was back to worrying about paying the bills.

While he was waiting for something better to come along, Mickey took a nightclub engagement at the Flamingo Hotel in Las Vegas. On the flight back to Los Angeles after a successful summer engagement, Mickey and Duke found themselves on the same plane with author James Michener, whose *The Bridges at Toko-Ri* had just been published and was about to be made into a major film, shot mostly aboard an aircraft carrier off the coast of Japan. "Michener took a liking to Mickey," Duke says, "and said he would see to it that a part was written into the script for him. It was a small part, and Mickey had to take short money for it, but he wanted to be in a major picture again."

Mickey had a lot of free time to kill while waiting for his scenes to be shot. To a restless, peripatetic character like Mickey, sitting around on an aircraft carrier in the middle of the Pacific with nothing to do but watch others work was a little bit like being in stir.

"One day I needed him for a scene," said George Seaton, who directed, in recalling the incident for some friends after returning to the States, "and I couldn't find him anywhere. We searched the ship but we couldn't find him. We thought perhaps he had fallen overboard. I spent the day shooting around him. Then, late in the afternoon, just as we were about to 'wrap' for the day, one of the carrier's planes landed on the deck, and out jumped Mickey from the copilot's seat. It seems that Mickey had bribed the pilot into flying him to Tokyo, so he could go to the horse races at the track there."

Despite his truancy from the carrier, Mickey turned in his usual competent performance and just missed winning an Academy nomination for Best Supporting Actor for his portrayal of Mike Forney.

In 1954, Mickey picked up another $75,000 for starring in his third B picture for Columbia, *Drive a Crooked Road*, another story about auto racing. Like the other two at Columbia, *Drive a Crooked Road* was scripted by Blake Edwards and Richard Quine, and directed by the latter. "Incidentally," says the producer of the picture, Jonie

Taps, "the picture was a milestone for Blake Edwards, because we let him direct the second-unit stuff. That was his first attempt at directing, and he turned out to be pretty good at it."

Although *Drive a Crooked Road* was a low-budget action melodrama and only mildly successful, critically and financially, when it was released later in 1954, Mickey's ability as a "thinking" actor never failed to impress the young man directing him, Richard Quine. "I did a scene with him in *Drive a Crooked Road*, Quine recalls, with genuine admiration in his voice, "and he's crying in the scene, which the script called for. And I was sitting there behind the cameras crying along with him because he was so convincing. In the scene he was working with a girl named Diane Foster. As he was doing the crying bit Mickey took Diane by the arm and gently moved her to a slightly different spot on the set. The tears continued to flow, however. And there was never a stop in the dialogue. I thought to myself, 'Gee, he hasn't done that before—why did he move her?' And then I realized what had happened. She had gotten out of her 'key' light, and he was putting her back in it. The facility of the guy is just staggering."

It was through working with Quine and Edwards that Mickey got his first television series, "Hey, Mulligan." Before "Hey, Mulligan," Mickey had already bombed in two attempts to get a series. He produced two pilots that didn't sell. One was on the life of Daniel Boone, with Mickey himself playing the legendary frontiersman and the other was based on the files of the Tokyo police called "Dateline Tokyo." CBS put up the money for both pilots, about thirty thousand dollars each, but when they couldn't interest a sponsor, they dropped the idea of doing a series with Mickey Rooney.

In his autobiography, Mickey begins to show the first indication of a growing paranoia about how TV has treated him, when he writes about the failure of the Boone pilot: "It wasn't a bad idea. That was the trouble. It was a good idea for the TV business, which had gotten rich on bad ideas."

Mickey was convinced that his future was in TV, "so he called Blake and me," Quine recalls, "and asked us if we could come up with a TV idea for him that was salable. We put our heads together and came up with an idea in which Mickey worked as a page boy for a broadcasting company like NBC while waiting to get a break as an actor in pictures." Edwards and Quine tentatively called the pilot "For the Love of Mike," but when it turned out that that title had already been registered by the then little-known radio announcer, Mike Wallace, it was retitled "Hey, Mulligan."

NBC liked the completed pilot film—in spite of the fact that

Mickey, at age thirty-four, was a little overage to be playing a page boy—and with the help of William Morris, who had put the package together, started offering it to the important advertising agencies in hopes of finding a sponsor.

When the Leo Burnett Company, one of the nation's most powerful agencies, liked the show and bought it for two of its biggest accounts, Pillsbury Flour and Jolly Green Giant Peas, NBC slotted "Hey, Mulligan" into their Saturday night lineup at eight o'clock, beginning September 4, 1954. This wasn't the most desirable spot in which to be, because it was opposite Jackie Gleason's big, hour-long variety extravaganza—the one that featured the June Taylor Dancers, the Honeymooners, and Frank Fontaine. But the network had enough confidence in the public's ability to remember Mickey as Andy Hardy to believe it had a chance to survive. And so did Leo Burnett and Peter Jurow, who was president of Pillsbury Flour, which owned Jolly Green Giant.

With a contract with NBC calling for $3,500 a week for thirty-three weeks, plus options if the show were picked up, Mickey was full of high hopes for his future when "Hey, Mulligan" went into production in the summer of 1954.

By now, Mickey was nearly out of the woods financially, thanks to his new employment and the hard work of his fourth wife, Elaine.

"I handled the finances for about two and a half years," she remembers. "Finally, the government was paid, all our bills were paid, and I took the envelope that had contained all our unpaid bills, and I said, 'Look, Mickey, no more debts.' "And what was the thanks I got? Two weeks later Mickey went up to Vegas to play a nightclub date. He went to the tables and lost fifty grand, just like that. We were back in the hole again. When I heard that, I threw up my hands and said, 'No more. From now on he can take care of his own finances.'"

Despite that setback, Mickey felt solvent enough to tell Elaine he wanted a new and larger house. "I saw nothing wrong with the place we were in," she asserts. "It was the nicest home I'd ever lived in, on a nice street, with nice people for neighbors. But Mickey thought the neighborhood was beneath him. The neighbors thought he was neat, but he couldn't stand them. He kept calling them a bunch of crows, and behind their backs he'd go 'caw, caw, caw!,' imitating the crow. I didn't like that, because they were nice people, even if they weren't in show business. So I'd say to Mickey, 'Well, if they're a bunch of crows, I'm a crow.' And Mickey would say, 'You used to be a crow, but not since you married me.' And he meant it.

"That's the way he'd act around autograph hunters, too. He'd be

195

nice as pie to their faces, and then after they left, he'd call them a bunch of crows behind their backs and go, 'CAW, CAW, CAW! so loud I was scared to death they'd hear him before they got out of earshot.

"But to get back to the house, moving into a new place was not my doing. The choice of the house *was* my doing. I spent a heck of a long time looking, because I was trying to find a house in the fifty-thousand-dollar range. Then they showed me the place we finally bought, and I flipped for it."

"The place" was a California ranch house, set about fifty yards back from Fryman Road, in the foothills above Studio City in the Valley. The house had only one drawback. "The asking price was eighty-five thousand dollars, and Mickey had told me we could only spend fifty," Elaine says. "But I just had to have it, so we reached out for this little bit more expensive home. Mickey was very nice about it, and so were the people we were buying it from. They came down to seventy-five thousand dollars, and let us have it for just twelve thousand dollars down and they took back the paper on it. That was April of '56."

The twelve thousand dollars down payment took most of Mickey's cash, but according to him it was important "to their relationship, and important to his own self-respect" to be able to buy Elaine everything she wanted to make her happy. The problem was (also according to him) that her requests for material things didn't stop there. After saddling him with a thirteen-room house, it had to be filled with furniture. What's more, they couldn't take their time about it, because they—and their home—were scheduled to be on the Edward R. Murrow "Person to Person" show in a few weeks. According to Mickey, all the furniture he and Elaine owned at the time were two mattresses; "a large one for Elaine and myself, and a small one for Elaine's father, Fred. We couldn't very well go on 'Person to Person' sitting on orange crates."

Today Elaine contends that it is "sheer nonsense" about not having any furniture when they moved into the house on Fryman Road. "We were not sitting on orange crates."

When they appeared on the Murrow show several weeks later, Mickey and Elaine seemed to be a very contented and happy couple. They were delighted with the house and garden, and their neighbors Sheila and Gordon MacCrae, who made a guest appearance on the Morrow show that night, leaning over the back fence, gnawing on chicken bones. So did Mickey's pet chicken, Miss Chicken, who was allowed to roam the premises of the Rooney estate, indoors and out, with no restrictions.

196

"Everybody loved Miss Chicken," Elaine remembers. "She laid an egg a day for eight years."

The rest of Mickey's family weren't around to make an appearance. Mickey Rooney, Jr., and Timmy were still living with their mother, Bety Jane Kassel, and Teddy was still a toddler and in the care of his mother, Martha Vickers.

"I wish Mickey had brought the children over more often," Elaine says, "because I liked the boys. They were only here a couple of times during our marriage. When I told Mickey to have them, he used to say, 'It's better not to confuse the kids . . . let them be with their mother.'"

One of the things that made this marriage different from Mickey's previous two was that he didn't get Elaine pregnant right away. In fact, not at all. "I was unable to have children of my own," Elaine states, "and as much as I would have liked to, I didn't want to adopt any, because of the raunchy language Mickey used around the house. His language was terrible.

"However, Mickey had a lot of nice points," Elaine continues. "He was very neat and clean around the house. Never had to pick up after him. And he could be a lot of fun, he could entertain you making a peanut butter and jelly sandwich. He could be sweet . . . I loved the gentleness of him. And he could be romantic . . . I still miss the way at night he would take my pajama sleeves and pull them down to keep my arms warm . . . He liked to let me sleep in in the morning. I'm a night person, so I'd stay in bed until nine or ten o'clock if I wasn't working on something. But he'd say to me when he had to go to the studio, 'Now you stay in bed, and come and meet me at the studio, and we'll have lunch together. Get yourself all dressed up and come meet me. I want to show you off.'

"Those times were nice. In the beginning he wanted me to go every place with him . . . Even if he went on tour, playing the nightclubs, he wanted me to go along. If he went to the races he wanted me there, too. And that was great, up to a point. The trouble was, I found I was spending all my time at the racetrack, and I really didn't care that much about watching horses run. I like horses, but to ride them myself, not bet on them. That was one of my dreams—to have my own horse.

"The nights we were home alone were wonderful, too. It was only when somebody came to visit, his cronies, I mean, or we went out that he had this thing going . . . of having to be 'on' all the time. But his friends were a problem when they dropped in. I'm not talking about Blake Edwards or Dick Quine. They hardly came over any more after they started to get successful. And I don't mean Les Martinson or Maurice Duke, either. But others I won't name. They'd always be dropping in, staying, and sitting around at the foot of our bed, on the bed. We hardly had any privacy . . . In the beginning, I would say nothing, because I knew it would start a fight. Mickey was very loyal to his friends, and always had to have a lot of them around. He can't stand being alone."

But there were other problems more serious than a simple lack of privacy. "Mickey wasn't faithful, almost from the beginning of our marriage, I found out later," Elaine says. "And he gambled and took too many sleeping pills . . . he nearly did himself in a couple of times. It's as if your mother told you, 'Don't marry a man who has such and such bad habits'—that would have to be Mickey. He had all of them."

17

WHEN "HEY, MULLIGAN" went into production in June approximately eight weeks before its scheduled air date, everyone was very high on the idea. If there was one thing Mickey wanted more than anything else at the time, it was to have a successful television series. However, because acting was second nature to him, "lots of days he'd be practically winging his scenes," Les Martinson remembers, who directed all thirty-three episodes. "You didn't take Mickey's time for a rehearsal or a reading. He was too busy fooling around in his dressing room, phoning his bookie or reading the racing form or working on one of his numerous projects that had nothing to do with "Hey, Mulligan," like writing a screenplay or trying to invent something he could make a million on. While he was doing his own thing, I'd be out on the set rehearsing the other actors and blocking without him. I'd have to block his moves with his stand-in, Sig Frolich. Sig would make all the moves, work with the other actors. Mickey wouldn't even know what scene we were working on, or the lines, either, when I called for him. Then Mickey would yell, 'Hey, Siggy,' and Sig would go running into Mickey's dressing room with the pages that we were doing turned down, and hand the script to Mickey. Mick would glance down the pages, to get a vague idea of what the scene was about, then hand the script back to Sig. 'Thanks, Siggy,' he'd say. And then he'd come onto the set and we'd do the scene. Those little beady eyes would glance down at the floor, see where the dolly marks were, and the tape marks, and then he'd look up at me and say, 'Okay, Les, let's make it.' Sometimes we'd do it in one take, too. Now I'm not saying that the other actors were getting the right cues, or anything, but it's remarkable how good a performance he could turn in, without really knowing the script."

Despite Mickey's lack of discipline, "Hey, Mulligan" had all the earmarks of a successful TV show when it aired September 4, 1954, with the pilot film that had been penned by Blake Edwards and Richard Quine: a world-famous star, good writers, and a funny premise. The story of the opening show had Mickey sneaking away from his page-boy duties to perform in a little-theater production in Hollywood, where he ultimately would be seen by a studio scout. "I remember one hilarious scene in it," John Fenton Murray recalls, who, with Benedict Friedman, wrote all the later shows. "Mickey had to put on lifts so he could be high enough to play a love scene in the little-theater production with a girl so he could kiss her on the lips. Mickey, or the character Mulligan, couldn't get used to walking on high heels and kept losing his balance and falling over. That was the highlight of the pilot, and it was probably what sold it to the sponsors."

The critics liked it, too, and "Hey, Mulligan" got good reviews and was hailed as a winner.

NOTWITHSTANDING, THE SHOW couldn't compete with Jackie Gleason at the height of his career. "Gleason got a 49 Nielsen, we got a 7," Maurice Duke grins today. "That meant that virtually no one out there in the great wasteland was watching "Hey, Mulligan," except maybe Mickey's mother."

After a few weeks of dismally low ratings, Mickey believed that the battle to survive was hopelessly lost. And when Mickey loses his enthusiasm and gives up on a project, he has a tendency to start behaving very unprofessionally. Often he'd resort to malingering. "For instance," Duke says, "they'd be down on the stage shooting the series, when I'd get a call from the assistant director saying 'Mickey doesn't feel good.' And I'd say, 'What's wrong?' And he'd say, 'Mickey's got a sore throat—laryngitis, he tells me.' And I'd say, 'Bullshit,' and I'd rush down to the set. And Mickey would be doing the laryngitis bit in his dressing room, lying on the couch looking like Camille and talking very hoarse and raspy. He'd even be able to work himself up to 101-degree temperature for the doctor we'd bring in. The doctor would examine him and say, 'Better send him home.' Which we would do, and Les would have to shoot around him all day. Then I'd bump into someone at Chasen's or somewhere that night, and they'd say, 'Hey, I saw Mickey on the golf course this afternoon. You guys on hiatus?' "I could tell by just reading the script when Mickey was going to play hookey," Duke says. "I remember a time when he was making some turkey with Jack Carson for Herman Cohn over at Allied Artists. I think it was *Magnificent Roughnecks*. I was no longer managing him, but I was on the lot, sharing an office with Mike Todd, when Herman Cohn came into my office one morning raving about Mickey. He says he doesn't know why I ever complained about Mickey. He says, 'That guy's a doll to work with. We're on our seventh day. He shows up every day early. He knows his lines. He does whatever we tell him. I can't understand this reputation he has. So I said to him, 'That's good. Let me see your shooting schedule.' He handed me the schedule, and I took a look at it. I saw that on the following night, they were supposed to do some night shooting. 'You mean, you're going to shoot all night?' I asked. 'Yeah.' 'Then Mickey won't show up,' I told him . . . And, of course, Mickey never showed, which completely screwed up their schedule."

AS THE SEASON wore on, with no improvement in the ratings, Mickey became particularly upset. Even on the nights the Gleason Show was pre-empted, the ratings remained low, because people weren't in the habit of tuning in Mickey. Paradoxically, Mickey's biggest fan was Jackie Gleason himself. He made it a point to stay home and watch "Hey, Mulligan" on the rare Saturday night that his own show was dark. But he would hold his compliments until about three in the morning, California time, at which point the phone in Mickey's bedroom would ring, rousing him and Elaine from a sound sleep.

Putting the receiver to his ear, Mickey would hear Gleason's mocking voice, "Hello, Spider"—Spider was his nickname for Mickey—"I want you to know, Spider, that one loyal American watched your show tonight." And then he'd laugh and hang up before Mickey could say a word.

Despite the show's low ratings, Mickey felt secure enough to think about acquiring a stable of race horses. Mickey would come onto the set in the morning, "worried about his jockey silks," John Fenton Murray remembers. "He was worried about the right colors. And he used to bring them in when we were trying to get rolling, and he'd start asking everyone what they thought of them. Did we prefer the green polka dots on a white background, or white polka dots against a green background? He even did it when Leo Burnett brought the sponsors on the set one morning to watch us shoot. Instead of talking about the show and what we were all trying to do to improve the

201

ratings, there he is shoving these jockey silks under the Pillsbury people's noses and saying 'What do you think of these—you like green polka dots or green stripes for the background?' And, hell, the show was slipping in the ratings pretty good by then. And the sponsors didn't look too pleased with Mickey showing so much interest in a racing stable."

The spring of 1955, however, Mickey was still a celebrity in the eyes of his sponsors. Consequently they invited him and Duke to attend the anniversary celebration of the Pillsbury Flour Company in Le Seur, Minnesota, which was the hometown of Pillsbury Flour and Jolly Green Giant Peas. As part of the celebration, Mickey was to play in a celebrity golf tournament, in a foursome consisting of Leo Burnett; Peter Jurow, president of the company; General Lucius Clay, and himself. But before the golf tournament, Mickey and Duke were summoned to attend a meeting with Peter Jurow in his private office. Jurow, a large, important-looking man, was sitting at his desk with a huge map of the United States on the wall behind him. There were different colored pins in it, indicating where Pillsbury sales were strong and where they were weak and needed bolstering. After explaining the meaning of the various colored pins, Jurow, who according to Duke was a staunch Rooney fan, turned to Mickey and said, "You can stay with us forever, Mick, if you can pick up the places where we're weaker."

For some reason, this made Mickey antagonistic. "I'm not supposed to sell your product, Mr. Jurow!" he exclaimed. "You hired me to be an actor!"

Duke nearly slid off his chair. "I could tell from the look on Jurow's face that we had blown the show right there," Duke says.

Duke smoothed over the contretemps the best he could with a line alluding to Mickey's "far-out" sense of humor and he kept Mickey from digging his grave any deeper by giving him a couple of sharp raps on his shin bone with the end of his cane. After that, they proceeded to a luncheon in the executive dining room, where Mickey managed to hold in abeyance any further insults, and spoke enthusiastically about the coming golf event, to which he seemed to be looking forward.

At the Le Seur country club, a large crowd of fans was waiting to watch Mickey tee off, never mind his lousy Neilsen ratings. Usually Mickey enjoyed playing in front of a crowd. But in the golf match at Le Seur, Mickey seemed to have a chip on his shoulder as he played the first three holes. He was in and out of the rough and struggling to remain two over par. "They were playing too slow for him," Duke recalls. "Mickey's a nervous guy. He can't stand to play slow. He has hyper metabolism. He likes to walk right up to the ball and sock it. But on the fourth hole, he takes me aside, and says, 'Let's get out of here, Duke. This is boring. I can't stand these guys."

Despite Duke's protestations, Mickey walked off the course, leaving his manager to cover for him with the weak excuse that Mickey had contracted a sudden stomach ache and couldn't continue with the match.

That night, Mickey and Duke attended a gala celebration at the Pillsbury mansion, which was about the size of Buckingham Palace. There was plenty of good food made of the company's products, lots of booze, and good music for dancing. In addition to the star and producer of "Hey, Mulligan," agency men, important company executives, and members of the local press, there were also a number of members of the Pillsbury family milling around the grand ballroom where the party took place. Mrs. Pillsbury, a well-powdered, regal-looking dowager type in a long dress, seemed delighted to meet the star of "Hey, Mulligan," remembered his *Andy Hardy* films with great reverence, and in general gave them a warm welcome. After she hurried off to greet other guests, Duke pulled Mickey aside and whispered to him, "We've got a good chance to keep the show going, Mickey. Mrs. Pillsbury likes you. So just be nice to everybody."

Mickey tried, but circumstances, not to mention his own giant ego, got in the way of the required diplomacy. Walter Pillsbury, the family's number-one son, had a few "and kept calling Mickey 'Charlie,'" Duke says. "This bugged Mickey terribly. He kept repeating, 'I'm not, Charlie,' 'I'm Mickey—Mickey Rooney.'"

Offended by what he considered to be a deliberate insult, Mickey kept nudging Duke in the ribs and muttering loudly, "Let's get the hell out of here."

For a while, Duke was able to handle Mickey and keep him from fleeing the premises. But all this self-restraint turned Mickey into a tinderbox ready to be set off by the slightest spark. What finally ignited him occurred after dinner when Walter Pillsbury jumped up from the table, grabbed Mickey by the shoulder, and started pulling him toward the piano.

"Hey, what's going on?" Mickey protested.

"It's time for you to do your act, Charlie."

"What act?"

"We want you to sing and dance for us."

"Thanks, but no thanks. I don't feel up to it right now."

203

"What do you mean, you don't feel up to it?" Walter said. "You're talking to Walter Pillsbury. We own you, Charlie."

"You don't own anybody, pal," flared up Mickey in a belligerent tone. "And for the last time, stop calling me, Charlie." Then, Duke says, Mickey turned to him and exclaimed in words loud enough for everyone to hear, "Let's go, Duke. I can't stand this bunch of crows another minute."

TO THE SURPRISE of no one in the business, least of all Duke, Pillsbury Flour dropped its sponsorship of the series. Mulligan uttered his last gasp over NBC on Saturday night, June 7, 1955. NBC sold it into syndication for a year of reruns and final oblivion.

WHILE "HEY, MULLIGAN" had been dying a torturous death, Mickey's and Elaine's marriage seemed to have come down with a terminal illness, too. According to Elaine's diagnosis, most of the trouble stemmed from Mickey's addiction to gambling and other women. From Mickey's point of view, she wasn't interested in him, only his money and what his name could do for her career.

Elaine admits that she was aware soon after their marriage that Mickey had never been faithful to her and that she couldn't ever believe what Mickey told her. "And if you can't believe your partner, what have you got in your marriage?" she adds. What kept Elaine from leaving Mickey after she realized he was afflicted with an incurable wandering eye was an earnest, almost-frantic, appeal from Mickey's psychiatrist to reconsider. "At the time, Mickey was going to a doctor who was trying to get him off pills—Seconals and Nembutals—on which he was heavily dependent, and had been since his Andy Hardy days at MGM, when he and Judy Garland were both on the stuff," Elaine reveals. "So the doctor said to me, 'Please stay with Mickey. I think I can help him if you do.' And so I did, but it was difficult."

Mickey's infidelity was apparently the hardest thing for Elaine— in fact, all his wives—to cope with. In a town like Hollywood, where everyone knows who's sleeping with whom, it's difficult for a wife to ignore rumors of her husband's philandering and still hold her head high.

Often Elaine couldn't.

Maurice Duke remembers a party he attended at the Rooney house on Fryman Road. There were a number of guests present, so they had brought in an extra serving girl to help. "She was a sweet little thing," Duke says. "Quite pretty, and you could see Mickey had his eye on her for something besides the hors d'oeuvres she was passing. When Mick thought nobody was looking, he wrote down his office phone number on a piece of paper and started to slip it to her. But Elaine caught him, and hit Mickey right across the mouth with all her might. Elaine was a lot bigger than Mickey, and took no shit from him."

MICKEY ALLEGES THAT all Elaine ever said to him was, "Let's buy." So, he contends, mainly to satisfy Elaine's craving for material things, he had to buy her a house at Lake Arrowhead, a Chris Craft speedboat, a Chrysler, and two horses. According to him, she wanted to live the life of a movie star's wife and completely disregarded the fact that he was a "has-been" movie star.

"Which is a crock," Elaine counters with indignation. "I had my dreams of course. But they were modest. I wanted a home, which we had; a cabin in the mountains; a small motorboat to use on the lake, and a horse. Those were my dreams . . . dreams I'd had since childhood. I liked the mountains and the streams and the lakes, and I couldn't have given a darn about city life or living like a movie star's wife. As for his being a 'has-been,' Mickey never made less than $150,000 a year the whole time we were married."

The cabin at Lake Arrowhead was actually paid for by Elaine. "I made the down payment, which was only a couple of thousand dollars, out of the money I had been able to save out of my monthly allowance. Mickey and I were both on personal allowances from his business manager—to do with what we pleased. He spent his at the races and on girls, but I chose to use mine to buy this cabin rather than spend it on a lot of fancy clothes and beauty parlors. I never went to a beauty parlor—my one extravagance was that I liked to get a manicure occasionally. I also made the down payment on a Century inboard motorboat, and was still paying for that when we got our divorce. The cabin was even in my mother's name, so since I had made the down payment, I can't say that Mickey *gave* me that."

After the Rooneys became a two-house family, Elaine began spending more and more time at Arrowhead. Her reason for this, she told Mickey, was that she became bored and depressed sitting around the big house, waiting for him to come home from wherever he happened to be—working at a studio, doing a nightclub gig in Vegas, or else running around Hollywood chasing women. Even between pictures, Mickey preferred life in Hollywood to going quietly mad staring at trees. He was also preoccupied with getting his career back on track.

205

"About the only time Mickey ever came to Arrowhead after we bought the cabin was when I told him I wanted a divorce, and he came up to talk me out of it," Elaine says. "That was toward the end of '57 or the spring of '58. But except for then, Mickey mostly stayed in town, doing anything he darn well pleased."

This, of course, included spending time with a number of girls around Hollywood. But the one he took the greatest fancy to was Barbara Ann Thomason (Miss Muscle Beach of 1954), whom he met in a nightclub early in 1958. Bill Gardner, a young, handsome auto salesman and a mutual friend, introduced them. "It was love at first sight for him," Gardner recalls.

Almost immediately, Mickey started squiring Barbara around Hollywood, and quite openly. An aspiring actress, Barbara Thomason was blonde, not much taller than Mickey, well proportioned and just twenty-one years old. When they met, Barbara was living in a small apartment off the Sunset Strip with a female nightclub singer named Pat Landers. That living arrangement didn't last long.

Pretty soon rumors started getting back to Elaine that Mickey had a new girl about whom he was apparently "serious." "By then, I knew I'd had it up to here with Mickey," Elaine delcares, indicating her elegant neck with her beautifully sculptured hand.

UNDER THE CIRCUMSTANCES, it was inevitable that a woman as attractive as Elaine would find someone for herself, too. And one glorious spring weekend at Lake Arrowhead, she did. "This was the first time in our marriage that I had ever seen anyone else," Elaine relates, "and at least I was honest about it. As soon as it happened, I told Mickey that I was going with a young man, that I had a boyfriend, so to speak, and that I wanted to leave Mickey. But Mickey begged me not to. So did his doctor. Mickey was still under the care of a psychiatrist. I felt sorry for him again, so I said, okay, I would stay, but I would not give up my young man. Mickey knew all that right up front, and he didn't care. He was all over the place with Barbara. He even bought her a fur coat for $4500. He felt so guilty, he even bought me one—and a more expensive one, at that." Here Elaine emitted a sardonic laugh. "I figured what was the difference? If it was the end of a marriage, it was the end of a marriage."

On June 15, 1958, Mickey and Elaine separated officially, and he rented a house belonging to Mayor Sam Yorty at 12979 Blairwood Road in Sherman Oaks. Sharing his new home, not surprisingly, was

206

Barbara Thomason. The night of August 12, Barbara took an overdose of sleeping pills and charged Mickey the next day with attempting to resuscitate her by pushing her into his swimming pool. According to Barbara's girlfriend, Pat Landers, who fished her out and called for an ambulance, Barbara's suicide attempt was the result of Mickey's refusal to marry her.

In a later version, Barbara recanted the part about Mickey pushing her in the pool, because in his plea of innocence he offered proof that he'd been at a party in Hollywood at the time. "The whole thing was a publicity stunt cooked up by the two girls," said Red Doff, who was acting as Mickey's spokesman to the press. Publicity stunt or not, there were at least two other instances on their rocky road to the altar when Barbara attempted to take her own life, according to Marge Lane, one of her best friends.

At any rate, the first tiff evidently wasn't serious enough to cause a breakup, because Mickey and Barbara continued to live together in Sam Yorty's hillside house. They must have had lots of lovers' quarrels, however, "because during the period that Mickey was living up on the hill with Barbara he was always phoning me and asking me to take him back," Elaine states. "But I told him, 'No, I have someone now, and have no intention of starting up with you again.'"

It seems that the next logical step would be a swift, painless divorce that both partners could live with. Unfortunately, that old stumbling block, money, stood in the way. After seven years of marriage, a track record for any of the Rooney wives, Elaine believed she was entitled to an equitable share of the community property and retained Max Gilford, a prominent Hollywood attorney, to represent her.

In the preliminary negotiations before she actually filed for divorce, Elaine indicated she would request a "fair share of the community property and $2,350 a month temporary alimony until we arrive at a permanent alimoney figure."

Mickey, on the other hand, didn't believe Elaine was entitled to anything approaching that, and instructed his own attorney, Dermot Long, not to capitulate to Gilford's demands.

With both sides at loggerheads, Mickey decided to play tough. "He cut off all my charge accounts and stopped my allowance," Elaine recalls. "Suddenly I had no money, no income. For a time I didn't have the money to buy food for my animals or pay the utility bills and make the car and house payments. Twice my gas and electricity were shut off because I was delinquent."

Because she was in such desperate financial straits, Elaine swallowed her pride one evening and phoned Mickey to ask him for funds. She caught him in the middle of dinner, she was informed by Barbara, who picked up the phone first.

"Well, I have to talk to him," Elaine said.

"What for?" demanded Barbara.

"I need money—to pay the bills and feed the animals."

"Who cares?" snapped Barbara.

"Look, you behave yourself or you're going to be sorry," Elaine warned Barbara.

What Elaine was alluding to was that she could still have Mickey back if she just said the magic word. "But I didn't want to tell her that. I wanted out myself."

The arcane threat brought Mickey to the phone, however, and he told her to stop calling him there. "I will, just as soon as you send me some money to live on."

Reluctantly, Mickey said he'd speak with his accountant in the morning. And he kept his word. Elaine received a few hundred dollars from Mickey to tide her over. That solved her immediate problem, but she still wasn't ready to accept the property settlement Mickey's lawyer had offered her.

Elaine finally filed for divorce in Santa Monica on February 5, 1959, charging Mickey with mental cruelty. They still were nowhere near agreement on a property settlement, however, and without that there could be no court date set for the actual divorce hearing. With Elaine refusing to cooperate, Mickey started making noises about running across the border and getting a Mexican divorce. But that, of course, was out of the question, because even in Mexico it is impossible to obtain a legal divorce unless both parties have signed a property settlement. Barbara was pressuring him to get some kind of divorce, because by the middle of March she was three months pregnant. She was, in fact, threatening suicide, if he didn't do something to make her baby legitimate.

On March 26, a hearing was held in the Superior Court in Santa Monica. This action was brought by Elaine's attorney, Max Gilford, in an effort to get her some "temporary alimony" to live on. All of Mickey's financial records were subpoenaed from MGM, as well as his business managers', past and present—Maurice Duke, Red Doff—and a couple of MGM lawyers. After getting an idea of Mickey's income, the judge awarded Elaine temporary alimony as well as the privilege of continuing to live in the Fryman Road house—at least until a permanent settlement was reached.

Until it was, Elaine would sneak off every chance she got to her

Lake Arrowhead hideaway. Things dragged on without a resolution until early spring. By that time Barbara was five months pregnant and unable to conceal the child she was carrying. At that point, ironically enough, Mickey was still "phoning me and asking me to take him back," Elaine says. "Finally I had to tell him, 'Look, Mickey. It's no longer just a question of you and me—there's a baby involved. So forget it!'"

How could he forget it? If something weren't done to break the deadlock fairly soon, the baby was going to be without a legal father. In 1959, Hollywood was a provincial town where it was no small thing to father an illegitimate baby. Mickey realized that a person could be drummed out of the business for it.

Desperate now, but still not willing to meet Elaine's demands, Mickey and Dermot Long devised another strategy. They sent detectives up to Lake Arrowhead to spy on Elaine. "Why he had to do this, I don't know," Elaine says. "I had told him all about my boyfriend and that we were living together up there. It was no secret. But he sent detectives anyway, and then came up with them and acted as if he had caught me doing something he didn't know about."

She soon found out his motive. The next time she and Max Gilford got together with Mickey and his attorney in the latter's office to see if there couldn't be a meeting of the minds, Long opened his desk drawer and pulled out some pictures of Elaine and her lover that the detective had taken.

"We'd hate to have to introduce these in court," he said smoothly.

From the surprised looks on their opponents' faces, it appeared that Long and Mickey had the upper hand and would be able to dictate any terms they pleased. But then, just when it seemed that Elaine would have to accept their terms, Mickey dropped to his knees in front of her, threw his arms around her legs and, after promising he'd never use the pictures in court, begged her to take him back.

With Mickey's guilt turning him into a pussycat, Elaine knew she had nothing to worry about and therefore was able to hang in. On May 1, she and Mickey were able to agree on a property settlement, leaving no impediment in the way of their divorce.

The formal divorce hearing was heard by Judge Orlando Rhodes in the Los Angeles Superior Court in Santa Monica on May 21, 1959, at which time an interlocutory decree was granted.

Most of the cross-complaints were well laundered by then. So what the press reported and what anyone still interested in Mickey Rooney's marital woes read in the public prints was pretty mild.

Elaine charged that her home life with Mickey was "disorganized," that he "was away from home a lot," and that he "didn't like my cooking."

"Which isn't true," Elaine smiles, who is actually a fine cook. "Mickey liked my cooking, but I had to charge him with something in court in order to get the divorce, and I didn't want to tell the world the real reasons."

According to the court approved settlement, Mickey was ordered to give Elaine: The house on Fryman Road; the furniture; the cabin at Arrowhead; a Century inboard motorboat; her Chrysler; the horses; assorted jewelry; fifty thousand dollars cash; and twenty-one thousand dollars a year for ten years at the rate of $1,750 per month.

Judge Rhodes also ordered Mickey to pay: Elaine's attorney fees, any outstanding or delinquent household bills, including $750 owed a maid, $1,250 for groceries, $150 for "horse board" at Pickwick Stables, and $144 to Lake Arrowhead Motorboat Company— totaling approximately $5,000; unpaid balances on car and jewelry loans, plus interest, and two personal loans—one from a friend in the amount of $800 and another from Elaine's aunt in the amount of $500.

According to Elaine, there was very little equity in the house when she was given sole ownership. There was a first mortgage of $24,760.28 and a second mortgage of $21,333.52. Mickey was ordered to refinance the house for Elaine, so her monthly payments would not exceed $450 a month.

Elaine did receive the motorboat and the Chrysler, both of which she continued to pay for, when Mickey didn't, on the installment plan. "The horses weren't even worth enough to mention," Elaine says. "And as for my assorted jewelry, that consisted of my engagement and wedding rings, and a small diamond cocktail ring Mickey had bought me when he was living with Barbara, and feeling guilty about it."

And, finally, she didn't receive the twenty-one thousand a year for ten years—it was more like a year and a half. "At that time Mickey decided he couldn't afford to pay me $1,750 a month, so he and three of his attorneys ganged up on me and my new attorney, Sy Taub,° one day. They claimed that Mickey and I had what's known

---

°Simon Taub took over Elaine's representation after Max Gilford, her first attorney, quit the case because he couldn't get Mickey to pay him the legal fees Judge Rhodes had ordered him to pay. "So I took over shortly after Gilford had arranged the original settlement, cited Mickey for contempt and finally collected every penny he owed her lawyers," Simon Taub today says.

as an 'integrated agreement,' and so they were able to knock me down from my good settlement to five hundred dollars a month. At first they wanted me to make it four hundred dollars, but Sy Taub told them they were taking unfair advantage of me and managed to get them back up to $500. The ironic part of it is I didn't get that, either. Sometimes, he would go month after month and never pay me anything. Finally, I had to rent the big house, and move into the guest house. I only lived in the main house when it wasn't being rented. It was a terrible time for me. I even did all the gardening and housekeeping. But finally I started getting some picture work pretty regularly and was able to meet my obligations. But what I resented is that Mickey tried to make everyone think I was just a gold digger."

ON FRIDAY, SEPTEMBER 13, 1959, at St. John's Hospital in Santa Monica, Barbara Rooney gave birth to a six-pound-ten-ounce daughter whom they named Kelly Ann. The blessed event occurred just four months after Mickey and Elaine were granted their interlocutary decree in Santa Monica. Under California law, neither would be eligible to marry until June 1960.

But good showman that he is, Mickey cleaned up his act for the press by announcing in *The New York Times* that he had divorced Elaine in Mexico in May of 1958 and had married Barbara the following December. "If he got a Mexican divorce, I was never aware of it," Elaine says. Mexican law being what it is, that in itself makes the Mexican divorce improbable.

ONE THING MICKEY can't be accused of is holding a grudge.

Several years later, after Elaine's "young man" had been killed in a freak horseback riding accident, Mickey dropped in on her late one afternoon when she was living by herself in the guest house. "I had a chicken in the oven," Elaine relates, "so I invited Mickey to stay and share it with me. He said, 'Sure,' and he enjoyed it, too, which proves he didn't hate my cooking. Anyway, we built a fire in the fireplace, and he talked about going back together with me again . . . he was married to *her* then. And I said, 'Mickey, I don't think so. But thanks, anyway.'"

211

18

WHILE MICKEY HAD been bouncing back and forth between wife and mistress in search of marital bliss, his career was also having its ups and downs. During a twelve-day hiatus while "Hey, Mulligan" was still being shown on NBC, Mickey produced, and also appeared in, a comedy called *The Atomic Kid* for Republic Pictures. It starred Mickey, Bob Strauss, and Mickey's then-wife, Elaine, who played a beautiful nurse. The film contained some amusing moments, but the major critics labeled it a "one-joke" idea. Nevertheless, it was fairly successful by "quickie" film standards, made back its costs, and still turns up every now and then on local TV channels.

In 1956, Mickey—ironically—replaced Donald O'Connor in the last of the *Frances* series, *Frances in the Haunted House,* for Universal Pictures. RKOs *The Bold and the Brave* also hit the nation's movie screens in 1956. This film was about three American GIs fighting in Italy, and although Mickey was hired only as a supporting player to Don Taylor and Wendell Corey, he wound up composing the theme song as well as directing the hilariously frenzied eleven-minute crap game, which gave the picture its high spot and won Mickey, as the leading dice thrower, a nomination for an Acadamy Award as Best Supporting Actor.The reviewer for *The New York Times* raved about Mickey's performance: "It is Mickey Rooney as Dooley who walks off with the show." Mickey was very modest about his personal contribution to the crap-shooting sequence. "How can you write a crap game? We threw out fourteen pages of script. There were thirty men before the camera. We roughly figured out how the game would play, and then we all chipped in to ad lib all over the place for fourteen minutes straight. Later it was cut to an eleven-minute scene."

With Mickey's acting star on the rise again, he found himself getting good parts in bigger and better films. In 1957 he appeared in Dick Quine's *Operation Mad Ball* along with its two stars, Jack Lemmon and Ernie Kovacs. Although Mickey was clearly not the star, he was, in the opinion of both the critics and the film's director, Richard Quine, responsible for keeping *Operation Mad Ball* from turning into a disaster. In Dick Quine's opinion, "Mickey made the ending for me. The whole picture builds up to this wild party, but the ending was pretty weak, as was the story, so I just turned Mickey loose and put four cameras on him. He went ape, ad libbing everything, and literally made the ending of the picture work. The guy's a genius, no doubt about it."

Mickey's name and talent couldn't do anything to help *Baby Face Nelson*, a gangster melodrama for United Artists and Al Zimbalist, in which he appeared in the title role, also in 1957. According to *The New York Times, Baby Face Nelson* is a thoroughly standard, pointless and even old-fashioned gangster picture, the kind that began going out along with the old-time sedans. As Mr. Rooney plays Nelson, or has to, he is nothing more than a rotten, sadistic punk, without one redeeming trait."

Interspersed with Mickey's attempts to become an important film star again were frequent sorties into the Las Vegas casinos as a floor show entertainer, which Maurice Duke had been able to obtain for him. At the time, Mickey was doing an act with Joey Forman, his sidekick on the Mulligan series. "I got him into the Riviera in Vegas right after the Riviera opened," Maurice Duke recalls. "We were about the third act to go in there. Hildegarde died there, Jeff Chandler, who was trying to become a nightclub singer, died there, so they were desperate. I sold them Mickey for seventeen thousand, five hundred a week. In those days that was a hell of a lot of money. But he was worth it. He packed them in. His show was a smash . . . You couldn't get near the place for four weeks. Then on the last day of the run, Mickey goes to the tables and loses about fifty Gs shooting craps. I was able—because the hotel wanted him to play there again—to go to the bosses and get some of it back for him.

"Anyway, Mickey was so disgusted that on the last night he gets up on the stage and announces that he's retiring. He makes one of those big dramatic speeches. He says this is the last time you'll ever see Mickey Rooney. He had the audience crying. 'I'm going to retire

214

to a farm and just take care of the cows and the chickens and the horses,' he told them. Then he turned around and walked sadly off to a standing ovation."

All the newspapers picked it up, of course.

MICKEY ROONEY RETIRES, screamed the headlines.

The next day comedian Wally Cox bombed at the Dunes Hotel in Vegas, and the management was dying to replace him immediately. As a result, they contacted Duke and asked him if he could deliver Mickey, who was already back in Beverly Hills.

Duke tracked him down at the William Morris Office. There he said to Mickey, "Is it really true, Mick, you're retiring?"

Mickey nodded, "Yes."

"How much money do you have left, Mick?" Duke asked.

"Nothing," Mickey replied.

"That's too bad," Duke said. "You know, I'm just managing you and I'm well fixed. I have a house in Beverly Hills, money in the bank, and you have nothing, and you're retiring."

"That's right," Mickey said. "I'm fed up."

"Too fed up to open tonight at the Dunes for $17,500 per week?"

After Duke's words sank in for a moment, Mickey sheepishly replied, "Okay," and left for the airport.

So much for Mickey's retirement from show business. Shortly after that, however, Maurice Duke retired from Mickey Rooney. "I just walked up to him one day, and told him that I quit," Duke remembers. "There was no particular incident. I just got fed up with him because he does stupid things. He's the greatest actor in the world—or one of the ten best, anyway—but he won't listen to you, and he thinks everybody steals from him and blames all his problems on them. No one ever stole from Mickey. Mickey steals from himself. Mickey's his own worst enemy. He has a fantasy about making two hundred million dollars a month. He's always going into all these crazy enterprises, and losing his money, like 'Mickey Rooney Macaroni' and 'Soda Pop for Dogs.' He goes into anything any promoter gives him a pitch on, but they all flop, and he winds up getting mad at his manager who advised him to stay out of them in the first place."

Mickey replaced Duke with Red Doff, his long-time press agent and confidant, with whom he had worked when he was making *Baby Face Nelson*, for which his salary was approximately $35,000. This wasn't much for an actor of Mickey's caliber, but it was a great deal more than the ten thousand dollars he received for playing the leading role in *The Comedian* on "Playhouse 90," over CBS on

February 14, 1957. *The Comedian*, however, did more for his status in the acting community than any of the so-called feature films he had appeared in lately.

In *The Comedian*, a TV adaptation by Rod Sterling of the Ernest Lehman best-selling novel of the same name, Mickey played a composite character who combined all the worst characteristics of almost every well-known comedian plying his trade at the time. The character was vicious, greedy, selfish, untrustworthy, a lecher, and an all-round son of a bitch, who abused his brother terribly and even made a pass at his sister-in-law.

Because none of America's leading comedians wanted to touch the part, for fear of being identified with the leading character, the script was passed around Hollywood from actor to actor until finally it wound up in Red Doff's hands for Mickey Rooney.

"I read the script," Doff recalls, "flipped over it and told Mickey, 'You've got to do it.'" After reading it, Mickey agreed, and the part of Sammy Hogarth, the comedian, was his by default.

That one exposure on "Playhouse 90," for which he received an Emmy nomination, proved what a fine dramatic actor he was—playing the role of a comedian. It was enough to make his name worth something again. As Mickey describes it in his autobiography, rather bitterly, "suddenly everybody decided that Mickey Rooney knew how to act."

He'd only been on the stage since he was two years old, twice had been nominated by the Motion Picture Academy for "Best Actor," and when he was only eighteen had been awarded a "special" Oscar for his contribution to the industry.

At any rate, Mickey was grateful for the new life the role gave his faltering career. Suddenly he wasn't getting the brush-off from important people he met around Hollywood, and there was more interest in making film deals with him. Mickey was able to go to MGM early in 1958 and talk the reigning heads there into letting him make another *Andy Hardy* film. This one, however, which was to be called *Andy Hardy Comes Home*, was to take into account all the years since Mickey was a boy. Mickey would play Andy Hardy as a young man.

Under new management, MGM sprang for the idea of bringing Andy Hardy back to Carvel as a grown man and on February 19, 1958, entered into a contract with Fryman Enterprises to make *Andy Hardy Comes Home*. Mickey was to get $35,000 for his services, payable to Fryman Enterprises, at the rate of $7,000 a week

216

for five weeks, commencing at the beginning of principle photography, which was to start on May 8, 1958.

The writers of the original story were assigned to write the screenplay, but before they completed it, they were to see several deviations from their original idea, which had Mickey portraying Judge Andy Hardy, married to his childhood sweetheart, Polly Benedict, to be played, they hoped, by a grownup Ann Rutherford. But that was not to be, much as Mickey wanted it. "I turned him down," says Ann Rutherford, who by then was married to Bill Dozier, a successful studio head. "I said, 'Mickey, in the first place very few people grow up to marry their childhood sweethearts. So that gets rid of me right away. And in the second place, you should not come back as Judge Hardy. You should come back as Andy Hardy; Andy Hardy would not grow up to be a judge. Andy Hardy would grow up to be Bob Hope or Red Skelton or a great radio performer.'"

Mickey Rooney, the producer, must have taken Ann Rutherford's advice to heart, for by the time Harry Ruskin, the veteran writer who had churned out many of the early classic Hardy films was called in to punch up the dialogue and reconstruct the script, Andy Hardy had become an attorney for an aircraft corporation seeking to purchase a parcel of land in Carvel, and his wife was a girl named Jane, whom he had met at work.

Among others in the cast was Teddy Rooney, Mickey's eight-year-old son by Martha Vickers. Teddy, with his sandy hair, freckles, and buck-toothed smile, bore a close-enough resemblance to his father to play Andy Hardy, Jr., in the film, in which Mickey was careful to preserve the "heart-to-heart" talk that audiences were so fond of in the early Hardy films.

Using Teddy to play Mickey's son was neither a mere gesture nor was it nepotism. Teddy, who resembled his father, was already considered an old pro by the age of eight, having appeared in a "Playhouse 90" with his mother; starred in an adaptation of O. Henry's "Ransom of Red Chief" for NBC; and appeared in a feature film, *It Happened to Jane*, featuring Doris Day.

Although Mickey was as qualified as anybody to direct an *Andy Hardy* film, the job was eventually turned over to Howard W. Koch. Today Koch is one of Hollywood's most important film producers. But in 1958 he was a relative newcomer at directing and had to take what amounted to a B-picture, with only an eleven-day shooting schedule.

217

What's more, he was burdened with having to direct a starlet named Patricia Breslin who couldn't act, but who was given the role of Andy Hardy's wife, Jane, primarily because she was the girlfriend of studio executive, Benny Thau. Pat had never been in a film before and, in Koch's opinion, didn't know the first thing about acting.

"I think we ought to test her," Koch said to Thau.

"Why?" Thau asked.

"Because I want to see if she can act," Koch said.

"Are you a director?" Thau asked.

"That's why I'm here," Koch replied.

"Well, if you're a director, make her act," Thau said.

Andy Hardy Comes Home went into production on May 7. "It was sad in a way," Howard Koch recalls. "On the sound stage next door, Paul Newman and Elizabeth Taylor were shooting *Cat on a Hot Tin Roof,* and here's Mickey, who'd been one of the world's biggest stars, and the fellow responsible for keeping Metro in the black all those years when he was a kid, and no one even knew he was alive. Nobody came on the stage to wish us any luck. Nobody sent flowers. Nothing."

Mickey maintained his enthusiasm for the project, however, and according to Koch not only contributed some good directorial touches but also wrote one of the biggest laughs in the film. It was in a scene that took place in the Hardy kitchen. Ma Hardy, Andy's mother, as played by Fay Holden, was talking with her sister, Aunt Millie, about the impending arrival of her son the lawyer in Carvel. From talk of Andy, the subject switched to a discussion about going on a trip. "The dialogue in the scene was pretty dull," Koch remembers, "so Mickey says to me, 'Why don't we have the two ladies say this?'"

AUNT MILLIE:	Why don't we take a trip?
MA HARDY:	Where?
AUNT MILLIE:	Let's go around the world.
MA HARDY:	No, let's go someplace else.

In his capacity of producer, actor, joke writer, and sometime director, Mickey did everything he could to insure the success of *Andy Hardy Comes Home,* including trying to invoke the spirit of the past by having the aging Andy daydream off and on about his youth. In these sequences, there were inserts from the early Hardy films showing the bumptuous young Andy with his old high-school flames—Judy Garland, Lana Turner, Bonita Granville, and Esther Williams. But despite all that, and a fairly good review by *Variety* when the picture opened in July, *Andy Hardy Comes Home* was neither a critical nor financial success, and wound up in most theaters on the lower half of a double bill. Moviegoers had outgrown Andy Hardy.

It's a tribute to Mickey's talent that despite his failures he continued to get picture work during the fifties. That same year, Mickey costarred with Tom Ewell and Dina Merrill in *A Nice Little Bank That Should Be Robbed,* which did nothing for the public or the critics, one of whom labeled it a "feeble comedy and a sad waste of its stars."

In 1959, Mickey played a condemned killer in a remake of *The Last Mile* for United Artists. The story took place on Sing Sing's death row, and one critic couldn't help calling it, "A cheerless, though literally electrifying, entertainment."

Mickey followed that one in 1959 with *The Big Operator,* in which he continued his tough-guy image by playing a vicious labor boss under investigation by the Senate Rackets Committee. *Variety* gave *The Big Operator* its endorsement as "a walloping labor rackets melo with enough stamina to carry it through general market to hefty grosses." Nevertheless, it disappeared rather quickly from theater marquees, though Mickey probably made a few bucks out of it.

Which is more than could be said about his short-lived stand at the Moulin Rouge Theater Restaurant in Hollywood in September of that year. Signed by the club's operator, Frank Sennes, to do two shows a night, Mickey quit after the first one and refused to come back for the second. His excuse was that he was dissatisfied with the failure of the management to provide him with "the proper staging and lighting facilities." Some insiders in the audience, however, believe that Mickey's refusal to do a second show probably had more to do with the lukewarm reception his act was given that night.

On the following day, Red Doff and Mickey's new agent, Milton Deutsch, notified the management that Mickey would not be returning. As a result, Frank Sennes presented Mickey with a bill for $5,917.67, which he claimed Mickey's failure to perform had cost him in lost revenue. A week later, Mickey announced to the press that he was suing the Moulin Rouge for a million dollars for damages he had incurred by the club's failure to present him properly during a performance. The suit never reached court, of course, and eventually Mickey and the nightclub owner settled.

If Mickey's career seemed to be on the down slope, his capacity for making headlines didn't diminish. In 1959, his name figured prominently in a number of headlines about his divorce and remarriage. A story in the Hollywood *Citizen News* on June 4 ran the headline:

ANGRY JUDGE TO PROBE
ROONEY MEXICAN WIFE SWAP

The story went on to say that Judge Orlando Rhodes, the judge who was on the bench during the MAHNKEN vs. ROONEY divorce hearing, threatened to investigate the circumstances in which Mickey Rooney quietly divorced Elaine Mahnken and married his fifth wife in Mexicao, five months before Miss Mahnken obtained a California divorce. Judge Rhodes said: "I was never informed of this during the hearing in my court and I intend to look into it and do whatever my legal duties call for." The same story added that Mickey appeared anything but worried about the judge's threat.

"We're happy," he said in Las Vegas, Nevada, where he was appearing at the Frontier Hotel. "She suits me," he added, noting that Barbara was the first of his five spouses to be shorter—by one inch—than he.

It was good that Mickey still had a sense of humor. He would need one after his appearance on the "Tonight Show" with Jack Paar on December 1, 1959.

For most of the year Paar did his show live from New York City, but for about two weeks every season he took his act to the City of Angels to make it more accessible to West Coast personalities.

According to what Jack Paar told me in a recent phone conversation, "I had never met Mickey Rooney before he was on my show that night. He was a legend to me, of course. I knew about him and liked his work very much. As a matter of fact, often on the 'Tonight Show,' we'd sit around talking about who was maybe the best motion picture actor who ever lived. And it would usually be Mickey Rooney or James Mason. Later when Mason was on, he was told that and asked who he thought was the best actor ever, and he replied, 'Mickey Rooney.'

"Anyway, we were out on the Coast, Mickey evidently heard we were in town, and he phoned us and wanted to know if he could go on the show. For what reason I don't know. He wasn't plugging anything, at least as far as we knew, and it certainly wasn't the money. Like everyone who appeared, I believe he got scale. When I

220

heard Mickey wanted to be on the show, I was delighted. And we booked him for December 1."

By an unhappy coincidence, December 1 happened to be the first anniversary of Mickey's marriage—the Mexican one, that is—to Barbara Thomason. Consequently, Mickey took Barbara to the Tail of the Cock restaurant on La Cienega Boulevard to engage in a little celebrating before it was time for him to go on the "Tonight Show." The "Tonight Show" was being broadcast live from NBC in Burbank at 8:30 P.M., Pacific Standard Time, but Mickey wasn't scheduled to go on until around nine.

Mickey was feeling pretty good by the time he arrived at NBC. But he was anything but "smashed," according to the way he remembers it. ("If I'd been smashed, Barbara never would have allowed me to go on the show.")

"Now ordinarily," Paar says, "whenever I would have a guest of Mickey's stature on the show whom I hadn't already met, I'd try to have lunch with that person so we could get acquainted beforehand. Well, that couldn't be arranged. Mickey evidently didn't have time, and just told my booker that he'd be there when we needed him for the show. So when we went on the air I still had never met Mickey. Well, I'd had that happen before, too, but when it did, I'd generally make a point of running back and greeting the guest during a two-minute commercial break just before he was to go on. I'd say, 'Hi, I'm Jack Paar. You're Mickey Rooney,' or whoever the hell the guest was, and we'd at least have a minute to shake hands and get acquainted. It just made it a little easier for everybody once we got on the air. But that night I was told by our booker who handled Mickey—his name was Tom O'Malley—that Mickey didn't want to see me, but it didn't bother me. I merely thought, that's the way he is—he just doesn't want to meet me first. Maybe he thinks it'll take away from the spontaneity. But I didn't read any hostility into it. I just didn't understand his attitude. As a result, I never actually met him until he walked out, shook hands with me, and sat down.

"Now in my opinion, you have to know a man very well to tell whether or not he's been drinking when you're first meeting him. I mean, unless he's staggeringly drunk, you can't tell what his style's like. If it's a close friend, or someone you know, you can tell instantly if he's had a few belts. So I didn't even have that advantage. All I knew was that he was terribly hostile—as if he had a very large chip on his shoulder."

As in the motion-picture classic *Rashomon*, there are a number of disparate versions of what happened after Paar and Mickey first

221

met, depending on which camp you're listening to. But after sifting through all the facts garnered from Jack Paar, Mickey Rooney's autobiography, Red Doff, and all the newspaper accounts in the following day's editions, the interview seems to have gone something like this: Mickey, in a state of high exhilaration from the martinis, swaggered on, and according to Paar kept mentioning over and over that he was now in the "tire business with some pro football player—I've forgotten his name. Anyway, Mickey kept mentioning the address of this tire company on Sepulveda Boulevard, over and over again, with absolutely no humor. There was no fun to it. He was really quite boring. At that point, I began to realize his redundancy was caused by his drinking, and the audience began to suspect that too."

Paar decided to change the subject. "What kind of a woman was Ava Gardner?" he asked.

Immediately, Mickey's back was up—probably because Barbara was in the audience.

"Ava," the Mick replied, leaning close to Paar and breathing heavily in his face, "Ava's more of a woman than you'll ever know."

Apparently, according to Paar, Mickey considered his relationship with Ava nobody's business. Paar contends just the opposite. "Ava was his first wife and an important part of his life, so I'm sure that I mentioned her, but not in any context that was unkind."

After the embarrassing lull that came over the studio following Mickey's belligerent reply, Paar asked Mickey if he had ever previously watched the "Tonight Show." Mickey replied that he hadn't. He said his favorite show at that hour was Tom Duggan's; he had a talk show on a local station. "And Mickey kept reiterating how great this Tom Duggan was and saying that I'd never be as good as Duggan. And I'm sitting there thinking how strange," Paar recalls. "He keeps mentioning his tire company over and over, and he keeps needling me about not being Tom Duggan. Then I suddenly figured this out. He and Mickey evidently were friends. And I could imagine what happened. One night they were sitting around talking and Mickey said, 'I'm going to go on the Paar show and tell him off, and make you look like a big man.' Up until then I had never mentioned Mickey with anything but great praise, but the audience was getting bored. And I'm an expert at when the audience has left you and the show is dying. And to die with Mickey Rooney on is pretty unusual."

Finally, Paar said to Mickey, "Are you enjoying my show tonight?"

"Not necessarily," Mickey answered.

"Then would you care to leave?" Paar asked.

At that point, according to Paar, the audience started applauding. "It was probably the first time in the history of this great actor that Mickey was applauded off the stage," Paar says. "And that's pretty hard to recover from."

Mickey stood up, shook hands with Paar, and departed.

Alone on the stage, Paar then took several shots at Mickey Rooney. Turning to the audience, he joked, "That was the only time I've ever got a hangover from just listening." And he followed that up by saying, "It's a shame. He was a great talent."

For the next two days the newspapers were full of headlines about the verbal shoot-out at the Jack Paar corral. Most of the stories emphasized the fact that Mickey was slightly inebriated before going on the air and, of course, tried to build what happened into a feud rivaling that of the Hatfields and the McCoys.

"Mickey got the worst of it in the press," Paar says today, not with malice but wonderment. "It's funny. In those days the press was generally hostile to me, because I never allowed myself to be interviewed by them. But in this case they took my side, because what Mickey had done was obviously so blatant. Frankly, he'd made an ass of himself on the stage. Which made me really feel sorry for him . . .

"Anyway, because Mickey had taken such a beating in the press, he came to my suite at the Beverly Hills Hotel the next day. Very belligerent, looking for a fight. There was no question about that. I saw he was unarmed when he came in, but noticed he was wearing gym shoes, and a Lacoste shirt. 'Oh, golly,' I thought. 'He's going to use judo on me.' But instead, he walked over, shook my hand, and much to his credit said, 'I'm sorry I was drunk.'"

Leaving Paar's suite, Mickey told the press and photographers waiting outside the door, hoping to see more fireworks, that everything was "fine," and that he was going to do a repeat performance on the Paar show that night—"without a precelebration."

Mickey couldn't help adding, however, that he would also appear on Tom Duggan's show on KCOP, Channel 13, that night and give Duggan equal time.

Neither of those appearances ever happened, and later in the day Red Doff dispatched a telegram to Robert Kintner, president of NBC, demanding a television apology from Paar on his coast-to-coast program for alleged slanderous remarks, including the dig at Mickey's talent ("He *was* a great talent.")

223

That never happened, either, but for years and possibly to this day Mickey has been bitter about his aborted appearance on the "Tonight Show," and believes that Jack Paar instigated the sparring match on the air purely for publicity purposes.

"I really think Mickey should understand that I didn't need publicity," Paar says. "I was rather successful."

19

IN RETROSPECT, THE incident was trivial. As Mickey himself expressed it to the press the following day, "So I made the unpardonable sin of having a couple of martinis before I went on the show."

And if that's all there was to it, it wouldn't have been worth mentioning. However, the incident does serve to illustrate how much hostility toward the world was bottled up inside Mickey's five-foot, three-inch frame. Even on the anniversary of his marriage to Barbara, which should have been a happy occasion, it took only a couple of martinis to uncover a side of him that only his wives, a small circle of close friends, and some of his co-workers knew existed.

The Ava exchange, with Mickey cracking at Paar that she was "more woman than you'll ever know," suggested two things: That Mickey was still carrying the torch for her and was still extremely sensitive on the subject; and that he may have been extremely envious of Paar's success.

If the fifties was a time Mickey Rooney would have liked to forget, he should have skipped the sixties altogether.

In September of 1960, Mickey was forty years old—growing bald, forced to wear glasses for reading, and with a slight paunch. "Let's face it," Dick Quine says, "it wasn't all that easy to find roles for a five-foot three-inch man who'd passed the age of Andy Hardy. And if Hollywood had Mickey Rooney typecast on screen, it also had him pigeonholed as an immature, temperamental womanizer— and a drinker and sometime pill taker.

Only his close friends knew Mickey wasn't a big drinker. "It was his metabolism," Red Doff explains. "One drink and he'd be looped. If he took a sleeping pill it would last twice as long as it would with anybody else."

Despite the fact that the name Mickey Rooney had lost most of its luster by the early sixties, there were a handful of producers still willing to take a chance on him—if the price was right and he would accept supporting roles. He did nothing for his reputation by turning up in such pictures as *Platinum High School, The Private Lives of Adam and Eve, King of the Roaring Twenties* (the story of gambler Arnold Rothstein), and *Everything's Ducky*, with Buddy Hackett—which *The New York Times* reviewer called "An ostensible farce in which Mickey Rooney is required to play straight man to Buddy Hackett and a talking duck."

However in *Breakfast at Tiffany's*, in which Mickey's friend Blake Edwards cast him as a Japanese fashion photographer, and again in *Requiem for a Heavyweight*, he made Hollywood sit up and take notice that if he was no longer exactly a leading man, he was at least a very fine character actor. Most of the raves were reserved for Audrey Hepburn in *Breakfast at Tiffany's*, but Bosley Crowther wrote that "Mickey Rooney's buck-toothed myopic Japanese is broadly exotic." Similarly, *The Times* found Mickey's delineation of the prizefight trainer in *Requiem for a Heavyweight* "as touching as Jackie Gleason's portrayal of a manager, and while he does not have Mr. Gleason's opportunities (except in a gin rummy game in which he takes honors hands down), he, too, is sad, defeated, and sentient without being lachrymose."

Because Mickey wasn't the star of either film, he hadn't been earning the kind of money he felt he deserved, or indeed could live on. So what did Mickey do under the circumstances? What he frequently did when faced with a career crisis: he fired his personal manager, replacing Red Doff with someone he felt had more clout—Bullets Durgom. Durgom had built a reputation managing some of the important names of the Big Band era, including the Dorsey Brothers and Frank Sinatra. More recently, until moving West, he had been Jackie Gleason's manager. It was those credits that attracted Mickey to Bullets, whom he had known socially for years.

"Things weren't going well for Mickey by 1962," Bullets recalls, "so he asked me if I could help him. I said I'd try, if he promised me he'd stop taking jobs in all those 'beach party' pictures like *Beach Blanket Bingo*. He was getting one and two grand for brief appearances in those pictures that he wasn't even getting credit on. So I said, 'Mickey, you have to stop lowering your price like that. Why do you take those parts, anyway?' And his reply was, 'Well, I had nothing to do that week, and they offered me a couple of grand, so I said, 'Why not?' 'But there goes your price,' I told him. 'I can't get any real money for you if you keep going in those things. Stay out of them!' So he promised, and for a while he listened to me, and for a while it worked."

Almost immediately, Bullets earned his twenty percent cut of Mickey's gross by getting him a job in the Stanley Kramer blockbuster comedy, *It's a Mad, Mad, Mad, Mad World,* a film about an assortment of people overcome by greed when they hear of buried loot, and, of course, all try to get to it first. "I got Mickey $125,000 for that picture," Bullets says. "That was the most he'd gotten in years, and Kramer didn't want to pay it. But he wanted Mickey real bad, so after I found out he was paying that to the other comedians, I held out and finally he gave it to Mickey, too."

IT'S A MAD, Mad, Mad, Mad World went into production on location in Palm Springs on April 26, 1962. During the six weeks Mickey was working there, he took a suite at the Riviera Hotel but occasionally commuted back to Sherman Oaks to be with his family.

Barbara had given birth by cesarean section to their third child, and only son, Michael Joseph Kyle, on March 30. Dr. Keith Wallace had performed the surgery and, while there were no complications, Barbara preferred to recuperate at home, because the weather in Palm Springs during May and June could be brutally hot.

After Mickey finished shooting his big comedy sequence with Buddy Hackett, he returned to Los Angeles, only to learn that he and Barbara would have to vacate the house on Blairwood, which they were renting from Sam Yorty, because the mayor wanted it for himself.

Although he owed a great deal of money, and creditors were pushing him toward the brink of bankruptcy, Mickey had enough cash left from his stint in *It's a Mad...World* for the down payment on a lovely house Barbara found for them on Magnolia Boulevard, in a lovely section of Encino. It was a rambling California ranch house with a sweeping front lawn and lots of play area for the children. Its price tag was forty-two thousand dollars—less than Fryman Road, but still a substantial sum for a place in the Valley in those days.

Strange as it may seem (at least in anybody's life but Mickey

Rooney's), Mickey closed the deal for the new house just a few days before his lawyer, Dermot Long, went to court in Santa Monica and filed a petition of bankruptcy for his client.

Judgment day had been a long time in coming, though it had seemed inevitable to those wives and friends of Mickey's familiar with his spending habits. A few days after Mickey returned from Palm Springs, Dermot Long sat him down in his office, picked up a pencil and a large lined yellow legal pad, and started to draw up a list of Mickey's debts. When Long finished, the grand total amounted to $464,914 while his assets amounted to only $500 plus clothes and household goods. These figures were pretty disheartening when one took into account that Mickey had earned more than twelve million dollars by the time he had reached the age of forty.

Seeing his debts in black and white, Mickey was stunned. It was one thing to have it in the back of your head that you owe some bills, and quite another to see it on paper: $464,914.

Panicky, Mickey asked his attorney what he should do. "Go into bankruptcy," Long advised. "It's the only thing you can do. You owe too much to too many people. I can't keep holding them off."

At first Mickey was fearful that the scandal resulting from a declaration of bankruptcy would drive the final nail into his coffin in Hollywood. How could he ever get his "price" for a film job if everyone knew he was virtually a pauper?

But after Long assured Mickey that many people declared bankruptcy and that it wasn't a disgrace, Mickey agreed that it was the only thing to do and told him to go ahead and file.

Mickey's bankruptcy made the headlines of course.

ROONEY BROKE

ROONEY UNABLE TO EXPLAIN WHERE IT ALL WENT; BLEW
TWELVE MILLION; FINANCIAL QUESTIONS STUMP MICKEY ROONEY

ROONEY CLAIMS "THE LADIES HAVE COST ME 5
MILLION DOLLARS TO DATE"

On the heels of Mickey's bankruptcy declaration, Uncle Sam stepped in and started demanding the one hundred thousand dollars in delinquent taxes he was owed by Mickey Rooney.

Mickey didn't have it to pay, but since he hadn't filed any phony forms or understated his income, the IRS didn't haul him into court. It simply did what it frequently does when dealing with celebrities who get behind with the government. It made itself a business partner of Mickey Rooney's. If not exactly a partner, at least the exchequer of his incoming funds. Under the government's rules, Mickey wasn't allowed to touch the money he earned. All his salary checks were to go directly to his attorney, Dermot Long. Long, in turn, was required to phone the man in charge of Mickey's account at the local IRS office. *He* would decide how Mickey's money should be spent. A percentage would go to pay back taxes, another percentage to cover current taxes. The remainder would be placed in an account that Dermot Long was charged with the responsibility of supervising. Checks would only be written if they were signed by Long and Mickey's latest father-in-law, Don Thomason, who was a successful furniture retailer in San Fernando Valley. For his own spending money, the government gave Mickey an allowance of two hundred dollars a month. He wasn't allowed to have his own checking or savings account, because it was obvious that he wasn't responsible enough to handle his own money. "Mickey wasn't deliberately irresponsible," says a former close business associate who wishes to remain nameless. "It was just that he always mistook his gross earnings for his real income."

Two days after Mickey's bankruptcy declaration, it was "yesterday's news," and he was his old devil-may-care self again, visiting the racetrack regularly, as well as being deeply involved in another project—getting his autobiography written with the help of Roger Kahn, one of America's leading sportswriters.

"Let me tell you how it came about," says Kahn. "I had just finished doing a piece on Jackie Cooper for *The Saturday Evening Post*, and that sort of made me an expert on people who had been child stars. So one day while I was in California—I believe it was in 1961—I got a call from an agent named Herb Jaffe, who told me he was representing Rooney. He said that Mickey wanted to do a book, and would I go meet him?

"During the meeting, Mickey gave me about a twenty-minute pitch, which was very good. His conception of his story was about a loud little guy like himself who didn't want to be loud—but who thinks well about twice a month. He was pretty eloquent, it almost sounded like a prepared speech, but nice construction for a book, however. He told me he'd gone through about twelve million dollars by then, was in bankruptcy, and not ashamed to admit it.

"Consequently, I did a little outline, and Walter Minton, who was then the head of Putnam, was interested in it. Not because Mickey was very hot here, but he was a big name in England, so it seemed that there was a big guaranteed sale to one of the English Sunday papers. Also, I think the publisher thought there would be a lot in the book about Ava and what she was like in bed.

"Anyway, they offered us fifty-five thousand dollars advance—twenty of which we were to get on signing, which we were to split fifty-fifty. But Mickey put on a poor-mouthing show, claiming he was desperate, facing bankruptcy, so we wound up letting him take a larger share of the advance than I got, out of sympathy for his position. However, we evened up down the road—exactly how, I don't remember.

"While the contracts were being drawn up, I went back East for a while. But when I came back to the Coast, to start working on the book with Mickey, he didn't want to see me. He'd gotten his share of the advance, spent it presumably, and so as far as he was concerned, that was it. He was full of excuses why he couldn't work. This literally went on for about three weeks . . . it was costing me money to be out in California not working. So finally I got fed up, went back to New York and told my agent, 'To hell with it. I'll take my expense, and give back my share of the advance.' But the publisher said, 'No, you can't do that.' He took the position that Mickey and I were business partners, and therefore I'd have to return his part of the advance as well. So now they were holding me responsible—whether it would hold up in court, I don't know. Nevertheless, I couldn't get out of this thing, so I wound up having to sue Mickey in order to get the thing going.

"Finally, my agent talked to Red Doff, or one of Mickey's people, who said I should please come back, that Mickey would cooperate and that everything would be fine. So I did and checked into the Chateau Marmont again.

"While we were working, we'd usually meet at Mickey's house in Encino on Magnolia—it was a nice house, with a beautiful lawn and grounds. We'd start around ten in the morning; often when I arrived there, Mickey would already be mixing martinis, and asking me if I wanted one. But even though we were there to write a book, Mickey didn't want to talk about his life, and unfortunately had very little to say. He didn't seem to remember. Especially about his wives. Although he did say Ava was a virgin when they were married, and that Martha Vickers was frigid. That's about all he could think of.

"In addition, Mickey was very restless. He said he couldn't work in a room because the walls 'closed in' on him. We wound up working in his car. I think it was a Corvair, or something very cheap. He was then paying about three years' back taxes.

"We were doing this thing mostly on tape, and I'd wind up having

230

to go to the track with him every day. We'd sit in the car on the way to Santa Anita, and he'd rattle on, not making too much sense when he talked. Then at the track, he'd bet, and then he'd come and borrow money from me. He was on his $200-a-month allowance that the government was letting him have at the time—that would take him to the third race. Anyway, this one time he borrowed six hundred dollars from me. When Dermot found out I loaned him that much, he said to me, 'Are you crazy?' He'll never let me pay you back.' Finally, he did repay me, but I never loaned him any more again.

"In the end I wound up having to go around Mickey to get information for the book. His mother, Nell, helped, for example. She was a tough little lady who went to the races every day too. She gave me most of the early stuff in Mickey's book—about his burlesque days . . . And she told me about his wives, most of whom she hated. I remember Nell showing me one of Mickey's canceled checks. It had a large imprint in lipstick of a girl's lips on it. She said the lips belonged to Martha Vickers. She said, 'See, the minute she married Mickey she's kissing his checks. That's all she loved about him.' Actually, Nell had a bad word for every wife.

"Dermot Long helped me, too. He was very cooperative. He thought the book had pretty big potential. He gave me all the stuff about Rooney's finances, and his mishandling of money.

"But it was very hard to get Mickey to talk without his going into a whole series of vaudeville routines, which had nothing to do with his biography. And he never let me go near any of his wives, so I never got anything from them about the marriages—only his side of it.

"But finally I had this huge mass of material, so I went back to New York, and began trying to make a book out of it, with as much verve as I could bring to it, without knowing whether any of the stuff I got from Mickey was true or just a bunch of bullshit from him."

AFTER ROGER KAHN returned to his home in New York to begin work on the first draft of what was allegedly Mickey Rooney's "true life story," the subject of that biography remained on the Coast, more idle than he was accustomed to being.

He did a little nightclub work; he made an appearance on the "Ed Sullivan Show"; and he played a little golf. But mostly, he was waiting impatiently for Bullets to bring him another film offer. While he waited, he filled in the time by playing the role of doting father and begetting still another child. He already had three children with Barbara—Kelly Ann, who was born in 1959, Kerry Yule, who was born in 1960, and Michael Joseph, who was born before he went to Palm Springs. By the spring of 1963 Barbara had conceived again. This one's due date was sometime in September. His two sons by his second wife, Mickey Rooney, Jr., and Timmy, who were seventeen and fifteen respectively, were now regular visitors to his and Barbara's new home.

Mickey Junior, who, along with his brother Timmy looked like a six-foot version of Andy Hardy, was an extremely talented guitarist—an instrument he'd been taught to play by his second stepfather, guitar virtuoso Barney Kessel—and seemed at the time to be well on his way to a career as a recording star. Timmy, on the other hand, wanted to follow in his father's acting footsteps, a career decision Mickey was encouraging. Mickey was even coaching him on the side. Teddy was still in the custody of his mother, who lived in Glendale, but was spending more and more time with his father.

From the publicity shots taken at home with his wholesome-looking and prolific wife and their brood, it would seem that Mickey had at last found domestic tranquility and happiness with Barbara Thomason.

BY EARLY SUMMER of 1963 there was activity on the business front, too. Roger Kahn had finally finished Mickey's autobiography and, despite the obstacles put in his way by his subject, believed he had written "a very decent book." *The Saturday Evening Post* also liked Kahn's first version, and offered him and Mickey $25,000 for a one-shot excerpt from it. That was a considerable sum for first serialization rights in those days, and Kahn was convinced Mickey would jump at the offer on the July afternoon he presented it to him and Dermot Long in the living room of Mickey's house in Encino.

But Mickey wasn't sure and went into the bedroom where Barbara was sprawled out on the bed, uncomfortably pregnant, and asked her what she thought of the *Post*'s offer.

"From the living room," Kahn recalls, "I could hear Barbara screaming at Mickey, 'Don't you dare take it—Cary Grant got a hundred thousand dollars from the *Post* for his story.'" Following that, according to Kahn, Mickey, and Dermot Long started doing their own negotiating with the magazine, whose managing editor finally became so fed up that he withdrew his original offer.

"Then *Look* agreed to take it in three parts for a lesser sum," Kahn continues today. "But by then, Mickey was fed up. He told me, 'I've changed my mind. I don't want the book to be published at all'—

even by Putnam, which had contracted for it. 'I'm too young to write my life story.'"

Kahn wasn't about to junk the book after investing so much time and work in it. So he returned to New York and sued Mickey for $75,000 for breach of contract.

A few weeks later, Dermot Long and Mickey's accountant, Sam Singer, went to New York and told Kahn, "We have to work this thing out. The legal fees are killing us. We'll release the book if you'll come back to California for a few days and go over the manuscript with Mickey."

Kahn said he would, for "fifteen hundred dollars a day expenses, plus first-class round-trip air fare." Long agreed to that, too, so Kahn called off the suit, returned to California, and started reading the manuscript aloud to Mickey in Dermot Long's office. "Mickey's not much of a reader, so I had to do it for him," Kahn says. "Mickey forced himself to listen for two days—I could tell from his expression he didn't like it—but then he grew restless, and I never did get to finish reading it to him; he left for someplace, probably the racetrack, and I turned the manuscript over to Long, who said he wanted to go over it. Later, after I want back to New York, he and Mickey proceeded to emasculate the manuscript, completely destroying any good writing in it, in my opinion. So after I saw what they had done, I told them to take my name off the book, took the next plane out for New York, and promised myself that never again would I write the biography of a celebrity."

When the book finally was published in December of 1965, under the title, *I.E.: An Autobiography,* Mickey's name appeared on the cover as its sole author. Judging by one review the book received from the *Los Angeles Times's* late distinguished book editor, Robert Kirsch, Roger Kahn knew what he was doing when he removed his name from the cover.

"Mickey Rooney's autobiography is written unfortunately in the language left over from a hundred Rooney scripts and interviews.

"This is a language which sounds better than it reads, filled with vaudeville gags, Andy Hardy sincerity, and the affected toughness of Baby Face Nelson. '. . . it isn't Hamlet, either,' Mickey writes. 'I'm sorry about that. I meant to write Hamlet, but somebody else beat me to it.' The Mick should have read Hamlet and let it go at that . . . It isn't that the story lacks potential. It has possibilities. Early success, disastrous marriages, bankruptcy, comeback—all the ingredients. But Rooney should never have written it. He shouldn't have, because with

233

a life like his the role becomes part of you. It takes some real perspective and writing ability to capture the dream and the nightmare of this life. This thing is soggy with sentiment, gritty with one liners. It's too bad. I think the material deserved a better writer."

In spite of the fact that Mickey and Dermot Long were the last people to have a hand in the book's editing, Mickey renounced its authorship after the generally bad reception it got, along with disappointing sales. "I didn't say those things, I did it for money—I was broke," he told George Colt, a writer for *The New York Times* entertainment section some years later.

Luckily for Mickey, books weren't his business. Show-business was. Bullets Durgom brought Mickey another picture offer. Roger Corman wanted Mickey to play one of the leading roles in *The Secret Invasion,* an adventure picture that the Corman Brothers were going to shoot in Yugoslavia in September. It was a small-budget action film, to be made for around five hundred thousand dollars, but Bullets managed to get Mickey $50,000 ($25,000 deferred), to play the part of an Irish resistance leader.

In addition, the ABC television network was showing interest in doing a TV series with Mickey as a result of the work he had done in *It's a Mad, Mad, Mad, Mad World.*

The critics weren't exactly overwhelmed by the concept of *Mad, Mad, Mad World* when it opened in 1963. Dwight MacDonald wrote "To watch on a Cinerama screen in full color a small army of actors inflict mayhem on each other with cars, planes, explosives, and other devices for more than three hours with stereophonic sound effects is simply too much for the human eye and ear to respond to, let alone the funny bone."

One thing everyone agreed on was that Mickey Rooney was very, very funny. In fact, *The New York Times*'s Bosley Crowther wrote, "one of the film's high points is when Mr. Hackett and Mr. Rooney are caught aloft in a plane in which they have to fly to an airfield when its pilot, Jim Backus, passes out."

But now it's time for Mickey and me to cross paths again, for the first time since we were teenagers.

20

I LEARNED FIRSTHAND of ABC's interest in doing a series with Mickey when my TV collaborator, Robert Fisher, phoned me in mid-July and said that our agents had got us an assignment to create, write, and produce a TV pilot for Selig Seligman, who had his own production company at ABC.

We had neither an idea nor a star in mind when we met with Seligman a few days later in his office at the American Broadcasting Studios. The only thing we knew was that, rather than write in the dark for an unknown star, it was better to have one in mind before we sat down at our desks to come up with a series idea. Seligman told us that the network had Mickey Rooney tied up and asked if we would be interested in creating a series for him.

We weren't that wild about using Mickey Rooney for in addition to feeling he was a little shopworn, we didn't think he'd be an easy sale on Madison Avenue, although we both felt that he was tremendously talented. Seligman, however, was high on Mickey and believed he could be sold in the "right vehicle." He suggested that we set up a meeting with Mickey as soon as possible, and he gave us a phone number where he could be reached.

A youngish-sounding man who said he was Bill Gardner, Mickey's personal secretary, answered our call.* After finding out what our business was, Gardner said he'd have to check with Mickey and get

---

*I later learned that this was the same Bill Gardner who had introduced Mickey to Barbara. Gardner was not a secretary by profession—but after Mickey and Barbara had been married a few months, he states, "I got a call from her saying I'd better come over and help out—Mickey's affairs were in a mess. So I said I would, for a few weeks, and I stayed six years."

back to us. Which he did, almost immediately, with instructions to meet Mickey in Rehearsal Hall 6 at CBS on Fairfax and Beverly Boulevard on Saturday morning at eleven o'clock. He was rehearsing to be on the "Judy Garland Show" and that was the only time he could talk with us.

When we arrived in the rehearsal hall, on the second floor of The Big Eye at Fairfax and Beverly Boulevard, Mickey, in slacks, a polo shirt, and tennis shoes, was rehearsing a dance number with three cute six year-old girls. To our disappointment, Judy Garland was nowhere in sight. I later learned she never came in before one in the afternoon, no matter how urgent the rehearsal, because she couldn't pull herself together before then.

We introduced ourselves to Mickey, who didn't remember me at all, and while the dance director continued to rehearse the kids, the three of us sat down on a bench in a quiet corner, and Bob and I told him our concept of a TV series for him.

The concept was very simple. We felt it should be a family show, with the father, played by Mickey, being an entertainer not unlike himself. That way we could get the fun of a family situation comedy, and also capitalize on Mickey's ability as an entertainer. It was the same format as the Danny Thomas show, which my collaborator favored, since he had written "Make Room For Daddy" in its first two years.

Mickey wasn't wild about that idea at all. And when we asked him why, he replied, "Because I think the Danny Thmas show was nothing."

After that, we kicked around a couple of other ideas, got nowhere with them, and finally, because Mickey was getting restless—you can't hold his attention more than ten minutes—we circled back to the Danny Thomas idea, which Mickey finally said "yes" to. At least, he said to put it down in outline form so he could see what it looked like on paper.

Before we could commit the idea to paper, we were called to a meeting at ABC with Seligman and Rooney, who informed us that he had come up with an idea himself that he preferred. In this conception, Mickey Rooney would be running a theatrical talent school. Obviously he had reached down into his memory bag for this one and had come up with Ma Lawlor's professional school that he and Judy and Dick Quine had attended when they were kids. We weren't too thrilled with this idea, feeling it was "old hat," but because it was Mickey's brainchild and he was enthusiastic about it—partly because Mickey would get part of the creator's percentage of the profits—Seligman more or less ordered us to play along with him. Obviously Seligman was afraid of losing Mickey if we didn't kowtow to him, so we agreed to try that format and promised to come up with a story line for the pilot script.

After we did, Seligman put his stamp of approval on it, and we were told to show it to Mickey.

By then it was mid-August, and Mickey was over at MGM shooting a "Twilight Zone" for Rod Serling. The episode was called "Tip on a Dead Jockey," and Mickey was the only actor in it. It was a real tour de force for him, and won him plaudits from the critics when it appeared on the air the following fall.

Mickey read our outline between takes and was so enthusiastic about the comedy bits we'd come up with that he went around telling them to the director, the stagehands, the cameraman, and anyone else he could buttonhole, including Judy Garland, who had just made a surprise visit to the "Twilight Zone" set.

While we were writing the pilot script, Mickey left for Yugoslavia to work in *The Secret Invasion,* the story of how five seasoned criminals were taken out of various prisons around the world and put together for the purpose of liberating an Italian general. Bullets Durgom, Bill Gardner, and Barbara Rooney, who was eight months pregnant with her fourth child, accompanied Mickey to Dubrovnik, leaving the other three children at home with a governess in their house in Encino.

Mickey played the role of an Irish resistance leader, and though he was not the star of the film, "Mickey brought a dimension to his role that was not in the script, and made the whole thing work," Gene Corman adds today. "Mickey was very good and so funny. Time and time again in the dailies I watched his ability to reach into a grab bag of comedy bits that he had done through his whole life, to make the character come alive. The picture only cost $500,000 but it made a bundle. And the critics liked it. Even today they're saying that *The Dirty Dozen* was just an expensive remake of our picture."

BECAUSE HER FOURTH child was scheduled to be born by cesarean section and she wanted her own doctor to perform the operation, Barbara kissed Mickey goodbye in early September and flew back to the States. She was admitted to Santa Monica hospital on the afternoon of September 12, and Kimmy Sue Rooney was born the following morning.

Mickey had two surprises in store when he returned to the States a few days later: his new baby; and the pilot script that Bob and I had written for him in his absence. Bob and I were worried about his reaction to our script. Not so much because we were aware of how critical Mickey could be of material—we believed we'd done a good job on the script, and were pleased with it—but because it was no longer about an acting school.

While Mickey had been in Yugoslavia, Seligman and ABC had got cold feet about the acting school idea, believing that the average TV viewer would not be able to identify with it, and paid us to write a second script. This one was set in Marina del Rey, and had Mickey playing a Midwestern family man who had inherited a motel on the harbor front, and who pulled up roots and moved West with his family to run it. The idea was about as far from an acting school as you could possibly get, and there was no telling how anyone as mercurial as Mickey, and with his hair-trigger temper, would react to the switch.

But when our executive producer Selig Seligman handed Mickey the script, along with the news of the change in locale, Mickey didn't bat an eye. He said he understood perfectly ABC's reasoning, and after a perfunctory reading, during which he reread some of the best jokes aloud and laughed it up at all the block comedy scenes, he gave our creation his approval.

And why not? If the pilot sold, he was to get $5,000 a show for a guaranteed twenty-three shows, $115,000 all told.

Mickey had only one suggestion. That a part be written into the script for his close friend and partner in his nightclub act, Bobby Van, who had taken the place of Joey Forman in his affections. As in his first series, he wanted a sidekick to bounce comedy off. He also had another request—that the part of the teenaged daughter be changed to a son, so that he could put his son Timmy in the role.

"Can he act?" Seligman asked.

"Yeah, I've been working with him," Mickey said. "He's pretty good."

Seligman acquiesced on both counts. It was no problem switching the daughter's role to fit Timmy, since it was just a small part in the pilot script anyway. But inserting a Bobby Van character did present a problem because the script was pretty tight and ready to be shot. In addition, there wasn't time to do any major rewriting because Seligman wanted to get the pilot film shot, edited, and on the market by January at the latest. That was the time networks and sponsors did their buying for the following fall. Since it was already mid-October and half of the pilot would have to be filmed on location at a marina in Newport, we had to go into production within the next two weeks to meet that schedule.

Since there's no shortage of actors or actresses in Hollywood, we had no trouble casting the parts. And when Richard Whorf, who had directed "The Beverly Hill Billies" for several successful years, said he wanted to do our pilot, everyone was convinced we had a hit.

Bob and I had never worked with Mickey before, but we knew he had a reputation, once he got his teeth into a project for wanting to take charge—from the writing to the directing, producing, editing, and even the publicity. But during the making of "Mickey," which was the only series title all of us geniuses could come up with, Mickey was pretty amenable, and his suggestions for improving a scene were usually very helpful. In one sequence, which was filmed on location in Newport Beach, he was supposed to escape from a rich woman's yacht—where she (played by Dina Merrill, the Post Toasties heiress) had stolen his clothes and tried to seduce him—in nothing but a short fur coat he had taken from her closet. He then rowed ashore in a dinghy and made his escape—as unobtrusively as possible—through the streets of Newport. On paper there wasn't much more to the scene than I have just described, but when Mickey finished putting his own comedy bits into it, including a confrontation with a funny cop (played by Peter Leeds, his straight man in *Sugar Babies*) who thought he was an escapee from a mental hospital, it was hilarious. He even had the staid Newporters, who had come from their luxurious waterfront homes to watch, in hysterics, as he ad-libbed and mugged his way down the town's main drag in the middle of the night.

That week Mickey also demonstrated his skill as a director in a scene involving Dina Merrill. It was the "seduction" scene, in which Dina wore a padded bra beneath her swimsuit. Dina didn't seem to understand what she was supposed to do with her built-up bosom to make the scene funny. At a critical point, when Mickey and Dina were snuggled up together on a couch on the fantail of her yacht, she was supposed to say:

"Mickey, it's such a beautiful, clear moonlit night. You can even see the Big Dipper."

As he asked, "Where?" she was supposed to twist around in her seat and point it out, while simultaneously thrusting her bosom right up under Mickey's nose.

However, Dina didn't seem to understand that "Big Dipper" was a double entendre, and consequently sat very straight and reserved as she spoke the line and pointed to the sky.

239

Moreover, because in person Dina presented a very dignified facade, Dick Whorf seemed afraid to be very explicit with her when he explained the scene. He intimated the joke but didn't actually spell it out.

Finally Mickey piped up impatiently. "Hey, Dick, what's the use of beating around the bush with this? We'll be here all day. Let *me* tell her."

Then turning to Dina, he put his arm around her bare shoulder, and said, "Look, Dina. The idea of this scene is very simple. When you say, 'Big Dipper,' you're supposed to shove your clydes in my face!" At which point he pulled her closer and buried his nose in her bosom.

"By George, I've got it!" Dina exclaimed with an amused giggle.

She did the scene perfectly.

There was only one hint of things to come. One day while I was standing outside the open door to Mickey's dressing room on the Paramount lot, I overheard a conversation between him and Dina. I don't remember the exact dialogue, but the gist of the conversation was that she was overwhelmed at Mickey's ability to do a scene without studying it at home the night before.

"It's easy," Mickey said. "I never do a scene the way the writers write it. I just glance down the page and get the gist of it, and make up my own words. I just use the script as a blueprint."

There's something to be said for extemporaneous acting, of course. Lots of performers make up their own lines and get away with it. But it also presents problems. The other actors in the scene don't get the proper cue lines, and if a joke isn't worded correctly, the rhythm is thrown off, and it won't get a laugh.

In the case of our pilot, however, what Mickey added far outweighed what he took away by destroying a couple of jokes.

On December 6, we had a running of the completed pilot at Consolidated Lab in Hollywood for everyone connected with the show—producers, the director, the actors and wives, including Mickey's lovely wife, Barbara, whom we had first met when we were on location at Newport. Mickey was his own best audience that afternoon, loudly guffawing at his performance, sometimes to the extent of actually rolling into the aisle of the projection room.

When the lights came up, the audience burst into applause and insisted that Mickey take a bow. Which he did. But following that he did something I've rarely heard a star do, except when accepting an Academy Award. He said, "Thanks, very much, but Bob and Arthur deserve the real credit for having done such a fine job of writing and producing."

With a star like that, Bob and I felt we could look forward to a long and fruitful relationship as Mickey's writers-producers. But first, of course, we had to get on the air.

The first step was for Seligman to take the completed pilot to New York and show it to Tom Moore and Ed Sherrick, ABC president and vice president respectively. He did that the first week in January, and when he returned he informed us that the network had "slotted" our show into their schedule on Monday night at eight o'clock. Evidently, it was well received. Now all we needed to nail down that spot permanently was a sponsor.

When we didn't find one in the next two months, we were told that the network was having trouble selling Mickey Rooney to the Madison Avenue boys because of our star's "bad image." What they were referring to specifically were his five marriages, the fact that his first child with Barbara had been conceived out of wedlock—which had been all over the papers—the Jack Paar incident, and a number of other headline-making antics, including the fact that Mickey's name had turned up in a call girl's little black book of customers during a trial in New York City in which a young playboy heir to a food industry fortune was being investigated for "procuring." (This lurid tale—and I use the word advisedly—had surfaced while Mickey was still married to Elaine. At that time Mickey admitted knowing the girl but claimed he had only "taken her to dinner.")

Another drawback to the sale of our pilot was that potential sponsors considered "Mickey" too sexy for family audiences because of the "Big Dipper" scene and the fact that we had too many pretty girls in bikinis lounging around the pool at the motel.

When the show hadn't sold by March 31, we were sure it was dead, because on April 1 ABC had to guarantee Mickey $100,000, or lose him. And losing him was a possibility, for Mickey was chomping at the bit to take a part in the new Jack Lemmon-Tony Curtis film, *The Great Race*.

On April 1, however, we received word that ABC was ordering eighteen shows and that we would be put on the air Friday nights at nine o'clock, sustaining. We didn't have a sponsor yet, but ABC had an opening in their schedule at that time because a show they had been counting on, a Rod Serling series, had fallen out. We would get his spot, and they'd worry about a sponsor later.

That was a lucky break, we thought, for there was nothing on the other networks at that time that could be considered serious competition to a Mickey Rooney series. Unfortunately, no network schedule is ever carved in stone. After we had written three scripts for the series, we were informed that ABC had scheduled another series for Friday night at nine and that they were switching us to Wednesday at nine, opposite Dick Van Dyke and Mary Tyler Moore on CBS, and the NBC "Movie of the Week" on the other major network.

Everyone felt it would be disastrous to put a new show like ours up against the most successful series in the country. What could ABC be thinking of? Later we discovered there were some network politics behind the move. A high ABC official liked another show better than ours and simply decided to give it the preferred time slot. At the time, however, we just attributed the switch in schedule to bad luck and, like most dreamers, told ourselves that if we turned out a really good series, it wouldn't matter who our competition was.

Mickey was full of confidence, too. He was also happy that he had just been relieved of a tremendous financial burden. Coming into 1964, Mickey had owed the government ninety-one thousand dollars in back taxes. This was one debt Mickey couldn't get rid of when his bankruptcy hearing had come to trial the previous summer. But thanks to Dermot Long, he was able to go to court in April of 1964 and get Superior Court Judge Ben Koenig to break the irrevocable trust fund that had been set up for him by Martin Gang when he was a child star. By April 1, 1964, the money in his trust totaled approximately $126,000. Under the terms of the trust, Mickey wouldn't be entitled to it until he was sixty years old. However, when Long pointed out to the judge that the interest Mickey was getting from the principle was considerably less than the 6 percent the government was charging him for his tax indebtedness, and furthermore that the larger interest would practically double his tax indebtedness, thereby wiping out the principle by the time he reached sixty, the judge felt sorry for Mickey and agreed to let him take $100,371 from his trust fund.

As a result, Mickey was able to pay off Uncle Sam, and still have seven thousand dollars left over to help him swing another real estate deal.

Because Barbara didn't like living in the San Fernando Valley, away from Beverly Hills, and Mickey was going to have to start shooting the "Mickey" series at MGM in Culver City, now that ABC had scheduled the show, Mickey traded the house on Magnolia for one closer to Culver City. This one, a Mediterranean villa, stood at

242

1100 Tower Road, in Beverly Hills, just a few blocks north of the Beverly Hills Hotel. Bill Gardner, Mickey's gallant man Friday, helped his boss swing the deal, which was no small feat considering that Mickey was technically in a state of "bankruptcy."

"Somehow I managed it," Bill Gardner says, who as an afterthought told me, "You know, Mickey did wonders to keep the real estate market active in those days. I don't think there was a house in the Valley that they showed that they couldn't say, 'Mickey Rooney lived here.'"

AS SOON AS we learned that we were on the network schedule, drop-dead time slot or not, Bob and I phoned Mickey to congratulate him. We also wanted to ask him if he cared to meet with us and kick around a few story ideas before we started writing the rest of the scripts. But he was either out of town or at the racetrack, I've forgotten which. We left word that we had called, but he never phoned back. As a result, we went ahead without his input and started writing as many scripts as we could before the series went into production in July.

We didn't hear anything more from Mickey until we'd written five scripts, and they'd been approved by the network. As we were about to quit work one day, we got an angry call from Bullets Durgom telling us that Mickey was "sore as hell" at us for not telling him any of our script ideas before we committed them to paper. We told Bullets that we had tried to include Mickey, but he seemed uninterested in getting together with us. But Bullets, normally an easy-going man, continued to berate us for neglecting a star of Mickey's stature and insisted that we set up a meeting with Mickey immediately so we could read him—or at least tell him—our story ideas.

Consequently, we showed up at Bullets's high-rise office on the Sunset Strip the following day with our first five scripts under our arms. We were full of trepidation about whether Mickey would, in his anger, dislike all of the scripts and throw them out, and maybe us too. When we arrived, Mickey was already there, sitting in a leather chair in front of Bullets's desk. He showed not the slightest sign of being a temperamental star. He was friendly and charming and, surprisingly, showed only a perfunctory interest when we told him we were there to get his approval of the scripts we'd written so far.

We handed him the first script, which had to do with his taking his kids on a Cub Scout overnight hike, but he handed it back to us and said we should just tell him the idea. So we gave him a thumbnail synopsis, after which we started to tell him the story line of the

243

second script. Halfway through he stopped us and told us an idea he had for a feature film, to star himself, which he claimed Walter Mirisch was interested in producing, if he could get someone to write the screenplay. Would we write it for him? For nothing up front, of course.

Aside from the fact that it wasn't much of an idea and we had no intention of writing a movie script for Mickey on spec, we didn't have time to take on additional writing. So as diplomatically as possible we told him we couldn't do justice to writing and producing his series if we also took on the movie script.

"Okay," he said, and we resumed telling him the story of our second script. We had barely reached the basic premise, when Mickey glanced impatiently at his watch, and announced that he had just a half hour to get to the first race at Hollywood Park. Then he borrowed some cash from Bullets, told us again what good work we were doing, and hurried out of the office.

After the door had closed, we asked Bullets why he had sounded so angry with us on the phone the night before, if Mickey weren't any more interested in the scripts than his behavior seemed to indicate.

"Mickey was standing right beside me," Bullets explained, with a sheepish smile. "And he was insisting that I chew you guys out for not showing him the scripts, or he'd fire me!"

"Why did he care then if he doesn't care now?" I asked.

Bullets shrugged and replied wearily, "That's Mickey, fellahs."

Well, we learned one thing from that meeting. If we didn't want to have long story conferences with Mickey we should always schedule them before the first race.

THERE WERE A number of minor crises before "Mickey" reached the public. I jotted down some of them in a journal I kept that summer. What follows are a few excerpts:

JULY 3. Had reading of first show, the Cub Scout one, today. We had it on the permanent motel set we have on Stage 16. Mickey was good and had only one request—that we not use live trout in the sequence where we pull him out of the lake in his sleeping bag and a dozen live trout fall out with him. "I may be crazy," he said, "but I can't stand the thought of those trout being killed if they're not going to be eaten."

"Okay, we'll eat them," Dick Whorf said jokingly after a lot of back-and-forth dialogue concerning whether or not if we used phony trout they would look phony on the screen.

Mickey wouldn't buy that, so we had to promise to use rubber trout, and Mickey left for a July 4 vaudeville date in the East, happy that he'd saved the lives of a few fish.

JULY 7. First day of shooting. No problems except that Mickey refused to wear the toupee the ABC brass insisted that he wear in order to look younger. We paid Max Factor three hundred dollars for it, but after Mickey put it on, he looked in the mirror and said, "That's not the Mickey Rooney I know." Then he went around the set asking everyone from the grips to the script girl, "Do I need this?" Knowing that's what he wanted to hear they all obsequiously said that he looked young without it, so he refused to wear it. He said he'd wear a hat instead to cover his bald spot. "Even indoors?" I asked. "Yeah, I'll keep my yachting cap on all the time. This is a marina I'm running, isn't it. Lots of yachtsmen keep their caps on indoors."

JULY 17. Today we got our daily call from Bullets. This time he informed us that Mickey doesn't want to attend any more readings. He feels it's a waste of time. I couldn't argue with that. At most of the readings Mickey has attended so far, he sits there with a racing form on his lap and a transistor radio on the table in front of him blaring out the latest results from the track. It's no wonder Mickey is surprised when he gets on the set and starts changing all the dialogue and pieces of business.

JULY 27. Bumped into Dick Whorf in the commissary this noon and asked him how the morning's shooting had gone. "Slow," replied Dick wearily. "Mickey's got a bug up his ass about building a theater-in-the-round in the Valley. He couldn't keep his mind on the script. He kept talking about the theater and how to raise money for its construction. He even had me draw a mock-up of it for him between setups. Said he had a great idea for the opening show. He and Judy would play *Girl Crazy.*

The trouble with Mickey Rooney, I decided, was that Mickey couldn't keep his mind on the main job at hand. He treats our series as if it's only a sideline.

JULY 28. Got to the set on Lot 3 early, on a hunch that the army camp sequence wasn't going well. And I was right. I found that when they were rehearsing it, Mickey was leaving out one of the best jokes in the script.

245

The sergeant in charge of the young recruits was supposed to say, "Strange that Schwartzkopf went over the hill. The recruits don't usually do that until after they've tasted the food here." When I asked Dick Whorf why Mickey wasn't doing the joke, he said that Mickey didn't want to shoot it because he didn't think we should insult the army's cooking.

JULY 29. Saw a real nice side of Mickey today. During a scene between him and an eighty-three-year-old character actress named Katherine Minner, she kept going up in her lines. Every time she said her line wrong, Mickey'd purposely say his line wrong, too. Then he'd hold up his hand to stop the camera and say, "Sorry, Dick. I fluffed. Let's try it again." Finally, he calmed her down enough to do the scene.

Mickey is also very helpful about giving his son Timmy acting tips. Timmy's not the greatest actor in the world, but with Mickey's coaching, he gets the right timing and seems almost natural. Apparently they have a very good relationship.

AUGUST 7. Bobby Van, whom we'd written into the series, showed up for his first day's shooting an hour late, claiming his alarm clock didn't go off. Well, the part of a lazy brother-in-law that we wrote for him certainly seems to fit today.

While we were waiting for Van to arrive, Mickey cornered us and started to tell a story for a script he wanted to write. "And I've got a great title for it," he said enthusiastically. "The Big Snatch!"

When we told him he couldn't get away with a title like that, he looked annoyed and said, "What's dirty about it? It's about a kidnapping. You guys just have dirty minds."

AUGUST 18. As I feared from Mickey's reputation, he s beginning to take over the writing and direction, when we're not constantly on the set. In the Cub Scout show, for example, he took out a piece of business that provided the motivation for why the electric hospital bed he's in suddenly tilts upward, causing him to slide out the window. When we told him it didn't make sense unless you knew that someone had short-circuited the electric motor, causing it to go berserk, he said, "Who cares? What's funny is that the bed did tilt up. No one has to know why. Who needs motivation in comedy?"

In this week's show, that has to do with an elephant that water skiis (we actually found one, which is why we wrote him into the script), Mickey's going wild with changes again. The idea of the show is that Mickey sees an elephant go by on water skiis in the marina. As a result, Mickey thinks he's seeing things and goes to an eye doctor, who assures him he's all right. When he's coming back from the doctor's, Mickey sees in the distance an elephant walk by pushing a baby carriage with a human infant in it. Again Mickey thinks he's seeing things. It's an old formula, but it works—until you start monkeying around with the mechanics of it. Mickey had put two elephants into the same scene—also using the spare animal that the trainer had brought along in case something happened to elephant number one. Mickey had moved the elephants within touching distance of where he was standing, when he spotted them in the scene. When we asked him why, he said he wanted to be able to see the elephants up close. They're funnier in a close up. Then we pointed out that if he could reach out and touch the elephants and also smell them (and boy did they smell), he would no longer be able to question his eyesight. So we might as well throw the whole script out the window because there was no motivation for anything. Mickey's reply to that was: "Who cares? Two elephants are funnier than one."

Furthermore, Mickey didn't want to admit he was wrong because his wife, Barbara, was on the set, watching, and he was showing off for her. He said to me, "Your way is okay for a Cary Grant picture, but this isn't that." Evidently he was trying to tell us that our brand of comedy was too subtle for Mickey Rooney. A water-skiing elephant subtle! Come on now.

Between Whorf, Bob, and me, we managed to wear Mickey down and get our way, but it took all morning convincing him (when we should have been in our office writing), and Mickey sulked through the rest of the water-skiing elephant segment.

AUGUST 26. Nothing but trouble from Mickey all day today . . . Little things he didn't feel like doing or saying he would argue about . . .

AUGUST 27. Another day of quelling minor rebellions on the set. These things are keeping us so busy that we finally had to give in and start hiring outside writers. Because between our production chores and trying to keep Mickey reasonably close to the scripts, we have no time to be writers.

AUGUST 28. While I was on our motel set late this afternoon between takes, I saw Mickey engage in a little group singing with some of the permanent extras on our set (these were people who are supposed to be residents of Mickey's motel). Although Mickey had complained earlier he was too tired to shoot any more today, he seemed to be full of life now, and paying particular attention to a very pretty young girl—kind of a Sophia Loren type—and showing off for her. When I asked Bobby Van where she had come from, since I didn't remember hiring her, he said that she was an ex-stripper, and that she was Mickey's latest girlfriend, and he'd put her on. He'd met her, according to Van, when he'd gone to Atlantic City over the Fourth of July, and brought her back out to be a permanent extra on our set.

AUGUST 31. Got a memo from Adrian Sammish, the ABC coordinator, evaluating the results of the ASI [Audience Sample Information] tests on two of our completed shows. The audiences we showed them to seemed to like them all right, but felt that Mickey was doing too much mugging. Could we please do something about it? That's a good one! Sammish is a laugh a minute.

SEPTEMBER 8. Shot car-wash sequence today, at real car wash, at Venice and Sepulveda. When we arrived at eight o'clock, Mickey was already in the midst of changing the action and the dialogue, and giving most of the best lines to himself. Bobby Van and Alan Reed took me aside and said they wished he wouldn't take lines away from them.

Later he made up for it by improving the car-wash sequence. The way we had written it, Mickey was supposed to go through the car wash in his car with the top down. But Mickey suggested he be out of the car and get his foot stuck in the conveyor chain and have to go through the wash on his own two feet. We admitted it would be funnier, but didn't think he'd want to take the chance of getting batted around by all those revolving brushes. But he did, although he nearly choked on the detergent as he went through the wash.

SEPTEMBER 14. Two days from D-day. When I phoned the set at nine o'clock, Harry Hogan, our associate producer, informed me that Mickey hadn't shown for his call yet. According to what he'd been able to gather from Bill Gardner, who had phoned Hogan, Mickey was having "wife trouble," and was still at home "having it out with Barbara." Around ten, Mickey and Gardner arrived. While Mickey slipped into his dressing room, Gardner took us aside and said that Barbara Rooney had found out about Mickey's new girlfriend and that the situation was very serious. Mickey and Barbara had mentioned calling in lawyers. Just what our show needs—a divorce announcement two days before we go on the air with a family situation comedy. "Why does he do this?" we asked Gardner. "He can't afford another divorce, either emotionally or financially."

Somehow, Mickey got through the rest of the day's shooting, but at five o'clock, when we were supposed to have a reading for next week's show, he said, "You'll excuse me if I don't read. But I've got a lot of *tsouris* at home."

"Well, I hope you get it straightened out," I said.

"Don't worry," Mickey said grimly, "I'll get it straightened out one way or the other."

"Don't worry about Mickey," Bobby Van said. "I've been through this hundreds of times before. He has to have a broad on the side, or he's just not happy."

Happy?

SEPTEMBER 17. Our show went on the air last night and was well received. The reviews were generally good and so were the ratings. We got a thirty-five percent share of the audience, as much as Cary Grant on NBC in *To Catch a Thief*. Fortunately, Dick Van Dyke and Mary Tyler Moore are not starting their show until next Wednesday. Our strong rating against Cary Grant bodes well for the future, however.

Mickey was upset. Because we didn't have a regular sponsor, there was room in our show for a one-minute paid political announcement by the Johnson for President Committee. Mickey is a Goldwater man, and even has a Goldwater sticker on his car bumper. When he saw the Johnson plug in one of our commercial spots, he was so furious that he phoned in this morning and refused to come to work. He said we had no business being political on our show. We were liable to offend all the Goldwater people and lose half our audience. After he heard about the reviews and the strong overnight ratings, he changed his mind.

TUESDAY, SEPTEMBER 22. After taking a long weekend, Mickey showed up for work on the MGM back lot this morning, an hour late and in a ugly mood. To get his mind off whatever was troubling him, I asked if he'd had a nice weekend.

"Any weekend's nice when you can spend it away from home," snapped Mickey.

"Kids can be a drag sometime," I commented.

"Kids, hell!" Mickey exclaimed. "It's my wife. I can't stand her, and she can't stand me. She's not even interested in my show any more."

Later, Bobby Van explained that Mickey had spent the weekend in Palm Springs with Peter Lawford, another fellow, and three high-priced young ladies at a friend's house—and that Barbara had found out about it.

AS THE TV season progressed and we steadily lost ground in the ratings race to the Dick Van Dyke Show, Mickey became extremely worried and started meddling more and more in the writing and directing. One morning when I criticized him for changing the ending of one of our scripts to something that he had just ad-libbed, Mickey became very sarcastic. "After all, these scripts aren't the Bible," he shouted in front of cast and crew in an effort to embarrass us. "It isn't sacrilegious to change your lines, is it?"

Whenever Mickey got like that, we found it simpler just to walk away and let him deal with it. Sometimes his own guilt would force him to return to the way it was written in the script. Sometimes it wouldn't. But either way, he was not going to be *told* what to do.

As if Mickey wasn't having enough trouble that fall between Barbara and the ratings, the past popped up to haunt him. On September 29, Timmy's mother served Mickey with a legal paper demanding twenty-five thousand dollars in back child support and alimony. And if that didn't put him in a dark enough mood, he saw in *Variety* on October 6 that "Mickey" wasn't listed in the first fifty popular television shows. That was just two weeks before option time, when ABC would have to make up its mind whether or not to drop us after we had seventeen shows in the can, or to try to hang in there for the full twenty-three.

To add fuel to Mickey's generally bad humor, he discovered that the show of ours that ABC had decided to air that night was one of his least favorite—one he had fought us and the director on tooth and nail all during the shooting.

"ABC is fucking me," he moaned. "They've fucked me about the music, our titles. They fucked me on our time slot. And now that we have a chance to get an audience, they throw in the wrong show and fuck me again."

It was a segment called "Children" and, strangely enough, in everyone's opinion but Mickey's it was the best we had shot to date. When we told Mickey this, he said, "Okay, show it to me." So we took him into a projection room that afternoon and ran it for him. Afterward, he said, "I have to admit I made a mistake, boys. It's charming." He was almost ready to resume shooting, which he had interrupted with his tirade, when he got into a fight over the phone with Barbara. This slowed things up for another two hours, which prompted us to call Seligman and ask him if he would phone Mickey and try to soothe him with some encouraging words about the fate of our show. But Seligman didn't even want to bother with Mickey. He said he didn't like the script we had just turned in and neither did the ABC brass. Moreover, they hated the last two shows of ours that they had seen.

It looked like curtains for Mickey's second series, especially after we read an announcement in *Variety* by Tom Moore, listing our show as one of several that were in trouble and would probably be canceled if the ratings didn't improve.

They did improve in next week's "overnight"—we actually beat out the "Dick Van Dyke Show" by a narrow margin. We were further encouraged by a poll that showed that Sammy Tong, the Chinese actor who played Mickey's handyman, had a bigger following than Mickey Rooney on TV because of his popularity on "Bachelor Father." As a result, ABC was considering picking us up for the last six shows. Their thinking was that we might catch on due to Sammy Tong's presence in the cast—especially if we would start building up his part in the series.

Accordingly, everyone but Mickey Rooney was pretty sanguine about the show's future when we wrapped the last sequence of the seventeenth show on October 22, and celebrated by having a "wrap" party prior to our taking a two-week hiatus while waiting for the "pickup."

Mickey was in one of his darker moods, however, and made a speech at the beginning of the party that was reminiscent of George Washington's "farewell to his troops." Waxing very dramatic, Mickey thanked everyone—the cast, the crew, the director, the extras, and even the writers, for the hard work they'd put in. "But it's hopeless," he added, predicting that because of the network's stupidity we probably wouldn't get picked up for the rest of the season. From this tone, you'd have thought he was burying his best friend. Mickey's sense of defeat was contagious, and by the time he finished, he had everyone on the set in tears.

Bob and I continued to work over the hiatus, for there were scripts to be written and rough cuts to be dubbed and edited for the final print. We still hadn't heard any word of a pickup from Seligman, but remembering what we had heard about Sammy Tong's popularity, we chose to be optimistic.

About eleven o'clock, on October 27, Harry Hogan phoned us and said, "I have bad news, fellahs. Sammy Tong is dead. He took an overdose."

According to Harry, who was the only one aware of it, Sammy had been an incurable gambler and owed a fortune to the Las Vegas and Reno mobs at the time of our hiatus. After hearing Mickey predict at the wrap party that the show would not be picked up,

Sammy apparently saw no possibility of ever being able to pay back his debts, and in a fit of depression took his life.

That was not only the coup de grace for Sammy, but for Mickey's second attempt at a TV series as well.

On November 12, the headline in *Variety* read: ABC AXES MICKEY.

Three days later, Seligman phoned us and said he'd just been informed by Adrian Sammish that ABC would have picked up our option if Sammy had been able to continue in the series. But with him gone, they figured, what was the use?

21

M IRACULOUSLY, MICKEY AND Barbara's marriage hung together, if only by a thread, for almost another year. No doubt this was due to the fact that Mickey was home so little during that period that they had few opportunities to get on each other's nerves.

Although it was a blow to Mickey to lose another series, he could take heart in the fact that it had nothing to do with his own talent, for his reviews had been generally good. Instead, so his thinking went, it was the network's fault for putting his show in such an untenable time slot. As a result he bounced right back up off the canvas and in November flew with Bill Gardner to Beirut, Lebanon, to costar with Lex Barker in *24 Hours to Kill*, a Seven Arts-Warner Bros., low-budget, action-adventure story that saw very little action at the box office when it was released in 1965. But the pay was good, and Beirut had a racetrack with "wonderful Arabian ponies running on it," remembers Gardner. Mickey even came out ahead.

When Mickey returned to Southern California in February, Bullets greeted him with the good news that he had just set him to star in a film for Aubrey Schenck, *Ambush Bay*, a World War II story to be shot in the Philippines the following fall. Mickey was to receive good money for that one, too—but not until it went into production. So Mickey did a little agenting of his own.

"One day I picked up a trade paper," says Bullets, "and read that Mickey was back doing a beach picture behind my back. I think it was *How to Stuff a Wild Bikini*. So I called up his house and asked for Mickey. And Barbara said he wasn't there—he was out at the beach shooting a picture. So I said 'Why did he do that?' and

Barbara said, 'Well, he was offered five thousand for a week's work, so he took it.' So I found Mickey and I said, 'Mick, it's no use. It's not worth it to me or you. I can't keep working to keep your price up, when you keep taking these lousy little beach pictures for a thousand or two a shot. 'But I can use the money,' Mick protested. 'I'd rather loan it to you,' I told him. But I just couldn't get him to understand. So I told him it was over, that I quit."

The following day Mickey bestowed on Red Doff the dubious honor of becoming his personal manager again.

To fill in the time and keep food on the table before going to the Philippines to shoot *Ambush Bay*, Mickey took his nightclub act, with Bobby Van, on the road. Mickey was still getting $17,000 a week for his nightclub appearances and usually managed to fill the room with his clowning. Mickey could always rely on the staples of his act—his singing, dancing, and imitations—to keep the audience entertained, but the bit that sent them rolling in the aisles was his "Look in the moose" routine, a burlesque of a "Candid Camera" producer (Mickey) trying to get a salesman (Bobby Van) in a sporting goods store to look into the camera, which was hidden in the moose's mouth. Unaware he was being filmed, Van kept looking everywhere but into the lens, prompting Mickey to yell, in ever-increasing volume, "Look in the moose!" until he was finally screaming it at the top of his powerful lungs.

Mickey's home life with Barbara was deteriorating rapidly. Very often Barbara couldn't find Mickey even when he *wasn't* on the road. Another source of conflict between them was Mickey's attachment to his stand-in, Sig Frolich.

Frolich worked as an extra when Mickey wasn't using him, but often he'd have long periods of unemployment, the way a lot of actors do. At these times, Mickey would invite him to stay at his house. Aside from the fact that Mickey frequently prefers the company of men to women, he felt a strong sense of loyalty toward Frolich because of the way Sig had stood by him after his marriage to Martha Vickers had gone sour. As a result, Mickey saw nothing wrong with putting Sig up in his home, for what to Barbara seemed interminable periods of time.

Because their relationship was pretty shaky, Mickey fell into the trap of believing that if he bought Barbara a new house in a different neighborhood it would somehow make her happier. As a result, he allowed Barbara to talk him into selling their Tower Road residence and buying one she already had her eye on in Brentwood, one of Los Angeles's most exclusive and "in" residential areas. The asking price

254

was a whopping two hundred thousand dollars, but because it had been labeled a "bad luck" house due to the demise, in freak accidents, of its previous two occupants, Mickey was able to buy it for one hundred thirty-five thousand dollars, utilizing the cash he had realized from the Tower Road sale to make the substantial down payment. Barbara and Mickey would have been smart to have paid attention to the "bad luck" tag.

Sometime during that period, Mickey and Barbara became friendly with the French film star Alain Delon, who introduced them to a twenty-four-year-old Yugoslavian named Milos Milocevic. An aspiring actor who'd done a few bit roles, Milos had worked in Paris as a stand-in for Delon, who then brought him to America.

On July 2, 1964, Milos married Cynthia Krensky Bouron, a Chicago socialite living in Los Angeles. On December 11 of that year he was admitted to the United States as a permanent resident. Although Cynthia was evidently in love with the handsome Slav, some of their friends claim that the only reason he married her was to gain entrée into the country. It seems a reasonable allegation, inasmuch as the two of them filed for divorce almost as soon as they became husband and wife.

By the time Mickey and Barbara met Milos, he'd become a member of the Screen Actors Guild and was trying to get film parts in Hollywood. But ruggedly handsome though he was, nobody was knocking down Milos's door.

"He was a devil-may-care guy, very pleasant but nuts," says an actor who worked with him once on location. "He loved to drive sports cars fast and aim them at pedestrians. They'd have to jump out of his way. This was always a big laugh to Milos."

On first meeting him, however, the Rooneys had no idea that Milos was such an erratic individual. Mickey thought he was fun, and Barbara was attracted to him. The three swiftly became close friends, with Mickey volunteering to help Milos get acting jobs. In the meantime, Mickey helped him out by giving him work as a chauffeur and "gofer."

Until it was too late, Mickey never suspected that there had been something between Milos and Barbara from the moment they met. Possibly he was just too busy trying to support five wives, seven children, a flock of lawyers, bookkeepers, and Uncle Sam to notice he was being cuckolded by his friend.

That fall Mickey made guest appearances on the Red Skelton show, the "Lucille Ball Show," and opened at the Valley Music

Theater for a three-week stand on September 1 as the star of a revival of *A Funny Thing Happened on the Way to the Forum.* Since film work was getting scarce, and his two TV series had failed, Mickey was now entertaining thoughts of an acting career in the theater. Certainly he knew his way around a stage, having started out in that medium when he was fifteen months old.

Mickey only had a week's rehearsal, but in spite of that, he managed to make the show "a Roman romp for Rooney," wrote Charles Champlin, entertainment editor of the *Los Angeles Times* in his review the next morning. "Rooney leers, chortles, giggles, struts, runs, dances, sings like a laryngical foghorn, and ad-libs all manner of regional and topical asides . . . The evening remains a largely personal triumph for Rooney . . . Rooney received a standing ovation, the first, he said with great emotion, he had ever received."

After a successful run at the Valley Music Theater, Mickey prepared to leave for the Philippines, where he was to start filming *Ambush Bay,* in mid-October.

The day Mickey left, Milos dropped in at their house to bid goodbye to "my good little friend." Before climbing in the front seat of the car with Barbara, Mickey shook Milos's hand and said, "Take good care of my wife while I'm gone."

Milos smiled and assured Mickey he would. And he did.

While Mickey was in the Philippines, playing the role of a spunky United States Marine trying to escape from a Japanese-held island during World War II, Milos landed a bit part as a submarine crewman in Norman Jewison's *The Russians Are Coming, The Russians Are Coming.*

Most of the picture was shot on location at Fort Bragg, California, which was about two hundred miles north of San Francisco, on a rugged and barren stretch of coastline resembling Cape Cod. So that Milos wouldn't be lonely, Barbara Rooney accompanied him to Fort Bragg and stayed there during the major part of the location filming. They returned to Southern California a few weeks before Mickey did, and though Milos kept his own small apartment in Hollywood for the sake of appearances, he spent most of his nights at Barbara's.

By the time Mickey returned home at the end of November, Barbara and Milos were in the throes of a very torrid love affair. Some of their friends believed they were even contemplating marriage, once she was free of Mickey. Naturally it was an inconvenience for them when Mickey returned and Milos had to move out.

By then, Mickey suspected from Barbara's coolness to him, plus a certain gleam in her eyes whenever she spoke of Milos or was in his company, what was going on between them. This in turn precipitated a fight that culminated in Mickey's moving out of the house and into the Bel Air Hotel.

After Mickey had been there a few days, Bill Gardner found Mickey a small house he could rent, across from his own home. Convinced it was over between him and Barbara, Mickey moved into the house with Timmy.

MICKEY AND BARBARA separated officially on December 22, 1965. At that point Milos gave up any pretense of living in his own apartment, and moved into the Brentwood house with Barbara and her four children.

The day after Christmas, Mickey and Bill Gardner left for New York City where Mickey was to open at the Latin Quarter on December 28 for a three-week engagement. When he returned to Los Angeles, around January 20, Mickey went straight from the airport to St. John's Hospital in Santa Monica. Ostensibly this was for treatment of an exotic blood disease called strongylosis, which Red Doff told the press he had picked up while making *Ambush Bay* in the Philippines. But others close to Mickey at the time, including Barbara's close friend, Margie Lane, are inclined to believe he was in the hospital "to try to kick his sleeping pill habit."

After Mickey had been in the hospital about a week, reflecting on the vicissitudes of love and marriage, he found out that Barbara had been seeing an attorney and was planning to file suit for separate maintenance. In retaliation, Mickey phoned his own attorney, Simon Taub, and told him to sue Barbara for divorce first and also to ask for custody of their four children, on the grounds that Barbara was an "unfit mother."

On Friday, January 29, Taub filed for divorce, charging "mental cruelty." In the same complaint he charged that Milos Milocevic was living in the same home with Mickey Rooney's wife and children and even giving the address as his legal residence on documents. Mickey was asking the court for a restraining order to keep Milos out of his house.

Of course Barbara was upset. She didn't wish to give up her children, or her lover, either. Milos wasn't too happy about this turn of events, either, according to Wilma Catania, a houseguest of Barbara's from New York, and Margie Lane. Margie had been an intimate friend of Barbara's even before she met Mickey, and became known as "Aunt Margie" to their children. As a result of

Margie's close relationship with Mickey and Barbara—"but mostly Barbara"—she had been aware for quite some time of what was going on between Barbara and Milos. She also knew that Barbara was terribly concerned about losing the children in a custody battle, and that this, in turn, was causing her to fight with Milos about whether or not he should move out. As much as she wanted him there, she was beginning to waver about the propriety of the situation. Her love for Milos was also beginning to waver a bit, and she was even considering returning to her husband.

Aware of this possibility, Milos was extremely jealous. "If Barbara even looks at another man, I'll shoot her and myself," he confided to actress Michele Lamour, another of Barbara's girlfriends, on the Thursday before Mickey filed his restraining order to kick him out of the house. "It'll be like a film. We'll be found sleeping like two lovers together." Feeling his words were just the bleatings of a jealous lover and that it was nothing to take seriously, Miss Lamour neglected to tell Barbara about Milos's threat. On Sunday afternoon, Barbara decided to visit Mickey at St. John's Hospital to discuss a possible reconciliation. If not that, at least she wanted Mickey to allow her to keep custody of the children.

Afraid that Barbara's maternal instincts might overpower her desire for him, Milos insisted that Barbara tell Mickey that she was not going to return to him. Because he didn't trust her, Milos wanted to hear it with his own ears. Since he wouldn't be along, Milos hid a concealed microphone in Barbara's bra so that her conversation could be recorded by a tape machine being operated in the adjoining room by Herman Schlieske, a private detective, who accompanied her to the hospital.

Unaware of any of this, Mickey talked with Barbara for about an hour and seemed to think they were close to a reconciliation. Especially when Barbara broke down and told Mickey, "I won't even see Milos as a friend if that's what you want." Remembering suddenly that the conversation was being recorded, Barbara surreptitiously snapped off the mike. Unfortunately, the damaging part of their talk had already been recorded, and the detective wouldn't give the tape to her after she'd left Mickey's room because his instructions were to play it for Milos.

After she returned home, Barbara, the detective, Milos, and Barbara's two friends, Wilma Catania and Susan Sidney, sat around in the den discussing Mickey's divorce suit and her suit for separate maintenance. They also listened to the tape. According to Barbara's two girlfriends, Milos became furious at her promise not to see him "even as a friend."

At seven-thirty, Wilma and Susan left the den and disappeared into the guest cottage outside the house. Barbara and Milos then decided to go out for an early dinner at the Daisy on Rodeo Drive. So Barbara showered and changed into tan capri pants, a flowered blouse, and pumps, while Milos put on black slacks and a white shirt.

They were about to open the front door when Margie Lane dropped in, and they invited her to go along to the Daisy with them. "They were still fighting over the custody suit," Margie recalls. "I had been with her the night before. At that point she had told me that she had asked Milos to leave, otherwise she would lose her children. But he had refused, and she didn't know what to do about it. She told me that again at the Daisy when he left the table for a few minutes to go to the washroom. At eight-thirty, Barbara said she was tired and wanted to go home early. So we drove back to Brentwood, and I said 'Good night' to them at the front door. Then I left. I was to call her the next morning. We were to make a plan."

While the three of them had been at the Daisy, Wilma Catania and Susan Sidney had decided to attend a dinner party in Hollywood to which they had been invited. Before leaving, Catania knocked on the master-bedroom door because she wanted to ask Barbara for permission to use her car. When there was no answer, Wilma assumed it was all right to take the car, borrowed the keys, and she and Susie drove into Hollywood. There was a maid in the house to take care of the Rooney's three children, who were asleep in their own rooms about thirty feet from the master suite. Two-year-old Kimmy Sue was visiting her grandparents in Inglewood.

Around two thirty in the morning, Wilma and Susan returned. The lights were still on, and Milos's blue Volkswagen bug was parked in the circular driveway. Wilma thought this rather unusual but, figuring it was none of her business, she said good night to her friend, who drove off in a cab. Then she went to bed in the guest house behind the garage and didn't awaken until noon the following day.

In the morning, Margie Lane had phoned the house to make a date with Barbara. "Kelly answered the phone," Margie remembers, "and when I asked for her mother, she told me, 'Mommy's still asleep—the door is closed.' So I hung up and went to take a bath."

WILMA CATANIA DRESSED and walked over to the main house to visit with Barbara. When the maid informed her that Barbara wasn't up yet, which seemed unusual to Wilma when coupled with the fact that Milos's car was still in the driveway, she knocked on the bedroom door. Alarmed at getting no response after she called out

259

Barbara's name several times, she tried the door and found it locked. She then got the maid, and the two of them jimmied open the bedroom door with a screwdriver. Seeing that the bedroom was empty and that the bed appeared unslept in, Wilma cautiously pushed open the bathroom door.

She nearly fainted at the scene. Barbara, still in her tan capris and flowered blouse, was lying on her back on the bathroom floor, with a bullet hole in her jaw. Milos, who lay face down, was dead of a bullet wound in his temple. Near him on the floor lay Mickey's chrome-plated .38 caliber revolver that the police later learned he had purchased in May of 1964.

After recovering her composure slightly, Wilma phoned the West Los Angeles Police Department, which dispatched two detectives and a coroner to the house immediately.

Following a lengthy interrogation of the maid and Wilma, who reconstructed for them the events of the night before, and an examination of the bodies by the coroner, Detective Sergeant Newstetter of the West Los Angeles Police determined that it was a simple case of murder-suicide, committed by a jealous lover.

According to Margie Lane, who heard the news over the radio, Milos had a couple of other reasons for not wanting to live. "There was a warrant out for Milos in Florida on a gun-carrying charge," Margie believes. "The federal police were after him and so were a couple of members of the Mafia. So he must have figured what was the point of waiting around for them to get him? Now that he couldn't have Barbara, he'd save everybody the trouble."

Mickey was still in his room at St. John's, but preparing to check out Monday afternoon, when his doctor told him about the murder of his fifth wife and Milos's suicide.

As the details were related to him, Mickey groaned, "No, no, God no," and collapsed in shock, necessitating another night at the hospital. There he remained in complete seclusion except for two visitors—Red Doff and his nineteen-year-old son, Timmy. According to Doff, Mickey "took it very badly. He kept repeating, 'My poor, four babies . . . my poor little girl Barbara.' He cried periodically. Nobody could describe what was in his heart that night."

If Mickey hadn't been filled with guilt as well as grief, he wouldn't have been human. His guilt was compounded by the news, which Red Doff had let slip, that the promise never to see Milos that he had extracted from Barbara had been tape recorded and heard by Milos—which no doubt led to his decision to take his and her life.

Still shaken by the news, Mickey's next concern was the children and what traumatic effect being in the same house as their mother when she was murdered would have on them. But fearing he'd already laid enough on Mickey for one night, Doff lied. He told him that all four children had been over at their grandmother's at the time of the shootings.

Mickey emitted a great sigh of relief and promised that from now on he would be a better father. According to Doff, Mickey said that the children had always been his prime consideration and the main reason he wanted the marriage to last.

By the time Mickey learned of the murder, the three children who had spent the night at the Evanston house had, in fact, been whisked away from the scene by Barbara's attorney in her divorce action, Harold Abeles, and deposited for safekeeping at their grandparents' home in Inglewood, where Kimmy Sue had already spent the weekend.

Mickey stayed in the hospital overnight, then went into seclusion in his home in Benedict Canyon until Friday afternoon, the day of Barbara's funeral. The services and interment were held at Forest Lawn, in Glendale.

Mickey's three eldest children, Mickey Rooney, Jr., Timmy, and Teddy were there to comfort him, along with Red Doff, Bill Gardner, and his close friends, Jonathan Winters, Red Barry, Bobby Van, and Joey Forman. Mickey's younger children didn't attend, but their grandparents, Don and Helen Thomason, did, along with Helen's sister, Sue.

The services, held in the Church of the Recessional, were conducted by the Reverend Douglas Smith, who had finally made Mickey's and Barbara's marriage legal in California by marrying them in his Los Angeles church in 1960, following Mickey's divorce from Elaine. Reverend Smith had also baptized their four children.

Helen and her sister sobbed throughout the ceremony, while Don Thomason remained sober-faced, alternating his glances between the bronze coffin of his daughter and Mickey.

Mickey, dressed in a business suit and dark tie, his red-rimmed eyes hidden behind dark glasses, his face somewhat puffy and lined, did his utmost to keep his emotions in check as he sat through the ceremony. But at intervals he couldn't help sobbing softly.

Meanwhile, on a mortuary slab in another part of town lay the body of Milos Milocevic, waiting to be shipped back to Belgrade, Yugoslavia, at the request of his mother who had claimed it. The solo he was doing in the mortuary was a far cry from the Romeo-and-Juliet tableau Milos had envisioned for himself and Barbara when he pointed the muzzle of Mickey's .38 at his temple and squeezed the trigger.

22

A S IF MICKEY needed anything else to make him feel bad during the days following Barbara's funeral, he had to read in the newspapers that Milos's mother was blaming him for her son's death. Mrs. Milocevic had told the Belgrade press that Mickey had "plotted to have my son killed." As false as her accusation was, Mickey still had to issue denials to the press through Red Doff, as well as cope with it in his dreams.

According to Doff, Mickey was in such a state of shock during the rest of 1966 that "he hardly knew what he was doing or even where he was living."

For a while he was in an almost catatonic state. But because of the children, Mickey pulled himself together, vacated his small house on Benedict, and moved his family into a much larger rental, on North Rexford Drive. Of course, he still owned the house on Evanston in Brentwood, but because it would be a constant reminder of what had taken place there, he put it up for sale soon after the funeral. Since it had been tagged a "bad luck" house before the twin killings, it was inevitable that its eerie reputation would be magnified tenfold after all the publicity. Its reputation scared off buyers, and Mickey wound up selling it for a "big loss," Bill Gardner says.

Getting rid of the "bad luck" house wasn't quite enough to stop the strokes of the grim reaper, however. Twice more that spring, Mickey was brushed by the deaths of people close to him. On March 3, Nell Pankey died of a heart attack, at the age of sixty-nine. The services, which were attended by Mickey, Fred Pankey and a few close friends, took place not far from the neighborhood where

Mickey and his mother lived when she put shoe polish on his hair to get him the part of Mickey McGuire.

No sooner had Mickey recovered from the shock of Nell's death than Red Doff's five-year-old daughter, Caroline, was drowned in a freak swimming-pool accident at the home of comedian Hal March. Red Doff and his wife, Marilyn, had given Mickey support during his bereavement following Barbara's death; now that the situation was reversed, it was Mickey's turn to lend comfort. "Nobody could have been a better friend at a time like that," Red Doff says. "He stayed by our sides night and day, helping out with the funeral arrangements and even paying for the catering after the funeral."

In addition to being saddened by these two deaths, Mickey had other problems. He hadn't had a picture offer since *Ambush Bay*, and except for a couple of nightclub appearances and one guest shot on a television show, he was unemployed. In addition, he was discovering it wasn't easy to rule over a houseful of kids and at the same time try to make enough money to raise them in the style to which they had grown accustomed. He had hired a housekeeper—a Mrs. Hogan—but since she had a drinking problem, it was a worry to leave them with her. What Mickey needed in his life was a good woman he could rely on. Not that another marriage had entered his head yet. But he did need somebody to keep things running smoothly. Which is why he welcomed help from an unexpected source.

"About a month after Barbara's death," Margie Lane relates, "I started going over to Mickey's house to see if I could help with the children—particularly the babies. It was a lot for a housekeeper to take care of, and Mickey was most receptive. In addition to helping out around the house, I'd sometimes do the grocery shopping, I'd take the children to church, or pick them up at their grandparents's house in Inglewood and take them to Mickey's when it was his turn to have them, and take them back again. They were back and forth between the two places a lot in those days. And Mickey didn't have time while he was working to drive them to school or to the doctor's. So it was up to me to do those things."

THAT SITUATION LASTED until Mickey had to leave for the island of Malta that summer to make a film with Vittorio Gassman called *The Devil in Love*, a fairly successful spoof of an Italian art film.

Since Margie couldn't devote full time to the Rooney household—she worked in real estate—Mickey had to find a reliable person to stay with the children while he was gone. He'd be away at least three months, and Mrs. Hogan refused to go that long without a day off. So, Mickey's trusted friend and man Friday, Bill Gardner, moved into the house to oversee everything. But Gardner, competent as he was as an executive secretary, was no match for five high-spirited kids and a drunken housekeeper. "It was a bad scene," he remembers. "I wasn't used to that sort of thing. When it got completely out of hand, I said, 'Oh, God,' and I called Barbara's parents, Helen and Don Thomason, and told them 'Come on over here and get these kids. You're the only ones who know how to take care of them. I don't know what will happen to them if you don't.'"

The Thomasons didn't have to be told twice. Within the hour, they were over at Mickey's house collecting their grandchildren and packing them and their belongings into their station wagon for the drive back to Inglewood.

When Mickey returned from Malta and found his children living with their grandparents in Inglewood, he was extremely upset. But after seeing how happy and secure they were with the Thomasons, and realizing that he couldn't as a single man take adequate care of them, and also pursue a career that sometimes took him halfway around the world, he was quick to concede that the new arrangement was best for their well-being. As a result he entered into a coguardianship arrangment with the Thomasons under which they'd keep the children; Mickey would pay approximately one thousand a month for their support, and in return he'd be given reasonable visitation rights. This left him free to work and to travel, and to see the children and even have them sleep over, whenever it was mutually convenient.

Without such a large ménage of children to care for, Mickey found his new place a little too much house for a bachelor. So when the lease expired in September he moved back into his former house in Benedict Canyon, which was about half as costly. In a lean period like the one he was going through cutting out a few dollars monthly was important to him.

Besides having little work, Mickey was once again in trouble with the government. Just two years after being permitted to take $100,371 from his "unbreakable trust" to pay back taxes, he found he was again in arrears to them, to the tune of $28,197, for the years 1961 through 1963. Fortunately, the judge hadn't permitted Mickey to empty the coffers completely the first time, so there was still enough money remaining in the trust to help him over the new tax hurdle. With Dermot Long arguing Mickey's case, Judge Scott once again took pity on the Mighty Mite and ordered the bank to release the necessary funds.

WITH SO MANY changes in his life, Mickey was in no mood for any romantic entanglements in the summer of 1966, though this was the longest period since he had taken up the idea of marriage and divorce that he didn't have an affair going.

Mickey couldn't afford a serious involvement, with all those alimony and child-support payments going out every month and so little coming in. But a widower, especially one as famous as Mickey Rooney, with a sometime houseful of high-spirited kids and a void left by the death of their mother, was more vulnerable to the attractions of a lady not uninterested in marriage than even a sophisticate like Mickey could have suspected.

Such a lady was Margie Lane, who, now that Mickey was home from his travels, had resumed her volunteer work at the Rooney household. Margie probably didn't give a moment's thought to the prospect of marriage when she started paying condolence calls on Mickey after Barbara's death and helping with the children. But after six months of being constantly available to him and his family, his dependency on her became so great that marriage to Margie was in some respects practically a fait accompli. As one of Mickey's associates who doesn't wish to be identified phrases it, "Mickey was in such bad shape in those days that he didn't know what he was doing. He'd have married anybody who looked at him—even an orangutan."

Not that Margie resembled an orangutan. But at the age of forty-five, with a tall, angular body and a not outstandingly beautiful face, Marge Lane was hardly the bathing beauty cutie that in the past had appealed to Mickey.

She was, however, extremely sensitive and intelligent; she was well educated, having studied accounting in junior college; she knew how to manage a household; she was extremely religious, which appealed to Mickey who had a new awareness of God now that she had introduced him to the Church of Religious Science. In general she had an air of middle-class respectability about her and could have played Andy Hardy's mother. Which, in retrospect, is what Margie Lane believes attracted Mickey to her.

"Our whole marriage was planned by Mickey and his managers in order to change his public image," she believes. "He needed work and had to show the world that he was dependable and respectable again, not running after young girls, and not on pills. I didn't know anything about the pills at the time. I was pretty innocent and just played right into their hands. I thought the world of Mickey, I really did, up until I discovered what was going on."

According to Margie, she and Mickey didn't live together before they married. In fact, "when Mickey proposed to me that September, he did it the old-fashioned way, on bended knee." As soon as she accepted, Mickey followed his usual pattern and chartered a plane to fly them and a small entourage of close friends to Las Vegas for the wedding.

After the marriage, which took place in early evening on September 10, Mickey and Marge checked into a suite at the Desert Inn. A large dinner party for the bride and groom and their friends was planned in the dining room downstairs afterward. "But as soon as we got up to the suite," states Marge, "Mickey went into the bathroom and started taking pills. He fell asleep immediately afterward, and was out until the next day. There was no consummation on our wedding night."

Back in Southern California after the wedding, Margie sublet her apartment and moved into Mickey's house, which now seemed inadequate. Basically a "couple house," it couldn't comfortably accommodate the two of them, a live-in maid, the four younger children when they slept over, and Timmy, who now resided with his father for approximately half the year.

Because Mickey and Bobby Van were booked to do three weeks of vaudeville in Australia in October, there really wasn't time to find a house to buy before they left. As a stopgap measure, they took a two-month lease on a contemporary home at the top of Trousdale Estates belonging to the pianist Byron Janis. Janis was off on a concert tour but would need his house again in December.

IN AUSTRALIA, MICKEY's vaudeville act played theaters in Sydney and Melbourne and made a little money for Mickey and his promoters. However, if Marge expected that touring with a movie star of Mickey's stature would be a glamorous life, she was deeply disappointed.

"Marge couldn't figure out why Mickey wouldn't go anywhere," Red Doff recalls, who accompanied them to Australia. "He never does when he's touring, unless it's to a sporting event or the racetrack. In Australia, where he was still a pretty good name, there were huge crowds to contend with and autograph hunters bothering him. He avoided them by staying in his room."

A month later, Mickey and Marge returned to Beverly Hills and settled into the Janis house to enjoy what appeared from the outside to be a very solid marriage. According to the publicity releases and magazine articles people were writing about him, Mickey had finally matured. He was no longer robbing the cradle for his brides, but sharing his life with a mature, church-going woman only a year younger than himself, known to his kids as "Aunt Margie."

According to "Aunt Margie," however, their marriage was nothing like what was depicted in the press releases. Mickey was a habitual taker of sleeping pills, which he obtained from various doctors around town. "He had pills hidden in different places in the house, like Ray Milland with his liquor bottles in *The Lost Weekend*," Marge declares. "If he took them, he couldn't go to work in the morning. So I had to stay awake all night to try to keep him off them. I finally wound up with nervous exhaustion from keeping an eye on him."

Mickey had other habits that a woman like Marge found difficult to cope with. "Even on my birthday, one month after we were married, he was up in Tahoe with somebody else." His girl chasing wasn't entirely inconsistent with what Marge had heard from Barbara, so that didn't surprise her. "All men do that," she says. "But she hadn't told me about some of the sexual things she had to put up with. Not just that he only satisfied himself, but the, well, you know 'imaginative' things he wanted to do. I truly believe he has an aversion to women—quite a complex about proving his manliness. I think he got this from his early years backstage at the burlesque house. Anyway, I finally told him, 'Look, Mickey, I'd have to lose my soul to do what you want to do. But we can stay married for the children's sake. I'll take care of the home. You can have another girlfriend, if you like. But I can't do these things."

As in his other marriages, Mickey was plagued by money problems. "He had so many bills you couldn't really keep track of anything. And his accountants didn't want me to look at the books. One day I did, though, when I was down at the accountants' office." Marge, with her own accounting studies background, says that she had a serious dispute with the accountants over the statement sheets they sent to Mickey. She says she pointed out to her husband what disturbed her, but that he "didn't want to be bothered."

In the midst of all this turmoil, Mickey and Margie had to vacate the Trousdale house four weeks before Christmas and move into another rented one, on Hazan Drive, just off Coldwater Canyon. "So between moving three times in the short time we were married and taking care of the babies and the marketing and the Christmas shopping and doing the hiring and firing of the help, it was almost more than a person could stand," Margie says.

As a result, she became rundown and caught a bad case of flu. "So," Margie continues, "because we were still sleeping in the same room, and I didn't want Mickey to catch it, I volunteered to move out and into my girlfriend's—until I was better. While I was over there, Mickey's manager, Red Doff, phoned my girlfriend and told her that Mickey was filing for a divorce, and that I shouldn't come back. There was no blowup, I never even got to talk to Mickey or anything after that. I was kept away from him."

Despite his threat, Mickey didn't file for the divorce first. Marge did—two days before Christmas and just three months and thirteen days after she'd said, "I do."

She charged Mickey with "extreme cruelty," which Mickey denied in his cross-complaint on December 30. The actual interlocutory decree was delayed for almost a full year while Margie's lawyer, Ralph Miller, and Dermot Long wrangled over a property settlement, which was finally reached on November 11, 1967. The case came to court on December 14, 1967. At that time Marge Lane was granted an interlocutory decree, by "default," and awarded $350-a-month alimony for only twelve months. In addition, she was allowed to keep her car, and Mickey had to pay all court costs, her attorney fees amounting to twenty-five hundred dollars, as well as "community debts" amounting to $5,348."

Compared with some of the gargantuan awards given wives today, the $350 a month Mickey had to pay Margie was veritable chicken feed. Nevertheless, there were times during that period when he was earning so little money that he couldn't even come up with that. Mickey became so remiss in his obligations, in fact, that in September of 1968 Margie's lawyer, Robert Gray, had him served with papers charging that he owed her $1,072 in alimony and community debts plus $2,500 in fees he still owed her lawyer. Gray also asked the court for an additional $2,000 for himself, explaining that numerous telephone calls for Mrs. Rooney to the couple's creditors entitled him to extra fees.

When Mickey didn't appear at a contempt hearing to answer those charges, a bench warrant was issued for his arrest. Bail was set at $625 by Judge MacFadden, who continued the hearing until October 16.

Jailing Mickey would have been difficult, however, because at the time of the arrest warrant he was in Las Vegas playing the

Flamingo. That was a little farther than the long arm of California law could reach. By the time he finished his gig in Vegas, Mickey had enough money to pay Marge the alimony due her, and as a result the judge took pity on Mickey, saying he was doing "the best he can," and dismissed the rest of the complaint brought by Gray.

23

THE BEST THAT can be said of Mickey's topsy-turvy life during the next ten years is that he tried. Desperately. Tried to find personal happiness. Tried to get back into the mainstream of show business. Tried to find that elusive pot of gold at the end of the rainbow.

Good reviews in pictures like the Italian art film *The Devil in Love*, and the action-adventure war story *Ambush Bay*, were offset by appearances in clinkers like *The Extraordinary Seaman* and *How to Stuff a Wild Bikini*. The former, a John Frankenheimer film, starring David Niven and Faye Dunaway, had all the earmarks of an important film. It was costly to make, was shot entirely on location in Mexico over an eighteen-week period, and had a good cast. But according to one of its actors, comedian Jack Carter, "It was so bad it was never released. I think it played a 'drive-out theater' in Philadelphia for one night before it was yanked." As for *How to Stuff a Wild Bikini*, the reviewers had nothing nice to say about it. "*How to Stuff a Wild Bikini*. Yep, that's the title that opened yesterday on a circuit double bill," *The New York Times* reviewer wrote. "And anyone expecting the worst won't be disappointed." As an alternative to film work, Mickey toured the boondocks in such Samuel French staples as *Luv, On The Way to the Forum, See How They Run, Show Boat, Good Night Ladies* and *George M*.

He continued to play nightclubs from Tahoe to Vegas to Houston to Miami. He did guest appearances on the "Dean Martin" and the "Carol Burnett" TV programs. He played barns such as the Municipal Auditorium in Kansas City and Busch Palace in St. Louis. And he

271

invested in all kinds of enterprises, lending his name to the promotion of the Downingtown Motor Inn, a moderate-priced resort in Pennsylvania-Dutch Country. According to the press release on that transaction:

> Mickey Rooney has purchased a part interest in the Downingtown Motor Inn and says he hopes to bring big-league golf there and build a motion picture studio.
>
> "We intend to build a motion-picture studio here and do three to five movies a year in this area," Rooney said.
>
> "We hope to bring a full-scale professional golf tournament here and we'd like to bring in top-level live entertainment."

Little of the foregoing ever became a reality, though Mickey is still vaguely connected with the resort, and his face, sporting a toothy grin still adorns the top of newspaper ads for what is now called "Mickey Rooney's Tabas Hotel" in Downingtown.

Another enterprise that was designed to make Mickey wealthy was the formation of Productions Eleven, Incorporated. This company was formed by Mickey, Red Doff, and Alexander O. Curtis, a Florida promoter who in 1968 succeeded Red Doff as his personal manager.

Productions Eleven was formed for the purpose of making movies for TV and theaters, and was even approved by the Securities Exchange Commission and certified to issue and sell stock to the public. "When we went public," Doff says, "Mickey had two million shares at a dollar, and I had a million, ten thousand of it tradable. Mickey had 20,000 shares tradable." Doff acknowledges differences with Curtis over the techniques the latter wanted to use to promote trading in the stock; and over accounting. Doff feels that he was forced out of the company, and at that point, everything fell apart and the company went bust.

So did Doff's relationship with Mickey. Curtis stepped in and took over full management of the Mighty Mite.

Mickey's and Doff's relationship deteriorated even further when the latter sued Mickey in 1970 for an eighty-eight hundred dollar debt that Doff claimed was due him as his percentage of a group of Rooney shows at the Fremont Hotel in Las Vegas and the Dean Martin and Carol Burnett television appearances. The two eventually settled the suit amicably, out of court, and they have been close friends ever since. In fact, Doff is Mickey's press agent today.

When he and Doff had their problems, Mickey was no longer

272

living in the house he'd been renting in Coldwater Canyon. Instead, because he was on the move so much, trying to hustle a living in nightclubs and dinner theaters, he had moved into a small apartment on Palm Drive near Third Street, in a commercial section of Beverly Hills south of the Santa Monica railroad tracks. (The Wonder Bread factory was within smelling distance.)

In 1969, Mickey was shaken to learn of the death of his pal Judy Garland, in a London hotel. According to Dick Quine, Mickey didn't attend the funeral when it was held a few days later in New York City, "but he wrote a song which was an ode to her called 'Judy' that was an absolute heartbreaker, and he showed up at my house one morning while I was still in bed to play it for me. Mickey often dropped in when I was in bed. He'd go right to my room, shake me until I was awake and say, 'I've got to play something for you.' And he'd sit down and play me something he had just written. This day it was this song called 'Judy' and it was really beautiful . . . You wouldn't think this about him, but his poetry is exquisite, and very revealing. I taped the damn thing when he was singing it . . . I wish I could find it. He cracked up twice in the middle of it, he was so broken up, and never could get through it."

Although Mickey didn't go to Judy's funeral, he'd do anything for her when she was alive. "Whenever Judy was in trouble," Quine says, "and he knew about it, he'd get on a plane and go to be with her.

"That's the kind of a friend Mickey is. If he likes you, he'll do anything for you . . . And he has a sixth sense, I swear to God, about knowing when you're in trouble. I remember I was directing a picture in Paris once, *In Paris When It Sizzles,* with Bill Holden and Audrey Hepburn. And everything was going wrong that could. And I was at the lowest of all ebbs. And the lady I was going with had walked out on me. I hadn't talked to Mickey in months . . . the whole time I was in Paris. And the night that I was really ready to take the gas pipe, the phone rang and it was Mickey phoning from the States, and he said, 'Are you all right, pal?'"

MICKEY'S DIVORCE FROM Margie Lane didn't become final until December of 1969. But there were indications that Mickey was at least thinking of a seventh marriage as early as April 17, 1968. At that time *Los Angeles Herald-Examiner* columnist Harrison Carroll wrote in his column that he'd been hearing rumors that Mickey and Jeri Green, Shecky Green's ex-wife, were getting serious about each other. But as usual, and despite his past record at the altar, Mickey was playing it pretty cool when Carroll asked him if they had set a wedding date yet.

"No, we're still [sic] very much in love, but that's a little premature. Actually my former wife, Marge Lane, hasn't picked up her final divorce decree yet. So I haven't married today. But give me time," Mickey chuckled. "It's only eleven o'clock in the morning."

That romance seemed to cool soon after the Carroll interview. But when it was over, Mickey didn't waste much time finding a new fiancée. While he was playing Miami that winter, he met Carolyn Hackett, a twenty-five-year-old secretary from Beverly Hills. Blonde, blue-eyed, taller than Mickey by about four inches, with two children of her own by a former marriage (Jonell, a girl, two years old, and James, a boy, five), Carolyn seemed to have everything Mickey needed at that point to make him happy—an instant family.

Because Marge hadn't bothered to get her final decree in court yet, Mickey was legally still her husband, though they'd been apart a full two years. To get around this sticky little problem, Mickey eloped to Mexico with Carolyn and married her on April 12, 1969. But just to make sure it was legal in the United States (everywhere except California, that is) Mickey married Carolyn again in Las Vegas on May 28, while he was appearing at a casino there.

There was a twenty-three-year age difference, but what's twenty-three years to a man wearing a long strand of love beads around his neck as he posed, hand in hand with his bride, for the photographers?

Still, plenty of bad and unkind jokes circulated in the industry. Such as "Mickey Rooney's been married so many times he has rice marks on his face," or "Mickey Rooney's another Elizabeth Taylor, only without the tits."

24

I N THE SUMMER of 1970, Mickey was touring the strawhat circuit in the musical, *George M.*, which had been produced on Broadway by David Black, whose one major success had been *The Impossible Years*. *George M*. had not been successful on Broadway, but in stock, with Mickey playing the colorful role of Cohan, it was a mild hit. Mickey was so good, that he won the Strawhat Award that season.

Sometime in late summer, Mickey's production of *George M*. wound up in a stock theater on Long Island. Having heard how wonderful Mickey was as George M. Cohan, David Black drove out to Long Island one night to see him in the play. "In the second act, Mickey put on a hat and coat to look like an older George M. Cohan," Black remembers. "But to me he looked exactly like W. C. Fields . . . and that's how I got the whole idea—to write a musical based on the life of Fields and get Mickey to play the led. I went backstage after the performance and proposed it to Mickey. He loved the idea. So then I commissioned Arnold Weinstein to do the book and lyrics and Larry Rosenthal, a Hollywood composer who'd scored lots of films, to do the music. We worked on it in Maine all that summer, but it didn't work out. It wasn't good enough to show Mickey, so I brought in Milton Sperling from Hollywood to do a new book and Al Carmine to write the music. We worked on it all that winter. It was much improved, so we showed it to Mickey in the spring. And he said, 'Fine.'" It was called *W.C.* After Mickey accepted, a then-unknown Bernadette Peters was cast in the role of W.C.'s mistress, and Ted Wanamaker was brought in to stage the vehicle. "We opened in Baltimore that summer with pretty good notices," Milton Sperling recalls. "Then we played New Haven, Westport, and a number of other stock theaters up and down the East Coast."

As with every Broadway-bound musical in the tryout stage, there were a number of problems—book problems that Mickey attempted to cure by "ad-libbing all over the place," remembers Sperling. And director problems: "Before the tour was over, we had to fire the original director and bring in another one. Which, of course, was unnecessary because by that time Mickey was doing most of the directing himself, as he always does."

Mickey was not the problem. "He was absolutely brilliant as W.C.," Black declares. "Without him we'd have had nothing on the stage. The problem was the book. It didn't seem to be going anywhere, and most of the songs weren't very good either."

Rudy Tronto, who played Mickey's agent in *W.C.*, remembers: "They couldn't make up their mind whether they wanted W. C. Fields to be a jerk, a letch, a juggler, a director, a drunk—I mean, they tried to get everything into the show. As a result, people would end up saying, 'What the hell is this? We don't want to see all this rotten stuff about Fields. We want to laugh.' Mickey said, 'Give me something funny to do. Fields was a funny man.'"

In spite of a shaky book and warfare among the participants, Mickey was a draw with middle-aged audiences—who remembered him as Andy Hardy. "So business was not a problem," says Sperling.

Still, David Black closed the show at the end of the summer bookings and abandoned his idea of taking it to Broadway. To begin with, in the shape the show was in, it was difficult to raise the three hundred thousand dollars needed to mount it in a Broadway theater. Backers weren't willing to risk that much money on Mickey's name. But according to David Black, the problem was that "Mickey wouldn't go in with the show. He was unhappy with the script and refused to play it on Broadway."

Mickey had struck out once again, and his future as a star, either in Hollywood or on the Great White Way, seemed very much in doubt. His confidence apparently completely eroded, Mickey escaped to Fort Lauderdale, Florida, where he and his new wife, Carolyn, had set up housekeeping in an apartment with her two children. The retirement city seemed a strange place for someone as peripatetic and high-strung as Mickey to settle down in. According to those who knew Mickey during that period, he seemed to be hiding out there.

He was literally afraid of any more failures and of being in California. It made him unhappy to be in Hollywood when he wasn't on top and couldn't get jobs.

The paucity of well-paying acting jobs wrought financial havoc on Mickey's life, too. Though his income was down considerably from the two to three hundred thousand a year he had averaged during his prosperous periods, most of his financial obligations continued, including having to write a check to the Thomasons every month for the support of his four children.

By 1972, Kelly was twelve; Kerry, eleven; Kimmy Sue, nine; and Kyle, ten. The four of them spent most of the year with their grandparents, who now had moved to a lovely estate in Rolling Hills, and to all appearances were content and secure there. However, in accordance with his joint-custody agreement, Mickey got to have them in Fort Lauderdale on holidays and vacations. These were always pleasant times for Mickey and his brood, which gave him and Carolyn the idea that he should seek sole custody of them. After all, he was their legal father, and it would relieve him of the almost unbearable financial burden of having to send the Thomasons money every month for their support. It couldn't cost nearly that much to house them under his own roof.

Consequently, Mickey retained Beverly Hills attorney Robert Neeb to represent him in an action to obtain sole custody of his children.

The case went to trial in Los Angeles Superior Court in Santa Monica the last week of August 1972. In his opening argument, Neeb contended that Mickey Rooney as the legal father of the four children was entitled to sole custody of them, and cited as the basis for his petition the Family Law Act of 1970, which stated that a natural father was entitled to custody of his children unless it could be proved that it would be detrimental to their health and happiness. Attorney Marvin Mitchelson, representing the Thomasons, argued that he would prove that Mickey Rooney was an unfit father.

Like most custody battles, this one was filled with emotional, self-serving testimony from both camps. Helen Thomason, the children's sixty-year-old maternal grandmother, started things off by testifying that she did not "dislike Mickey Rooney, only his actions." To bolster her contention, she started referring to notations in a diary she had kept of Mickey's behavior as a father since Barbara had been murdered. For example, when Mickey Rooney was leaving to go to Malta in 1966 to make a film, Mrs. Thomason went to his house to pick up the children. According to her diary,

"Mickey didn't even bother to come out of his bedroom to tell them goodbye." In another bit of testimony, Helen Thomason said, "He has broken promises and appointments, and things haven't been much different over the past three years." Bill Gardner also testified for the Thomasons, stating on the stand that he thought the children would be better off with their grandparents.

Mickey's side countered with big guns of their own. Robert Neeb put the Reverend William Hornaday, pastor and one of the founders of the Church of Religious Science, on the stand to testify on Mickey's behalf. Mickey had been a member of Hornaday's congregation for thirteen years. His pastor testified that three years of marriage to his sixth wife, Carolyn, had changed Mickey Rooney very much. "The present Mrs. Rooney is a fine Christian girl and has helped him to become much more stable and responsible."

To prove what a good mother she would be, Carolyn took the stand and said that she was the eldest of six children and frequently looked after her younger brothers and sisters when her mother, a registered nurse, was on duty.

Last to take the stand was Mickey himself, casually dressed in slacks, turtleneck shirt, and sweater. Looking tan and fit from his residency in Florida, and somewhat distinguished with his hair totally white and a grandfatherly smile on his face, Mickey rebutted some of the earlier testimony with avowals of how much he loved his children, declarations of what a good and caring father he'd been to them, and statements espousing his belief that the only remaining natural parent of the children was entitled to sole custody of them.

When Marvin Mitchelson asked Mickey if it was true that he had an explosive temper, he replied, "Yes, I did have a bad temper, but I curbed it through Christ. I am a member of the Science of Mind Church now, and I live a Christian life."

After three days of testimony, Judge Mario Clinco continued the case over until September 29, at which time he said he would render a decision.

When the case was reconvened in September, both sides in the family drama looked apprehensive and fell silent as Judge Clinco sat down on the bench and prepared to read from his fifteen-page decision. In essence, Judge Clinco said that he was "keenly aware of Mickey Rooney's expressed feelings of love for his youngsters. However, it is not Mr. Rooney's feelings which control, but rather what is best for the children is and should be the principle concern of the court."

Clinco went on to say that he hoped "Mr. Rooney and the children would get to know each other better, with a greater opportunity to develop stronger ties and a better and healthier relationship.

"The entire record is devoid of any evidence that Mr. Rooney gave, or attempted to give, his children paternal guidance during the past six years, particularly during the past three years."

Judge Clinco said that the children's life at the Thomasons had been one of "regularity, reliability, stability, love, strong emotional ties, and dependence and companionship. To award Mr. Rooney sole custody would be detrimental to the children."

In making his decision, the judge observed that the children themselves had, in chambers, expressed a preference to remain with their grandparents.

Arguing for Mickey, Robert Neeb pointed out that the Thomasons had not proved that his client was an "unfit" parent. Judge Clinco's reply was that the "court notes that the language of the 'code' does not include the word 'unfitness,' nor does this court believe that a finding of personal unfitness is required under this section. This court must be guided only by the paramount consideration of the best interests of the child. I'm therefore denying Mr. Rooney's petition seeking sole custody of the children, and ruling that they should remain with their maternal grandparents with whom they have lived since 1966."

Under the decision, Mickey would remain a coguardian of Kelly, Kerry, Kyle, and Kimmy Sue, with full visitation rights—which is just where he was before, only slightly poorer.

25

THINGS COULDN'T GET much worse. For anyone but Mickey Rooney, that is. Mickey seemed to specialize in excesses. This time he plumbed the depths of failure and somehow was able to dig himself in a little deeper.

After losing the custody battle, Mickey returned to Florida and several months of unemployment. In the preceding year, his agent, Milton Deutsch, who had been getting Mickey what little work he was obtaining, died suddenly. And since Mickey wasn't exactly in demand in show business, it wasn't easy to find another agent willing to take on a middle-aged, pot-bellied has-been. As a result, there was a period when he didn't even have an agent.

As often happens when money becomes a problem, Mickey's marriage to Carolyn started to fall apart after three years. According to Timmy Rooney, Mickey believed his wife's spending extravagant. In Mickey's shaky financial position, their disagreements over money caused violent arguments, culminating with Mickey storming out of their home and pulling his famous disappearing act—the one that all of his past wives had complained so bitterly about in court.

It had to have been the absolute nadir in Mickey's life when friends finally talked him into signing with a new agent, Ruth Webb, in 1971. Webb operated out of her home in Nichols Canyon in Hollywood and other than Mickey and Gene Barry, did not have many "name" clients.

Mickey had never had a woman agent before. For most of the years he'd had the power of an important agency like William

281

Morris behind him, plus well-known personal managers like Bullets Durgom and Maurice Duke. But what did he have to lose? He called on Ruth and offered to dump what was left of his career in her lap, if she was willing to take him on.

Middle-aged but dynamic, with an abiding faith in God, Ruth Webb refused to believe that Mickey was "yesterday's mashed potatoes. I knew that talent such as his never goes stale."

Once Mickey put his career in her hands, Webb worked zealously to make over Mickey's career and image. "We started with the dinner theaters," Webb says, "and we were doing very well with them, until one day Mickey went home to Florida. There wasn't any home, there wasn't any marriage, there wasn't anything."

It was October of 1974 when Mickey returned to Fort Lauderdale and discovered that Carolyn had left him and filed for divorce. Under Florida's "no fault" divorce law, Carolyn did not have to specify any charges against Mickey. She was only required to state that their marriage was "irretrievably broken." But those people who knew the couple well believe that the marriage suffered from the usual complaint: Mickey's fiery temper and his habit of staying away from home for long stretches.

"Mickey was pretty much down to his last dollar,' Webb continues, "when I booked him in Houston. I came to Houston to see him, and I was told that he had collapsed on stage. I stayed with Mickey for ten days. I took care of him. I read the Bible to him. I read *Science and Mind.* Then I had to go back to my office on the Coast. So I said, 'Mickey, any time you can come to California, my home is yours.' Three days later Mickey showed up on my doorstep, and said, 'I'm here. I'm cured!'"

While Mickey was recovering at Ruth Webb's house from the trauma of the end of a seventh marriage, his new agent threw a cocktail party for him and invited, among a great many others, his number-one son, Mickey Rooney, Jr. Mickey Junior brought along as his date country-and-western singer Jan Chamberlin. Blonde, statuesque, and just thirty-five years old, but with a very independent mind, she had been doing some country-and-western singing with Mickey Junior at small clubs.

"At the time we were very good friends as well, so Mickey suggested that we go to Ruth Webb's party to meet his father," Jan recalled in a TV interview with Marilyn Funt. "I really didn't care to go, but he somehow talked me into it. And I'm very glad now, because in the course of the evening, Mickey and I got to know each other very well. He was playing the piano, and I sat down and sang 'I

Can't Last a Day Without You.' I felt like Judy Garland in the 'barn' show. It was fun, and I got to see a side of Mickey that I had never even thought about. He's so sensitive, energetic—a caring human being. The other fellows I was dating at the time, well, they were kind of lackadaisical. They didn't care whether tomorrow came or not. But Mickey was out there really doing it. That energy, I really loved it."

And at the age of fifty-four, his divorce from Carolyn not even final yet, Mickey loved Jan almost at first sight. "He was hoping," Jan continued, "that I would go back to Florida with him. But I felt that wasn't the answer. I felt that if he stayed in California and kind of faced up to where he belonged, jobs would start coming in again. Well, he would say, 'I'm not in the clubhouse. They don't want me . . . they're not interested in me.' And I said, 'I don't think that's true. You've kind of turned your back on them.'

"To this day I don't know what he thought the pull was back there in Florida. There was a manager back there that I felt wasn't good for him. And as time went on I dragged him away from that fellow . . . We had an awful lot of fights about that man. But finally one day Mickey woke up and it paid off."

With the help of Jan Chamberlin, who soon gave up her country-and-western singing career to travel and live with Mickey, and Ruth Webb, who waged a tireless campaign to book Mickey into the nation's dinner theaters, the Mighty Mite began the slow road back to the top again.

Mickey crisscrossed the nation, playing in every shopworn stage vehicle from *Luv* to *George M.* to *Show Boat* to *Good Night Ladies*. But the play he took over and made into his own was a trifle by Woody Kling and Robert J. Hilliard, called *Three Goats in a Blanket*.

Except for the fact that the character played by Mickey Rooney was a down-on-his-luck TV producer instead of an actor, *Three Goats in a Blanket* might have been the story of Mickey's married life. The kind of bedroom farce that, because of the critics, disappeared from Broadway about forty years ago, the vehicle dealt with a man trying to cope with burdensome alimony payments while pursuing a new love.

As one *Los Angeles Times* reviewer put it after catching the play at Sebastian's Dinner Theater in San Clemente, "the hair around Rooney's bald pate is white and he's developed a pretty good-sized pot. Otherwise, age is an entirely negligible condition. The windup doll moves are as abrupt as ever and the delivery is still crackling.

What remains tiresome about Rooney is his way of jamming into jokes and other people's rhythms. But he effectively uses every trick in the book to snare his laughs. He's the oldtime boffo comic, faintly salacious (he claps his hands on his mistress's cheeks and declares, 'The Andy Hardy days are over'), with a positively ruthless desire to please."

It may not have been Broadway material, but audiences ate it up, and Mickey was making anywhere from $2,500 to $5,000 a week in it. In fact, he soon became such a regular on the circuit that he was rapidly becoming known as "The King of the Dinner Theater Circuit."

Mickey was making such a name for himself that Ruth Webb was able to obtain work for him in Hollywood again. In 1976 he appeared with Gene Hackman and Candy Bergen in *The Domino Principle* for Stanley Kramer; and he costarred with Helen Reddy and Shelley Winters in *Pete's Dragon* for the Disney Studios. In 1977 he costarred with Jimmy Stewart (and Lassie) in *The Magic of Lassie* for Jack Wrather Productions, which Bonita Granville, who played Mickey's girlfriend in *Love Laughs at Andy Hardy* produced. None of these was an Academy Award contender, but Mickey received good money for them, and his name was in the Hollywood trades again as a working actor.

With all this activity in Mickey's career, it was time again for some TV producer to think of doing a series with Mickey. This time the producer was no less than TV kingpin Norman Lear.

For sometime now, Lear had been working on a concept for a TV series called "A Year at the Top." Another switch on the well-worn Faust legend, this was the story of four old vaudevillians who swapped their souls to the devil for "a year at the top." Lear signed Mickey to play the lead vaudevillian. CBS ordered six segments, and the series went into production in the fall of 1976 at Tandem Studios in Hollywood.

The opening segment of the series was to go on the air January 19, 1977. But there were script troubles resulting in constant changes in the show's format. In addition, several segments had to be junked altogether. Consequently, the first show didn't go on the air until August 5, 1977—a time of the year when networks, stuck with products they have to amortize, broadcast series segments that they knew aren't going anywhere except to the Sargasso Sea of unsold pilots.

Disappointing though this third stab at a series was, Mickey could take satisfaction in still being "King of the Dinner Theater Circuit."

284

Moreover, by 1978, love had come to Andy Hardy once again. There was even talk of an eighth marriage. Mickey had moved back to Southern California a few months after meeting Jan Chamberlin, and while he was shooting "A Year at the Top," he and Jan shared an apartment in Hollywood. But after the series folded, Mickey bought another house in Westlake Village, a community in the San Fernando Valley.

They hadn't been residents of Westlake Village long when they quietly took out a marriage license in the Valley city of Thousand Oaks. Mickey was becoming gun-shy about making wedding announcements. He had become so paranoid about their treatment in the press, in fact, that he now was beginning to see the humor in the situation and was starting to make jokes about his love life.

When asked by a reporter in the summer of 1978 if he was going to marry Jan, Mickey replied that it wasn't necessary for them to get married, because they had already become man and wife two and a half years before when the two of them were in Hong Kong, where he was making a film.

Jan was beginning to see the humor in it, too. "I personally don't believe in marriage because it wrecks a good relationship," she laughingly told a reporter who was inquiring about the possibility of marriage in San Fernando Valley. "However, Mickey believes so much I can't disappoint him. Poor Mickey. All his previous wives didn't understand him. I'll be different for him. Understanding is so important."

Mickey and Jan tied the knot in August of 1978. The ceremony took place in the Conejo Valley Church of Religious Science. Sig Frolich was Mickey's best man, and Chris, Jan's teenaged son by a former marriage, gave the bride away.

Immediately after the ceremony, Mickey left for Sacramento (and points east) to appear in *Show Boat*, in the part of Captain Andy, at the Music Circus. Although he didn't know it at the time, it was to be his last year on the road as King of the Dinner Theaters.

26

Mickey Rooney probably would have lived out his life on the dinner circuit—making a comfortable living in parts for older and older men until he was ready for retirement to the Motion Picture Country Home—had it not been for a small newspaper story in the *Los Angeles Times* in 1974 that piqued the eclectic interests of veteran TV director Norman Abbott, nephew of Bud Abbott of Abbott and Costello.

The story said that the Burbank Burlesque Theater on Main Street in downtown Los Angeles had closed its doors permanently and that all of its furnishings and interior decorations were going to be auctioned off before the building was razed. Anyone interested in bidding on any of the furnishings was invited to go through the theater.

A collector of antiques and an aficionado of burlesque, Abbott drove downtown with his wife, Ann, and spent the afternoon going through the fusty, dusty, cobwebbed interior of the Burbank Theater—former home of some of the sleaziest bump-and-grind strip artists ever to arouse the puritanical instincts of the Los Angeles Police Department's vice squad.

"While my wife and I were looking around," Abbott recalls, "I noticed a lot of old theater placards and posters advertising the appearances of some of the burlesque stars who had played the Burbank—Rose La Rose, Rosita Royce and Her Pigeons, Tempest Storm, and some of the well-known top bananas, such as Rags Ragland, and, of course, Joe Yule."

Suddenly Abbott had an inspiration. "Hey, Ann," he exclaimed, "wouldn't it be a wonderful idea to do an old-fashioned burlesque show for Broadway?"

Ann was equally enthusiastic.

"But it would only work with Mickey Rooney starring in it," said Abbott, who was familiar with Mickey's work, having directed him in a number of TV segments over the years, as well as in a series pilot for ABC in 1963 that didn't sell.

Abbott was aware that it would take a unique sort of performer to bring it off—one who knew all the classic burlesque bits, and who was still young enough to perform them. Rags Ragland, Joe Yule, Sr., and Gus Schilling were all dead. The living top bananas of yesterday, such as Phil Silvers and Jack Albertson, were either too old or too sick to face the rigors of going back to Broadway.

He also knew that it would take a very daring kind of producer to chance such a risky venture on Broadway. The first person who came to mind was Harry Rigby. Not only did Rigby specialize in producing revivals, his most successful one being *No, No Nanette*, starring an aging Ruby Keeler, but Abbott had already met him at the home of a mutual friend, a prominent Beverly Hills doctor with whom the producer stayed whenever he came to Southern California.

By a strange coincidence, Abbott learned from his doctor friend that Rigby was in town that week in order to get Debbie Reynolds's name on a contract for the revival of *Hello Dolly* he was planning to produce in the fall. Abbott's friend put Rigby on the phone, and the two made a date for lunch at Abbott's house the following noon.

Over lunch on the patio of Abbott's picturesque Spanish hacienda on Camden Drive, Abbott told Rigby his idea. He showed him a collection of Abbott and Costello burlesque sketches, including their classic "Who's on First," which he had inherited in manuscript form from his uncle, and said that if it ever became a reality, he would like to direct the show.

Rigby said, "Fine. You've got yourself a deal."

"There's just one hitch," Abbott added. "You have to get Mickey Rooney for the top banana or it won't work. "Mickey knows all the bits, and there's a certain innocence in his face that will keep the show from being dirty."

FROM WHAT ABBOTT remembers of that meeting, the notion of doing a Broadway show that would be a tribute to burlesque—the innocent kind of burlesque that was on the boards before the strippers

288

came along to stop it from being "family" entertainment—had not occurred to Harry Rigby until he told him about it that day at lunch.

"He liked the idea and said, 'You're right—Mickey Rooney would be very good for Broadway.'"

For some reason—perhaps he was busy with other projects—Rigby did nothing to activate Abbott's idea until after he attended the "Conference of American Pop Arts" at New York's Lincoln Center in 1977. "Various professors were there talking about carnivals, minstrel shows, and other forms of popular entertainment, Rigby recalled, "when Ralph G. Allen, a professor at the University of Tennessee, came out and gave a lecture on burlesque that had the audience rolling in the aisles. I thought if he could get that kind of reaction from that audience, then a burlesque show should do well."

It was shortly after Rigby heard Allen's lecture that he phoned Mickey to ascertain his interest in doing a Broadway show about burlesque.

Mickey's initial reaction was not encouraging. He told Rigby over the telephone from whatever dinner theater he was playing that week that he thought it was a "bullshit idea," and that burlesque would never go on Broadway today.

Rigby believed quite the contrary. He told Mickey that he felt Broadway was ready for some old-fashioned family entertainment like the vintage burlesque shows: plenty of good-looking dancing girls, adequately costumed; sketches that were funny and only slightly risqué; and lots of good music from the twenties and thirties.

Rigby didn't get a commitment from Mickey that day, but he did manage to persuade him to keep his mind open about the project until Rigby had something on paper to show him.

ONCE MICKEY GAVE him that much of an opening, however, Rigby got in touch with Ralph G. Allen, the professor he'd heard lecture at Lincoln Center and whom he had met through Josh Logan, and asked him if he'd be interested in working on the book. Allen said he'd be delighted to, Rigby signed him to a contract, and the two of them went to work writing the libretto. It wasn't so much a question of *writing* a musical book, however, as it was of sifting though the over-six thousand burlesque sketches that Ralph Allen had compiled on tape and from various comedians's collections, plus the material Norman Abbott showed them, and choosing the ones that they believed would amuse today's audiences and then shaping everything into some kind of manageable form for Broadway.

After a first draft was completed, Rigby sent the book to Mickey, who still wasn't sure. At that point Mickey was playing in Louisville, and Ralph Allen went to see him. "I introduced myself," says Allen, "and literally talked him into doing the show."

According to a small item in *Variety* Mickey officially committed to do the play in October of 1978.

> Ruth Webb pacted Mickey Rooney with Harry Rigby for B'way-bound Sugar Baby, a look at burlesque from 1898-1935.
> Rooney would play a Joe Yule, Sr.-like performer. Rehearsals are skedded to start in March . . .

Harry Rigby phoned Norman Abbott shortly after that and said enthusiastically, "Well, I've got Rooney," and made a deal with Abbott to stage the musical.

Now that Rigby had a star and a director, he set about getting a musical score of standard songs that would be of the same vintage as "family" burlesque. Rigby wanted the kinds of songs one could hum going into the theater.

Not being a piker, Rigby started at the top, and tried to get the complete library of the old maestro himself, Irving Berlin. But Berlin turned him down, saying he didn't want his songs associated with burlesque.

The next person Rigby approached was Sheldon Harnick, who wrote the lyrics for *Fiddler on the Roof*. A pretty fair second choice—but Harnick also passed, claiming he was working on another show.

Finally, Rigby, whose idea it was to get Ann Miller to costar with Mickey in the show, remembered that she used to go around with the late Jimmy McHugh, one of Tin Pan Alley's greats. Moreover, she always used to sing "Don't Blame Me," one of McHugh's tunes, at Hollywood parties that Rigby attended. Besides "Don't Blame Me," the McHugh catalogue could boast such standards as "I Can't Give You Anything But Love, Baby," "I'm in the Mood for Love," and "On the Sunny Side of the Street."

Checking with the Jimmy McHugh estate, Rigby also discovered that in his trunk the dead composer had about seventy tunes that had never been published or even had lyrics written for them. Since Rigby wanted some new songs to go along with the standards in the show, he tied up the Jimmy McHugh catalogue and on the recommendation of Ernest Flatt, whom he had signed to do the choreography, hired Arthur Malvin to write the lyrics for the unfinished

McHugh songs and to compose any other special material that might be needed. Both Flat and Malvin had worked on the "Carol Burnett Show," Flatt as choreographer and Malvin as orchestra conductor and composer of special material, so they had a good record of being able to work well together.

When Rigby first announced that he wanted Ann Miller to costar with Mickey, "a lot of people thought he was crazy," remembers Malvin today. "But Rigby had a strong hunch that the combination would be good. He felt that both of them being former musical MGM stars—having been in that period together—would make something happen."

At first Ann Miller resisted the idea of doing burlesque. According to Arthur Malvin, "She had some other revival in mind—*DuBarry Was a Lady*, or one of those shows. It wasn't until I went over to her house in Beverly Hills with a pianist the following February and played the score for her that she agreed to do *Sugar Babies*."

Sugar Babies, incidentally, was not the show's original title. When Ralph Allen first submitted his libretto, it was called *The New Majestic Follies and Lyceum Gardens Review*. But Harry Rigby said he thought *Sugar Babies* would entice more people into the theater, *Sugar Babies* being what the Stage-door Johnnies of the burlesque era called the chorus girls they dated. And in the end, Rigby being Rigby, he got his way.

WITH THE CAST, music, choreography, and director set, all that was needed to make *Sugar Babies* come true were the $1.3 million necessary to put it on its feet. That sum was slightly more than most musicals were costing in 1979, but Rigby was planning to break the show in during a five-city road tour that summer before taking it into Manhattan in October. Because shows don't always make money, or even break even, during their pre-Broadway tryouts, and there are always unexpected expenses—new costumes that have to be made or new sets constructed—a producer has to have extra money in the kitty to meet every contingency. Hence the extra-high budget. Even so, an additional three hundred thousand had to be raised while the show was on the road that summer, which meant that when it finally came into New York its cost had risen to $1.6 million.

Luckily, Rigby's partner in the venture was a woman named Terry Allen Kramer, whose husband, Irving Kramer, was on the board of Columbia Pictures. Before the show went into rehearsal in March, Terry Allen Kramer had persuaded Columbia Pictures to invest $500,000 in *Sugar Babies*, had wangled another $300,000 out of another investor, and guaranteed the remaining $500,000 herself. With that much already in the coffers, Rigby had no trouble getting other investors.

Once the money had been raised, and *Sugar Babies* was sure of at least opening, Mickey and Jan moved into a motel suite in Fort Lee, New Jersey, just across the Hudson River from Manhattan. Fort Lee wasn't exactly handy to the Michael Bennett Studios in downtown Manhattan where six weeks of rehearsals were scheduled to begin in the middle of March, but the motel was near an eighteen-hole golf course.

The first two weeks of rehearsals were mainly devoted to the dance numbers, which were being choreographed by Ernest Flatt, and to readings of the sketches by the actors involved. The readings were presided over by Norman Abbott who had made the mistake of flying into Manhattan to begin his directing chores without a signed contract, just what he believed to be Rigby's word that they had a deal.

Although it's not unusual for there to be some firings during the opening stages of putting on a multimillion-dollar musical, the first two weeks of rehearsals were complete chaos. They went through three different straight men. The "satellite" bananas who had worked with Mickey before, or had never worked with him, all threw up their hands and said they'd never work with him again, because Mickey was being very difficult. "He didn't like the material . . . He didn't think the show had a chance . . . He absolutely resisted everything," says Rudy Tronto.

To Mickey's credit, he was right about most of the sketches; they were ancient examples of burlesque that needed updating and sharpening to make them palatable to today's sophisticated audiences. Ralph G. Allen, though a learned lecturer on burlesque, was not an expert joke writer. When Mickey complained about the sketches, Allen's answer was usually, "Look, if these sketches aren't right, I've got trunksful of them." His trunks didn't contain a lot of new and funny punch lines to "button" many of the sketches, however, and later, during the show's San Francisco stand, two TV gagmen, Ralph Goodman and Paul Pompian, had to be called in from Hollywood to punch up the sketches.

Besides finding fault with the material, Mickey was growing impatient about the fact that Norman Abbott hadn't put any of the sketches on "their feet" yet. This wasn't exactly Abbott's fault, however, because by the middle of the second week of rehearsal, they were still without a straight man to work with Mickey.

As a result, Abbott had to read the sketches, playing the part of the straight man, with Mickey. Finally, at Abbott's suggestion, Rigby phoned Peter Leeds on the West Coast and asked him if he'd be interested in joining the cast. Leeds had worked with Mickey many times in the past, and Mickey felt comfortable with the tall, gangling man with the rubbery face that could be twisted into all kinds of funny reactive expressions.

Leeds said he was excited about the prospect of working with Mickey again, but by the time he and Rigby finished haggling over what his weekly salary would be, it was Friday afternoon and the producer said he wanted Leeds in New York, to begin rehearsals, by Monday morning.

There just wasn't enough time for Leeds to pack and close up the house for what could be an extended stay away from home. "So I told him I couldn't possibly get there until Wednesday," Leeds recalls.

Meanwhile, Abbott continued to read the sketches with Mickey who was becoming increasingly impatient to get them on their feet. Mickey was edgy over the delay and for some reason, according to Abbott, blamed him for the fact that they were going to be without a straight man until the following Wednesday.

"So at the beginning of rehearsals on Monday," relates Abbott, "Mickey came to me and said, 'I love you, baby, but this isn't going to work out. You just can't control the actors.'"

If Mickey was being unreasonable, he was probably being motivated by a severe attack of the jitters. After all, he was staking his whole future on the success of this one show. If it failed, he'd be back on the dinner theater circuit again—probably for the rest of his life.

In addition he probably felt, deep down inside him, that he was a better director of burlesque than Norman Abbott, most of whose directing exprience had been in TV doing filmed sitcoms and variety shows. Mickey, on the other hand, had been brought up in burlesque and unquestionably knew more about that kind of show business than any other living director.

As a result, Rigby bowed to the wishes of his star, without whom there'd be no show, and fired Norman Abbott, without whom there'd probably never have been a *Sugar Babies* in the first place.

Disappointed as he was, Abbott had no choice but to accept the firing, especially since he'd made the mistake of coming to New York without his contract being settled. Without a signed contract, he had no recourse except to sue for damages, a decision he didn't make until months later.

After the second week, Rigby hired Rudy Tronto, on the recommendation of John Kennelly, known for operating the Kennelly Theater circuit in Ohio. Kennelly felt Tronto was the man for the job because he had a working relationship with Mickey from the past—he'd played W. C. Fields's agent in *W.C.* for an entire summer with Mickey, and they'd become very good friends, and in 1959, Tronto had directed *The Best of Burlesque,* a show glorifying burlesque, with Tom Poston, Sherry Britton, and Joey Faye. "*The Best of Burlesque* was very much like *Sugar Babies,* except it was more formal," Tronto says today. "Anyway, John Kennelly knew my work, knew I had worked with Ann Corio, knew I was familiar with burlesque material, and knew I could handle Mickey.

"So I walked into the Michael Bennett Studio and into a den of crazy people, really crazy people. The first person who got me was Ann Miller. She said 'Ernest Flatt's trying to ruin me. He's starting to give me all this shit dancing. I hate this. Why did I ever let myself get involved in this? Please help me.' And I said, 'Ann, I can't help you. I have nothing to do with the dancing. I'm here to do the sketches.'

"Then Mickey grabbed me and said, 'Rudy, we've got to get rid of all this shit. This stuff is terrible. My father did it fifty years ago.' And then he proceeded to do two sketches for me, which he used in *Three Goats and a Blanket.* One was The-Bridge-on-the-River-Kwai bit, and the other one was from 'Candid Camera'—the "Look-in-the-moose's-head routine.' He did both sketches for me, and he was hysterical, and we were both screaming with laughter. But I said, 'Mickey, this isn't 1950 with television. This show takes place in 1926. There is no television, no 'Candid Camera,' and they didn't know those Japanese words in the River-Kwai routine.' So I had to talk him out of those sketches.

"And then what happened next—which was all in the very first day of rehearsal—was I said, 'Okay, give me all my sketch people. We'll sit down and we'll read through the sketches.' At which point, Mickey hit the ceiling, and said, 'I'm so goddamned sick of reading these sketches. That's all we've done. We haven't put one sketch on its feet for two weeks. What the hell are we doing here?' Anyway, we read some of the sketches, and I realized Mickey was getting more and more agitated. So I said, 'Listen, we don't have to read any more. Let's put them on their feet.' And a good thing I did. Later that day, I was informed that we were having a run-through of the entire show on Saturday. At that point there were about twelve sketches in the show, as long as seven and eight minutes each. So I had no choice . . . I had to start putting the sketches on their feet right away. By Saturday we had a run-through, hell or high water. The few people watching—Rigby, Terry Allen, Ruth Webb, and a few others—in the rehearsal hall started to laugh. And at that point the whole thing started to come together . . .

"Mickey still didn't feel the sketches were ever going to work. So then we would go through hours of sifting through the old sketches. And yes, we even wrote some new ones. Mickey would come in with an idea . . . I would come in with an idea. And we'd sit down for four hours, instead of rehearsing, and write sketches, and some of them were funny. And then we started rearranging sketches and pruning them down, and that was basically the process . . . weeding out the ones that were no good, and pruning down the ones that were too long, and giving them a good payoff. Because Mickey was screaming, 'We have to have buttons, we have to have buttons.'"

Once in a while, according to Tronto, "there would be an artistic flare-up. Peter Leeds, for example, started to sulk because we took a sketch away from him. Or Mickey didn't like a piece of material, or a song, and would refuse to do it. Then there'd be big meetings between Rigby and Ruth Webb and Mickey and Terry Allen Kramer in a back room. But finally they'd get it worked out, and Mickey would be his old self again."

One musical number that Mickey was dead set against doing involved his having to roller skate on stage while singing the Jimmy McHugh tune, "I Just Want to Be a Song-and-Dance Man," to a group of pretty girls. If roller skating were one of Mickey's specialties, he might have been able to bring it off. "But Mickey was none too secure on the skates," Arthur Malvin remembers, "and not very good. But Ernie Flatt said 'Roller skating is in, it's going to be very effective and he'll learn it.' But . . . he couldn't do anything fancy or spectacular, and so, to me, the number was just barely okay, and *not* worth having Mickey break a leg over. Then Mickey fell once at rehearsal, and I got really nervous, and I said, 'You know, you lose him, and you lose the whole show.' 'But Ernie kept saying, 'No, it's going to work, it's simple, he'll learn it.'"

"As a result, the roller-skating number was still in the show when the *Sugar Babies* company arrived in San Francisco the end of April to begin two weeks of previews at the Curran Theater before officially opening on May 13."

The cast and most of the company were staying at the Cliff Hotel, which was just up Geary Street from the Curran Theater. Despite San Francisco's reputation for being a tough theater town, the advance ticket sales were "surprisingly good," Arthur Malvin says, "and by the time we started previewing business was excellent."

The audience's reaction at the first preview is generally a pretty good barometer of the show's future. In San Francisco there might have been some jokes that didn't get laughs, some props that failed to work, but *Sugar Babies* was obviously an "audience pleaser" from the moment the curtain was raised, with the spotlight focused on the back of a huge brown coat, marked here and there with floating black triangles. When the coat finally turned around, the audience saw that the somebody inside was Mickey Rooney, grinning a rubbery grin at them. After milking that moment for all it was worth, Mickey started stripping away articles of clothing to a Jimmy McHugh tune appropriately called "A Good Old Burlesque Show," until he was finally down to his bright red long johns.

At that moment, the audience couldn't have been more delighted if he had been the reincarnation of Gypsy Rose Lee clad only in a bejeweled G-string. That magical time in a stage actor's performance when he knows that he and the audience are at one with each other and that he has them in the palm of his hand to do with what he pleases—make them laugh, cry, applaud, whistle, roll in the aisle, or all five simultaneously—had come earlier than Mickey could have dreamed. And as he looked out at the delighted audience, it made all the bitterness of the years before evaporate in a cloud of warm feeling for his fans.

Mickey took eight curtain calls that first preview, and by the next morning word of mouth was so good that a line started to form at the Curran's box office even before it had opened at ten o'clock, and it remained there during *Sugar Babies*'s entire San Francisco run.

Opening night, May 13, went even better; and the reviews the following morning ran the gamut from good to raves. For the next four weeks, *Sugar Babies,* starring Mickey Rooney and Ann Miller, those two old "has-beens," did spectacular business in the City by the Bay, and the ticket speculators had a field day.

Even Mickey's roller-skating number seemed to work. It wasn't a showstopper, but the audience didn't throw tomatoes at it, either. Then, one night, Mickey took a spill while doing the skating number and "really banged up his knee," Arthur Malvin recalls. "It was swollen and hurt him, and he kept saying, 'I'm not going to do this fucking number again. I don't give a shit how much the audience likes it. That number goes.'"

Faced with such resistance, and well aware that it wouldn't be worth it to have Mickey break his leg with his show beginning to "smell like a hit," Rigby and Tronto took out the roller-skating number and decided to replace it with a medley of McHugh favorites that Arthur Malvin had arranged for Mickey and Ann Miller to sing.

Mickey didn't want to do the medley, either. He felt the show was already a hit, so why should he bother to learn anything new? But Rigby, insisting that the show had a hole in that spot, which the medley would fill nicely, ordered Mickey to do it. Without committing himself, Mickey agreed to listen to it, then make up his mind. "So he came up to my room in the Cliff," Malvin says. "But before he'd listen to the medley, he did fifty-five minutes of saying, 'I'm not going to learn a new number, so why bother?'"

"Because Rigby wants it in," Malvin said.

"If Rigby wants it in," Mickey said, "let him sing it."

With that, the phone rang, and it was Rigby on the other end. Malvin held the receiver out to Mickey, and said, "Tell him yourself."

Not quite ready to bite the hand that was feeding him, Mickey recoiled from the phone and said meekly, "I'll tell him later."

"Okay," Malvin said, putting down the phone. "Just do me a favor. Listen to the medley. If you don't like it, you'll tell him no, but at least I'm off the hook. I told him I'd play it for you."

The fight out of him, Mickey sat there while Malvin's piano player/arranger, Stan Freedman, played the medley for him, and Malvin sang the lyrics. After Malvin sang the last word, Mickey sat there quietly for a moment and then said, "It's good, it's very good. Let's do it."

Once Mickey decided to do the number, he wanted to put it in the show right away, that night, despite Rigby's protestations that the number couldn't be done before an audience until costumes were made for him and Ann, and orchestrations written and learned.

"We don't need costumes?" Mickey exclaimed. "Let's do it. I'll find something to wear."

"So Mickey wore a maroon turtle neck sweater and a pair of old pants, and Ann found some old dress in the wardrobe mistress's trunk, and we put the number in the show that night," Malvin remembers. "And without costumes they stopped the show cold, the two of them on stage alone, singing those Jimmy McHugh standards. I mean, the dog act, which followed them and which was the 'eleven o'clock number' had to be taken out—because it died there—and spotted earlier in the show. The audience just flipped. It was magic."

Despite the magic evoked by Mickey and Ann doing a number of nostalgic tunes, there were moments of friction between them. "If one upstaged the other, for example, there'd be a terrific argument," Malvin says. "But generally they liked each other. And if Mickey did something like get a little too rough, like step on her toes, he'd apologize to her later. I remember one time when we were on the road, he started to ad-lib like mad, leaving her with egg on her face. She became so furious that she walked off the stage right in the middle of the routine. Later, when he went backstage to apologize, she said, 'Mickey, don't ever do that to me again, or I'll quit the show.'"

FROM SAN FRANCISCO, *Sugar Babies* moved into the Pantages Theater in Hollywood. Opening on June 19, *Sugar Babies* received rave reviews from every critic except Sylvia Drake of *The Los Angeles Times*, who wrote that it was for "the Magic Mountain crowd." She also believed it was basically a very "sexist" show, a slap in the face to all women, who would like to be considered more than mere sex objects. Sylvia Drake's chauvinistic carpings notwithstanding, *Sugar Babies* did capacity business in Los Angeles. The theater critic on the *Hollywood Reporter* took a shot at Sylvia Drake for insulting the Magic Mountain crowd. "Personally, I've had some very good times at Magic Mountain. Just as I did at *Sugar Babies*."

THE ONLY THING marring the success of *Sugar Babies* in Los Angeles was that three days after it opened at the Pantages, Norman Abbott filed a breach of contract suit against its producers for nine hundred thousand dollars in Los Angeles Superior Court. A year later, Abbott settled out of court for a figure he is not permitted to disclose under the terms of his settlement agreement. However, it's understood to be well up in the six-figure range.

From Los Angeles, *Sugar Babies* went on to play Chicago, Detroit, and Philadelphia with the same satisfying results. Everywhere it was an unqualified hit, and by the time it was ready to open at the Mark Hellinger Theater in New York City on Friday evening, October 9, 1979, it already had a million dollars in advance ticket sales.

Notwithstanding, everyone connected with the show was nervous and apprehensive about the New York opening. It was one thing to be a hit in Philadelphia, quite another to overwhelm the New York critics.

"It was impossible to tell whether Mickey was nervous," Rudy Tronto says. "He never seems to be on the surface. He . . . sent flowers opening night to all the ladies in the cast. He even went around to all the dressing rooms and told the actors there was nothing to worry about. But underneath it all I'm sure he was as nervous as the rest of us. He wouldn't have been human if he hadn't been."

Although Mickey told Ann Miller after the performance that he thought "We both were rotten tonight," the first-nighters apparently never noticed. Every sketch and number in *Sugar Babies* knocked the audience dead—Mickey alone; Mickey and Ann; Ann alone; Mickey, Ann, and the entire leggy ensemble. By the time Mickey was on stage alone, taking his final bows, the entire audience rose to its feet.

Backstage in Mickey's flower-filled dressing room, the scene resembled a scene from a forties' MGM musical. All kinds of celebrities were there to congratulate the aging Mighty Mite, and, later, at least a hundred fans were waiting for autographs as Mickey and Jan made their way out the stage door to the sidewalk.

"I'll sign as many as I can," Mickey grinned, as the crowd engulfed him. Finally, Mickey and Jan jumped into a waiting limousine for the short ride to New York, New York, the restaurant-disco where Harry Rigby was hosting the opening night party.

The photographers' strobe lights winked a welcome as Mickey entered the disco, his arm linked with Jan's. A hundred hands were extended for Mickey to shake. Mickey seemed to bounce through the room, grinning victoriously as he took his seat at his table, which was a level below the one reserved for Ann Miller, who would make her entrance last.

Mickey ordered a soft drink for himself, explaining to an interested member of the press that the bad old days of gambling, alcohol, and compulsive marriages were long behind him. "I've even quit smoking," he explained, adding that he had found a measure of acceptance of himself through the Church of Religious Science.

"To sum it up, living with Mickey Rooney hasn't been easy," Mickey told the reporter. "I haven't always liked Mickey Rooney. There have been crevices, fissures, pits, and I've fallen into a lot of them. But the crux of it is, you can't quit on life, you've got to keep going."

By now the reviews were beginning to come in. They were read aloud to Mickey and his well-wishers by Terry Allen Kramer. "The *Times* loves us," she cried out, and the room rang with cheers, as she started to read aloud from Walter Kerr's review:

> The occasion is essentially a Rooney occasion (it seems to me extremely unlikely that anyone would have shaken the mothballs off sixty-year-old routines, and done them, throttle open and with all flags flying, without him) and the indefatigable Rooney is exactly as energetic, exactly as talented as he was when at the age of three or four, he rammed a cigar into his mouth, raked a Derby over his brow, and made a star of himself. Which is, very, very energetic, and even more talented.
>
> Liked Miss Miller, too, in stunning shape at whatever age she must be, ready to leap from a baggage cart, whip off gloves and overskirt, and tap as though there'd been no yesterday. And I had a grand time, thank you.

Clive Barnes, writing for the *Post*, gave *Sugar Babies* another rave:

> The show is solidly on the shoulders of Broadway's most promising newcomer, yes, oddly enough, it is a first for Mr. Rooney. Rooney delivers with manic grace . . . he is the glorious epitome of the clown. With his lopsided grin, his geriatrically boyish air, his warmth and total naturalness, Rooney is something to experience. Rooney is the true icing on *Sugar Babies*, a Top Banana if we ever had one.

The Daily News also gave it a "money" notice, as did NBC, CBS, ABC, and "Today."

AFTER ALL MICKEY's struggles, how sweet it was that somebody up there had decided to touch him with the wand of success again. Maybe there was something to that Church of Religious Science stuff after all.

300

27

Over the next three weeks, rave reviews continued to roll in for *Sugar Babies*.
From *Time*, October 22, 1979:

Nostalgia shows do not flourish on gilded memories alone. They remind us of things that we miss on the modern stage. We miss chorines who look smashingly lovely. The chorus line in *Sugar Babies* could qualify for the Miss America Pageant. We miss the assured versatility of a show-biz veteran. Mickey Rooney has grease paint in his blood and the house in his pocket.

He has lungs of iron and feet that skitter like a sandpiper's. When he beams, the sun comes out. When he is troubled, the sky falls on Chicken Little. And when he leers, he is the naughtiest boy in class. Class is also the word for his partner and co-star, Ann Miller. When haven't we missed her long lithesome legs? The years have left them far sounder than most currencies.

A follow-up in *Time* on October 29:

These days the sun is shining almost constantly at the Mark Hellinger Theater. At 59, Mickey once again has the approval he needs and demands. "The audience and I are friends," he says. "We're family. They grew up with me. They allowed me to grow up with them. I've let them down several times. They've let me down several times. But we're all family, and it's time for a reunion. What warmth comes over you when they laugh! It's as if they're saying, 'It's all been worth it, thank you.'"

301

From *The New Yorker*, October 22, 1979:

Surely I am not alone in my conviction that Mickey Rooney is among the three or four greatest men of the Twentieth Century. One thinks of Einstein and Freud, but after them whose name leaps more readily to the lips than Rooney's. Half a century ago he was an exceptionally gifted child star in the movies; now he is an exceptionally gifted middle-aged star on Broadway, where he belongs . . . His skills as a performer are greater than ever. I would have been content if the opening night of *Sugar Babies*, at the Mark Hellinger, had lasted until morning; when that prospect dimmed I resolved to make do with repeated visits to the production just as it stands.

From *Newsweek*, October 22, 1979:

At last Broadway has been slipped a Mickey, and the explosive dose is just what it needs. At the age of 59, Mickey Rooney is making his Broadway debut in *Sugar Babies*, a welcome attempt to restore some of the simple virtues of good, not-so-clean fun to the over-intellectualized spirit of the Broadway musical . . . Mickey is the heart, soul and body of the enterprise; not even eight tall wives have exhausted that heart, which for 57 years and 8 months has belonged to show business. As for the soul, only a boundless and rebounding one could have kept Mickey going through the professional and personal ups and downs that life and Louis B. Mayer devised for him. And it's all writ large in the small body: at five feet, three inches, Mickey isn't short, he's just transcendentally truncated.

From Rex Reed in the *Daily News*:

Mickey Rooney and Ann Miller . . . finally made it to Broadway Monday, and although Louis B. Mayer might be turning over in his grave, the rest of us have something to live for. They knocked me senseless with their dazzle, turned their new home at the Mark Hellinger into New Year's Eve on Times Square, and sent show business soaring into orbit . . . If Burlesque or even vaudeville was ever this good, then we were dumb losers to let it go.

With reviews like that from some of the toughest critics in the land it was no wonder the lines at the box office extended clear around the block, and over to Ninth Avenue.

Assured of at least a year's run on Broadway, Mickey and Jan set

302

up housekeeping in a temporary home in Fort Lee. With everything he needed to make him happy—a hit show, a golf course within a ten-minute drive, and the Garden State race track only twenty miles away—Mickey settled down to the pleasurable life of a successful and suddenly wealthy actor.

Mickey played golf or went to the races by day and enthusiastically commuted into Manhattan by night, and twice weekly during the daylight hours, for Wednesday and Saturday matinees.

Have little doubt, Mickey was enjoying his new title as "King of the Broadway Hill" tremendously. There might have been classier shows on Broadway, but none that entertained audiences to the degree *Sugar Babies* did. Audiences of all ages, from eight to eighty, were discovering Mickey Rooney all over again. In his first year in the show, Mickey took a straight salary of $10,000 a week. "He didn't want a percentage deal," states Alan Wasser, the show's general manager. "Later, after he saw the grosses, he realized he was better off with a percentage, he changed it to a guarantee against 10 percent of the gross." With the show grossing $300,000 a week, most weeks, Mickey was earning about $30,000 a week, ample for even Mickey to struggle along on.

He even had enough money left over to invest in some of his favorite money-making enterprises: Act-O-Lab, a mail order acting school; a racing stable; a soft drink company called Thirst Come, Thirst Serve; a whole line of fast-foods—Mickey Rooney's Star-B-Que, Rooney Shortribs, Rooney's Weenie World Hot Dogs, Mickey Rooney Macaroni. A cosmetic company in his wife's name that manufactured a product called Foundation of Youth, a formula cream that "makes plastic surgery unnecessary." According to Jan Rooney's newspaper ad, featuring a large photo of her head in the center, her "Foundation of Youth" formula cream is "only available through the mail, for the astonishingly low price of $2.50."

Whether Mickey is making the millions he envisioned from all these enterprises is a well-kept secret among him, his accountant, and the IRS. No matter. Whether Mickey is dissipating his income on an off-the-wall investment, or socking it away in T-Bonds, there is one thing about him that success on Broadway hasn't changed. He was just as conscientious about giving the audience his best every night as he was before all those smash reviews. And this included never missing a performance and being at the theater on time for the *Sugar Babies* eight-thirty curtain. This doesn't mean, however, that he didn't sometimes take his success with the nonchalance of the veteran trouper he is. For example, it wasn't unusual

303

to see Mickey, at a quarter to eight in the evening, scurrying up and down the stairs backstage at the Hellinger, in his jockey shorts, to place bets with the doorman—or eating his fifth bowl of chili in his dressing room while phoning a bookie or a friend on the West Coast, as the overture began. Then, in one frenetic but far from frantic motion, he would tug on his costume (he wears no makeup in the show and only polo shirts, because he can get in and out of them quickly), skip downstairs, wave to the stage crew, greet the cast while gabbing about a horse he just bought, pull back the curtain to peek at the house. As the overture ended, he'd step into position on stage in time for the spotlight—and the delighted audience—to find him hidden behind his giant brown overcoat.

During the three years that *Sugar Babies* packed them in on Broadway and the four years the show has been playing on the road, Mickey has always showed up, on time. To those directors who've worked with him in the past, in Hollywood, and who have had to shoot around the Mighty Mite on the days his moodiness prevented him from reporting for work and propelled him out to the golf course instead, it's a complete reversal of form.

"I can't imagine how he's done it," Dick Quine says. "It's incredible—something for 'Believe It or Not.'"

MICKEY ALWAYS HAD a zest for life and for his acting career. But it had petered out during the bad times. Now that he was on top again he'd regained his enthusiasm. And, of course, there's nothing like success to beget success. No doubt, Mickey's career was on the ascent, and by the end of 1979, it appeared that nothing was going to stop him ever again.

In 1980 he received a Tony nomination for his work in *Sugar Babies* and in the same year his film career received a shot in the arm when he was nominated for an Oscar for his performance as the feisty horse trainer in Francis Ford Coppola's, *The Black Stallion*. Unhappily, he didn't win either award, but in 1982 he proved his comeback was no flash in the pan by winning both an Emmy and a Peabody award for his TV performance as a retarded lunchroom operator in "Bill."

ONCE AGAIN IT was time for some television producer to exclaim, "Hey, why don't we do a TV series with Mickey Rooney?" And so in 1982, "One of the Boys" came to pass. In this creaky vehicle, Mickey played Oliver Nugent, a restless retiree sharing a New York apartment with his grandson, Adam, and a young pal—its comedy derived from their age differences.

Since Mickey was still starring on Broadway, the series was shot on tape during the days Mickey didn't have matinees. It was a pretty heavy schedule for a man sixty-two years old: golf in the morning, shooting a TV series in the afternoon, and starring in a demandingly heavy role in a Broadway show six nights a week. But that was no problem for someone with Mickey's inexhaustible energy. What was a problem was Mickey's old nemesis—the Nielsen ratings. Although Mickey was frequently hilarious playing Grandfather Nugent, the show failed to capture a large segment of TV viewers and was canceled after the first season. Mickey blames this not on the show, but on the network executives who were "stupid enough" to air it on Saturday nights when nobody stays home.

To the ordinary mortal, starring on Broadway every night would be enough to keep one's ego fed. "But Mickey . . . can't turn anything down," Dick Quine says. "While he was in New York doing *Sugar Babies*, he actually commuted to Canada to play a part in some B-movie he was offered. On the days he wasn't doing matinees, he'd fly up in a Lear jet, do his scenes in the movie, and then fly back to New York just in time to make an eight-thirty curtain. Then he'd do the show, grab a few hours sleep, and jet back to Canada the next morning."

THE AWARDS TO Mickey Rooney kept coming. In 1983 the Academy of Motion Picture Arts and Sciences bestowed on him the highest honor of all—a "Special Oscar for Lifelong Career Achievement."

According to Mickey, none of these achievements would have been possible had he not discovered God and become a born-again Christian. "I don't mean to be philosophical," Mickey told the audience when he was being honored on "This Is Your Life" the same year, "but I want to say, if I may, one should never be afraid to fail in life, because you pass failure on the way to success. And if you trust in the Lord, you can get up off the canvas of life and you're going to be able to finish out what He intended for you to finish out."

28

SUGAR BABIES PACKED them in on Broadway for three straight years, ending its run there on Labor Day, 1982, after 1,208 performances.

By then Mickey had hoped to have another high-flying musical on the runway, ready to take off. This one was to be based on the comic strip characters, Maggie and Jiggs, with Mickey playing Jiggs, of course, and possibly Martha Raye in the role of Maggie. But to date, no writer—and Mickey has gone through a number of them—has been able to come up with a book to satisfy him.

Meanwhile, Mickey took to the road with *Sugar Babies* after it closed on Broadway, and except for a few weeks off for vacations, he's been in it every night since. Moreover, as this book goes to press, Mickey has just signed for another year. Following that it'll probably be Europe, Asia, Australia, South America—and possibly the moon.

And no wonder the producers keep re-signing Mickey, and vice versa. In the great heartland of America, *Sugar Babies* has racked up staggeringly high grosses—$535,000 for one week in Orlando, Florida!

All told, to date *Sugar Babies* has grossed approximately seventy million dollars, according to Alan Wasser, the show's general manager. What's more, Ray Stark is considering making it into a film—if he can figure out how to do it. At any rate, he bought the film rights for a reported one million dollars, and is paying it off at the rate of two hundred thousand a year for five years. By then he ought to know if there's a movie in it or not.

307

All of which is a tribute to the tremendous drawing power of Mickey Rooney. When Joey Bishop substituted for Mickey for four weeks on Broadway several years ago, "the grosses dipped to practically nothing," Arthur Malvin recalls. Moreover, when a second road company was sent out starring Carol Channing and Bobby Morse, it was a total disaster. It folded in Boston, and Harry Rigby took a one-million-dollar bath.

It isn't surprising then that the show's producers want to keep re-signing Mickey for the road, no matter how high his price is getting to be. And it's getting pretty high. "On exceptionally good weeks," Alan Wasser reports, "Mickey can earn, between his guarantee and his percentage, maybe seventy thousand dollars."

But as satisfying as it is to be making that kind of money, Mickey probably wouldn't have remained with *Sugar Babies* this long if he also weren't having fun being its top banana.

As he's always done ever since the night young Mickey uncorked the ad-lib about a "jock strap" to a shocked audience, Mickey still takes great delight in straying from the script when he's in the mood, even if it upsets the actor he's working with, and perhaps confuses the audience. "When *Sugar Babies* was playing at the Pantages in Hollywood," recalls Bullets Durgom, "I went to see Mickey in it. Knowing I was in the audience, he started calling the people in the show—not by their character names but by the names of people we used to know and deal with when I was managing him . . . Sam Stiefel, Maurice Duke, etc. That night, he kept referring to Ann as Sam Stiefel. 'Hey, Sam,' he'd say to her . . . 'Come over here.' The audience was completely confused. But he was getting a kick out of it for my sake."

Mickey also enjoys holding court in his dressing room after a performance, and everyone is welcome, even those he's had differences with in the past. People like Nick Sevano, for example. Even though their parting had been none-too-friendly, Mickey got him and his family hard-to-get tickets when *Sugar Babies* played Los Angeles, and joked around with him backstage afterward.

Ava Gardner also saw the show in Los Angeles and dropped into Mickey's dressing room after the final curtain to congratulate him. "He's still the same beautiful clown," she told a friend afterward. "I'm very proud of him."

How long Mickey will be able to continue the pace, no one knows. According to his close friend Richard Quine, who received a phone call recently from Mickey from the dressing room of some theater on the road, "Mickey admitted to me that he's finally getting tired. But even as he said it, I could hear the assistant stage manager yelling in the background, 'Five minutes to curtain, Mr. Rooney.' Mickey answered him, 'Yeah, yeah,' and kept right on talking with me. And I said, 'Mickey, don't you think you'd better go?' And he said, 'Don't worry about me, Dickie. I'll make it.' And then we talked some more, with Mick asking me how I was doing, and then he exclaimed, 'Okay, Dickie, got to go now . . . Take care of yourself.' And off he went, as enthusiastically as if it were opening night, despite his statement that he was growing tired."

And so life is still continuing at hurricane speed for Mickey Rooney, even at the age of sixty-six. The pace would no doubt kill a younger man. But with Mickey, who knows? He'll probably still be taking pratfalls in *Sugar Babies* when he's a hundred, which is about as long as the show will run if the Mighty Mite chooses to remain in it.

Index

Crawford, Joan, 46, 112
Crowther, Bosley, 123, 125, 127, 149, 155, 226, 234
Curtis, Alexander O., 272

Dailey, Dan, 74
Daily News, 300, 302
Daily Variety, 54, 58, 164
Damone, Vic, 178
Darrow, Frankie, 132, 149
Dead End Kids, 114
Death on a Diamond, 45
de Havilland, Olivia, 47, 49, 50
DeHaven, Gloria, 124
Delon, Alain, 255
Deutsch, Milton, 219, 281
Devil in Love, The, 264, 271
Devil Is a Sissy, The, 61
Disney Studios, 284
Doff, Marilyn, 264
Doff, Red, 207, 208, 269, 272; M.R.'s manager, 215, 216, 219, 223, 226, 230, 254, 257, 260, 261, 263, 264, 267
Domino Principle, The, 284
Donat, Robert, 83, 84
Dorsey, Tommy, 114
Douglas, Melvyn, 84
Drake, Sylvia, 298
Drake, Tom, 112, 113, 152
Drive a Crooked Road, 193, 194
Ducich, Don, 186, 187, 191
Duke, Maurice, 192, 193, 198, 200-201, 202-3, 204, 208, 214, 215, 282
Dumont, Margaret, 74
Dunaway, Faye, 271
Durbin, Deanna, 37
Durgom, Bullets, 282, 308; M.R.'s manager, 226-27, 231, 234, 237, 243, 244, 245, 253-54

Eagle-Lion, 180
Edwards, Blake, 180, 181, 193, 194, 197, 200, 226
Eisenhower, Dwight, 120, 140, 145

Estabrook, Howard, 125
Every Sunday, 37
Everything's Ducky, 226
Ewell, Tom, 219
Extraordinary Seaman, The, 271

Family Affair, A, 57-59
Fast Companions, 41
Feldman, Charlie, 95, 95n, 110
Fields, W. C., 46
Fireball, 174, 175
Fisher, Robert, 235-37, 238, 239, 240-44 passim, 247, 251
Flamini, Roland, 136
Flatt, Ernest, 290, 291, 292, 294, 295
Forman, Joey, 214, 238, 261
Francis the Mule, 165
Francis in the Haunted House, 213
Frankenheimer, John, 271
Friedman, Benedict, 200
Friedman, Harry, 61
Frolich, Sig, 70, 75, 76, 147, 182, 199, 254
Fryman Enterprises, 216-17

Gable, Clark, 46, 59, 62, 83, 89, 124, 156
Gaiety Girls, 18, 19, 20
Gang, Martin, 61, 63, 173
Garbo, Greta, 46
Gardner, Ava
    Artie Shaw and, 146; Frank Sinatra and, 114; Howard Hughes and, 136, 137; MGM and, 88, 94, 102, 111, 112, 118, 122, 127; M.R. and, 70, 87-99 passim, 101-8 passim, 109-18 passim, 121-22, 126-27, 133, 135-36, 154, 308; Monogram and, 113-14
Gardner, Beatrice "Bappie," 89, 90, 91-92, 101, 105, 113, 126
Gardner, Bill, 206, 235n, 235-36, 237, 243, 248, 253, 257, 261, 263, 265, 278
Garfield, John, 149

313

imitations and, 39–40, 77; income of, 43, 61–62, 63, 129, 130, 131, 132, 141–44, 145, 148, 159, 160, 178, 185, 192, 193, 214–17 passim, 230, 234, 238, 241, 254, 277, 284, 303; IRS and, 182, 195, 228–29, 242, 265–66; "jeep show" and, 140–41; "King of the Dinner Theater Circuit," 284, 285, 287; "Mickey" (television series), 235–52 passim; as Mickey McGuire, 32–39 passim; military service of, 94, 118–21, 123, 130–33, 135–41 passim, 145–46; music and, 38, 38n, 71, 75, 114, 137, 187, 213, 273, 282; nightclub performances of, 193, 214, 215, 219, 231, 254, 257, 269–70, 271; politics of, 249; products of, 215, 303; racing/gambling of, 54–55, 78, 109, 110, 115, 116, 129–30, 148, 151, 166–67, 169, 183, 190, 193, 195, 201–2, 231, 244, 245, 299; radio and, 143, 144, 150, 156–57; reviews of (films), 41, 56, 58, 81, 83, 87, 123, 124, 125, 126, 128, 149, 155, 175, 180, 213, 214, 226, 234, (plays) 50, 56, 256, 283–84, 296, 298, 300–302, (television) 237, 252; Rooney, Inc. and, 129–31, 148, 151, 160, 161, 164–65; sports and, 41–42, 51–56 passim, 70–71, 104, 105, 148, 163, 177, 183, 186, 202–3; television and, 196–97, 215–16, 220–25, 231, 271, 304–5; tours of, 79–80, 81, 85, 105–7, 115, 128–29, 267; with USO, 190; vaudeville and, 39–40, 153; at White House, 80–81, 107. *See also* specific individuals and film titles
Rooney, Mickey Jr., 139, 141, 146, 147, 153, 197, 232, 261, 282

Rooney, Teddy Michael, 175, 180, 181, 197, 217, 232, 261
Rooney, Timothy, 153, 197, 232, 238, 257, 260, 261, 267, 281
Roosevelt, President Franklin, 80–81, 105, 107
Rosenstein, Sylvia, 187
Rosenthal, Jerry, 118
Rosenthal, Larry, 275
Rouverol, Aurania, 67
Ruskin, Harry, 217
Rutherford, Ann, 56, 57, 59–60, 217
Ruthless, 171

Sabu, the Elephant Boy, 193
Saroyan, William, 124
Schary, Dore, 82–83, 160, 172, 172n, 178
Schenck, Aubrey, 253
Schenck, Nicholas, 160
Seaton, George, 193
Secret Invasion, The, 234, 237
Seitz, George, 59, 60
Seligman, Selig, 235–38 passim, 250, 251, 252
Selznick, David, 41–43, 57
Serling, Rod, 237, 241
Sevano, Nick, 151, 158, 161, 162, 165, 192, 308
Seven Arts-Warner Brothers, 253
Sherman, Eddie, 129
Showboat (musical), 283
Sidney, George, 88
Sidney, Susan, 258, 259
Silvers, Phil, 72–73, 288
Sinatra, Frank, 114, 158
Singer, Sam, 233
Skidding (play), 57
Slave Ship, 61
Slight Case of Larceny, A, 192
Small, Eddie, 179
Smith, Alfred E., 23
Sobel, Bernard, 16
Sothern, Ann, 124
Sound Off, 180, 181, 185

320